New Directions in East Asian History

This series addresses the ways in which history influences the political, economic and social development of East Asia, a region which now plays a pivotal role in our world's multipolar international system. The series provides new perspectives on East Asia's distinctive economic and political situation through the lens of 20th century history, with a particular focus on Pre-War and Cold War periods. It argues the need to re-examine the history of East Asia and provide new historical approaches to a vibrant and constantly changing region.

Highlighting that history is at the root of many modern day conflicts in Asia, this series provides a global forum for rigorous academic research and timely debate by scholars worldwide, and showcases significant new research on East Asian history and politics in the contemporary era.

The series will appeal to specialists in the history and politics of Asia; international history; scholars of modern and contemporary Japan, Chinese and Korea as well as international relations.

More information about this series at
http://www.palgrave.com/gp/series/15870

Hitoshi Suzuki

Japanese Investment and British Trade Unionism

Thatcher and Nissan Revisited in the Wake of Brexit

palgrave
macmillan

Hitoshi Suzuki
Ministry of Foreign Affairs of Japan
Tokyo, Japan

ISSN 2522-0195 ISSN 2522-0209 (electronic)
New Directions in East Asian History
ISBN 978-981-15-9057-3 ISBN 978-981-15-9058-0 (eBook)
https://doi.org/10.1007/978-981-15-9058-0

This Palgrave Macmillan imprint is published by the registered company Springer Nature Singapore Pte Ltd.
The registered company address is: 152 Beach Road, #21-01/04 Gateway East, Singapore 189721, Singapore

In memory of Sir Hugh, who bridged the two countries

Acknowledgements

In the wake of Brexit, many have debated Japanese industry in Britain, both past and current standoffs, let alone its future. For me, the issue first arose during my time as a Ph.D. candidate at the European University Institute in Florence up to December 2007. My research topic was German trade unions and the Schuman Plan. During a tutorial, the late Alan Milward, as supervisor and official historian, mentioned foreign direct investment and multinational overseas plants as a trade union issue. At the moment, for shame, Alan's comment did not strike me. However, when Pascaline Winand arrived as my new supervisor and focused on the EC/EU's relations with Asia/Japan, what Alan meant gradually came into focus. Why would Europeans (or Americans) want to "welcome" Japanese plants to their country? If I were in their shoes, I would not wish to work "like the Japanese do in Japan." My answer remains negative as long as my employment is secure. If it were not, the answer could change. It became the topic of this book, thanks to both of my supervisors.

As a motorcyclist and slight petrol-head, I have always been fascinated by cars and motorcycles. Shortly after leaving Florence, my topic naturally shifted from coal and steel to trade negotiations on cars between Japan and Europe. Despite possessing a Honda VTR SP1 and a modified Jazz/Fit, I chose Nissan as my next research topic. The story of the Nissan–Sunderland deal was first published as a Japanese article in 2013. I thank Jyunko Tomaru, Yuichi Hosoya, and Toshiro Tanaka for their guidance and help. A Japanese monograph followed shortly from Yoshida

Publishing, for which I owe thanks to Shinya Yoshida, Naotaka Kimizuka, and Yuko Hosoda. Throughout my research, I am heavily indebted to the archivists in Europe and Japan who kindly guided me to useful sources. After publication, I received helpful comments and encouragement—including book reviews by the EUSI, *The Japan-British Society*, and *Diplomacy* (Gaikou)—from Izuru Makihara, Harukata Takenaka, Yoichi Kibata, Ariyoshi Ogawa, Oliviero Frattolillo, Toshio Masuda, Tomoichiro Aoki, Susumu Sato, and Michiru Ishihara, who was kind enough to deliver his grandfather's book.

Shortly before the June 2016 referendum on Brexit, the JSPS funded a year's leave (No. 15KK0126), enabling a stay at the Department of International History, LSE. Thanks go to Antony Best, Janet Hunter, and Piers Ludlow for their warm hospitality and academic input, and especially to the late Sir Hugh Cortazzi, who was energetic and passionate in sharing his thoughts. From the beginning of his career as an RAF officer in occupied Japan, Sir Hugh's memories of Tokyo and elsewhere were surprisingly clear, considering that his age was not far from reaching a century. This book is devoted to his memory. During my stay in London and afterwards, I was provided with numerous occasions to present my research and receive helpful comments. I thank Wilfried Loth, Antonio Varsori, Christophe Bouneau, David Burigana, Jan van der Harst, Anjo Harryvan, Marie Conte-Helm, Frances Lynch, Paul James Cardwell, Patrick Fridenson, Tommaso Pardi, and Yoshimi Igawa. Special thanks go to Connie Lie, who kindly guided me to publication. The usual disclaimer applies.

Last but not least, I would like to thank my family, Yuki and Hana, for their company and warmth. Driving from home to a university three hundred kilometres away after every weekend was not always easy but never failed to be rewarding on the way back. The analyses of this book are those of the author himself and do not represent the official position of the Japanese government.

Praise for *Japanese Investment and British Trade Unionism*

"Fascinating account of an important economic relationship. Invaluable contribution to our knowledge of contemporary political economy and the EU's external relations."

—Finn Laursen, *Honorary Professor, University of Southern Denmark, Denmark*

"A ground breaking book focusing on one of the most important issues, setting new standards for multi-archival research on Japan-EU relations."

—Katsuhiro Shoji, *Professor of European Union Law with the Jean Monnet Chair ad personam at Keio University Law School, Japan*

Contents

1	**Introduction**	1
2	**Japan's Post-War Reconstruction, the Car Industry, and Nissan/Datsun**	9
	1 Introduction	10
	2 Reconstruction and Nissan	10
	3 Nissan and JAMA	17
	4 Japanese Trade Unions	19
	5 US Plant Project	21
3	**The British Car Industry and Anglo-Japanese Relations in the Post-War Period**	25
	1 Introduction	25
	2 British Leyland, the "British Disease," and EC Membership	26
	3 The Queen's Visit to Japan	29
	4 The Labour Government's Response to the Japanese Challenge	32
	5 The CBI's Japan policy and Margaret Thatcher	34
	6 Power Change in Nissan	36

4 Negotiations over Financial Assistance and Local Content 39
1 *Introduction* 40
2 *Thatcher Comes to Power* 40
3 *The Fraser Tornado and Nissan's US Plant Project* 42
4 *The First Encounter* 44
5 *Nissan-Alfa Romeo, Volkswagen, and Motor-Iberica* 49
6 *The Announcement* 51
7 *The First Feasibility Study* 57
8 *The SMMT and the TUC* 60
9 *Trade Unions and Plant Location* 65
10 *Lobbying Brussels* 69
11 *Negotiating Financial Aid* 71
12 *The Second Round of Talks* 76
13 *The Falkland Crisis* 78
14 *Thatcher Visits Japan* 82
15 *Ishihara's Call at No. 10 Downing* 87
16 *The Poitier Incident* 90
17 *Another Retreat* 93
18 *The G7 Williamsburg Summit* 95

5 The Deal: Financial Aid and Local Content 99
1 *Introduction* 99
2 *The 1983 General Election and Kawamata's Compromise* 100
3 *The Breakthrough* 102
4 *The Final Round of Talks* 105
5 *The TUC Approves* 108
6 *Shioji's Turn* 110
7 *The JAW and the TUC* 114
8 *The Deal* 116

6 Plant Location Sunderland 125
1 *Introduction* 125
2 *Sunderland* 128
3 *The Single European Act* 130
4 *Recruiting Workers* 132
5 *Signing the Single Union Agreement* 134

6 *The Royal Couple in Japan* 139
7 *The First Bluebird Assembled* 140
8 *Honda and Toyota Catch up* 144
9 *Single Union Agreements in Britain* 145
10 *Retaliation from the Continent: The Elements of Consensus* 150

7 Epilogue 155
1 *Nissan's Fall* 156
2 *The Nissan-Renault Alliance* 158
3 *Brexit, the Japan-EU EPA, and Carlos Ghosn's Fall* 161

8 Conclusion 169

Bibliography 175

Index 183

About the Author

Hitoshi Suzuki has taught international relations and European integration since April 2009 at the Faculty of International Studies and Regional Development, University of Niigata Prefecture (Niigata, Japan), as Associate Professor. His research interests are the history of European integration and how it was influenced by pressure groups, industry, and trade unions. He received his Ph.D. in history and civilisation from the European University Institute (Florence, Italy) in December 2007. He has written articles on the historical process of how the EC negotiated trade conflicts with Japan, including "Negotiating the Japan-EC Trade Conflict: The Role and Presence of the European Commission, the Council of Ministers, and Business Groups in Europe and Japan, 1970–1982," in Claudia Hiepel (ed.), *Europe in a Globalising World: Global Challenges and European Responses in the "Long" 1970s*, Nomos, 2014, and in 2015 published a Japanese monograph, *Thatcher and the Nissan Sunderland Plant: The History of Negotiations, 1973–86*. He has been Associate Researcher of the Keio Jean Monnet Centre for EU Studies (Tokyo, Japan) since 2008, international visiting fellow at the Monash European and EU Centre (Melbourne, Australia) in 2009, and visiting fellow at the Department of International History, LSE, in 2016 and 2017. From June 2020 he is Deputy Director of the Economic Partnership Division at the Ministry of Foreign Affairs of Japan.

Abbreviations

ACAS	Advisory, Conciliation, and Arbitration Service
AEEU	Amalgamated Engineering and Electrical Union (see also AUEW and AEU)
AEU	Amalgamated Engineering Union (see also AUEW and AEEU)
AUEW	Amalgamated Union of Engineering Workers (see also AEU and AEEU)
BL	British Leyland
BLMC	British Leyland Motor Corporation
BMH	British Motor Holdings
CBI	Confederation of British Industry
DoI	Department of Industry (see also DTI)
DoT	Department of Trade (see also DTI)
DTI	Department of Trade and Industry (see also DoI and DoT)
EC	European Communities
EEC	European Economic Community
EETPU	Electrical, Electronic, Telecommunication, and Plumbing Union
EFTA	European Free Trade Association
EP	European Parliament
EPA	Economic Partnership Agreement (between Japan and the EU)
EU	European Union
FCO	Foreign and Commonwealth Office
FDI	Foreign Direct Investment
GATT	General Agreement on Tariffs and Trade
GM	General Motors
GMB	General, Municipal, Boilermakers, and Allied Trade Union
IBB	Invest in Britain Bureau

ICFTU	International Confederation of Free Trade Unions
IMF	International Metalworkers' Federation
JAMA	Japan Automobile Manufacturers' Association (*Jikoukai*)
JAW	Japan Automobile Workers' Unions (*Jidousha-souren*)
JETRO	Japan External Trade Organisation
JIL	Japan Institute of Labour (*Nihon roudou kyoukai*)
JNR	Japan National Railway
JR	Japan Railway Company
LDP	Liberal Democratic Party (of Japan)
MITI	Ministry of International Trade and Industry
MOFA	Ministry of Foreign Affairs (of Japan)
NEDC	North of England Development Council
NETC	Nissan European Technology Centre
NMUK	Nissan Motor Manufacturing (UK) Ltd.
NRC	Northern Region Council (of the TUC)
NUM	National Union of Mineworkers
OECD	Organisation for Economic Co-operation and Development
RDG	Regional Development Grant
RR	Rolls-Royce
SEA	Single European Act
SFA	Selective Financial Assistance
SMMT	Society of Motor Manufacturers and Traders
TGWU	Transport and General Workers' Union
TUC	Trade Union Congress
UAW	United Auto Workers
UNICE	Union of Industrial and Employer Confederations of Europe
VER	Voluntary Export Restriction

List of Charts

Chapter 1

Chart 1 Japan's outward FDI by Country/Region (Balance of Payments Basis, Net and Flow) Unit: US$ million (*Source* https://www.jetro.go.jp/ext_images/en/reports/statistics/data/country1_e_17cy.xls. Accessed on 4 May 2014 and modified by the authour) 4

Chapter 6

Chart 1 Annual output of Nissan Sunderland (units) (*Source* Industrial Journal [*Sangyou journal*]. 2018–1992. *Nissan; Group Activity of 2018–1992* [Nissan-jidousha group no jittai 2018–1992], Nagoya: IRC) 127

List of Tables

Chapter 2

Table 1 Nissan sales records by region (million yen) 15
Table 2 Nissan exports by region (units) 15

Chapter 7

Table 1 World car production (1,000 units) 167

CHAPTER 1

Introduction

Abstract Literature on Anglo-Japanese relations have centred on diplomacy, industry, and culture, but failed to incorporate the EC/EU dimension. In this book the Nissan-Sunderland deal will be thoroughly addressed with an eye on the negotiations of the Thatcher administration and Nissan's European strategy. Britain's EC/EU membership was at the core of both parties. Another crucial missing piece was trade unions and its misunderstood role in the negotiations, which was the key for both Nissan's choice of plant location and its "successful" operation. The Brexit referendum of 2016 and Carlos Ghosn's fall have put the future of Sunderland in uncertainty.

Keywords Anglo-Japanese relations · European Community/European Union · Brexit · Foreign direct investment · Car exports · Nissan · Trade unions

The Nissan plant in Sunderland was launched in September 1986, and although its future was brought into question by the Brexit referendum in June 2016, it remains the largest car plant in Britain and has achieved one of the highest productivity rates among European assemblers. This book aims to examine the history of the negotiations between Margaret Thatcher's administration, Nissan, and trade unions of both countries.

H. Suzuki, *Japanese Investment and British Trade Unionism*,
New Directions in East Asian History,
https://doi.org/10.1007/978-981-15-9058-0_1

Due to its flood of exports, Japan faced trade conflict with European Communities (EC, from 1993 European Union, EU) member states during the 1970s and 1980s. Britain took the unique position of both criticising Japan's aggressive export drive as an "abuse of free trade rules" and simultaneously inviting Japanese industry to build its first European green-field plants in Britain. Due to its ambition to overtake its major rival, Toyota, Nissan reached an agreement with the British government in February 1984. It did so regardless of the costs and risks: the overall investment cost of 380 million pounds, the shortage of financial assistance, the need to draw on high levels of local content, doubts about the reliability of British-made components, labour disputes in both countries, and Nissan executives' own conflict over whether to prioritise the USA or EC market. Soon after Nissan successfully concluded this agreement, Toyota and Honda followed suit and launched their own plants in Burnaston and Swindon, respectively, in 1992. These events created a new dimension in Anglo-Japanese relations, with the EC/EU clearly uppermost in Japan's mind.

To focus on the details of the negotiations and their wider implications for Anglo-Japanese relations, the history of Japan's post-war reconstruction and its relations with Britain and the European Economic Community (EEC) will be reviewed together with Nissan's corporate history and European strategy. Britain's membership in the EC heavily influenced Japan's relations with it because the Japanese government and industry started to view Britain as a gateway to the EC market. This shift is not sufficiently illustrated in the current works by Keck and Gilson that focus on Japan's relations with the EC/EU[1] because they tend to categorise this period as a transition from an era of trade conflict to the current improved relationship between global partners; therefore, the outcomes and lessons of trade conflicts are underemphasised. The Nissan negotiation was first analysed by Conte-Helm.[2] However, her focus was on local exchanges between the North East and Japan; thus, she mostly neglected the EC/EU factor. This lacuna has been overcome to some

[1] Jörn Keck, Dimitri Vanoverbeke and Franz Waldenberger (eds.), *EU-Japan Relations, 1970–2012: From Confrontation to Global Partnership*, Abingdon: Routledge, 2013; Julie Gilson, *Japan and the European Union: A Partnership for the Twenty-First Century?*, Basingstoke: Macmillan, 2000.

[2] Marie Conte-Helm, *Japan and the North East of England; From 1862 to the Present Day*, London: Athlone Press, 1989.

extent in recent works written by eyewitnesses who served the British government. For example, Sir Hugh Cortazzi and Robin Mountfield testified to the details of the negotiations.[3] These contributions, however, lack the Japanese side of the story, namely, the perspectives of Nissan's management and trade unions and the Japanese government trade policy. To illustrate these points, this book consults the memoirs of Takashi Ishihara, the president of Nissan, and Ichiro Shioji, the leader of the Japanese trade unions, together with the archival materials of the Japanese (and British) trade unions, with which the English audience is not familiar. This book therefore provides a clearer and fuller picture of the negotiations and explains how, why, and when Japanese industry chose Britain as its gateway to the EC/EU market, how and why Britain "welcomed" Japanese industry, and the wider implications of this development for Anglo-Japanese relations in the wake of Brexit (Chart 1).

Works on the history of European integration have extensively examined transatlantic relations, but few have systematically analysed relations with Japan. Lord Francis Arthur Cockfield recalled as an eyewitness that economic competition with Japan, along with the US, was the main focus of the EC during the late 1980s and influenced the creation of the EU in 1993. This book widens the scope of integration history by describing how Anglo-Japanese relations helped to shape the present-day EU and its policies and aims to indicate how and in which fields Brexit could affect Britain, Japan, and, last but not least, the EU itself. Among the nine EC member states, why did Britain become the main gateway for Japanese industry to operate plants and export to the single market? Member states and the European Commission jointly criticised Japan's flood of exports for being concentrated in very specific sectors, constituting an abuse of free trade rules.[4] This was damaging for declining sectors and

[3] Robin Mountfield, "Nissan Investment in Britain: History of a Negotiation 1980–84," in Hugh Cortazzi (ed.), *Britain & Japan: Biographical Portraits* Vol. 6, Honolulu: University of Hawaii Press, 2007a; Hugh Cortazzi (ed.), *Britain & Japan: Biographical Portraits* Vol. 4, Abingdon: Routledge, 2002.

[4] Hitoshi Suzuki, *Thatcher and the Nissan Sunderland Plant: The History of Negotiations 1973–86* (Thatcher to Nissan eikoku koujyou), Tokyo: Yoshida Publishing, 2015a; Hitoshi Suzuki, "Negotiating the Japan-EC Trade Conflict: The Role and Presence of the European Commission, the Council of Ministers, and Business Groups in Europe and Japan, 1970–1982," in Claudia Hiepel (ed.), *Europe in a Globalising World: Global Challenges and European Responses in the "Long" 1970s*, Baden-Baden: Nomos, 2014a; Keck et al., 2013; Gilson, 2000; Toshiro Tanaka, *Politics of the European Union* (EU no

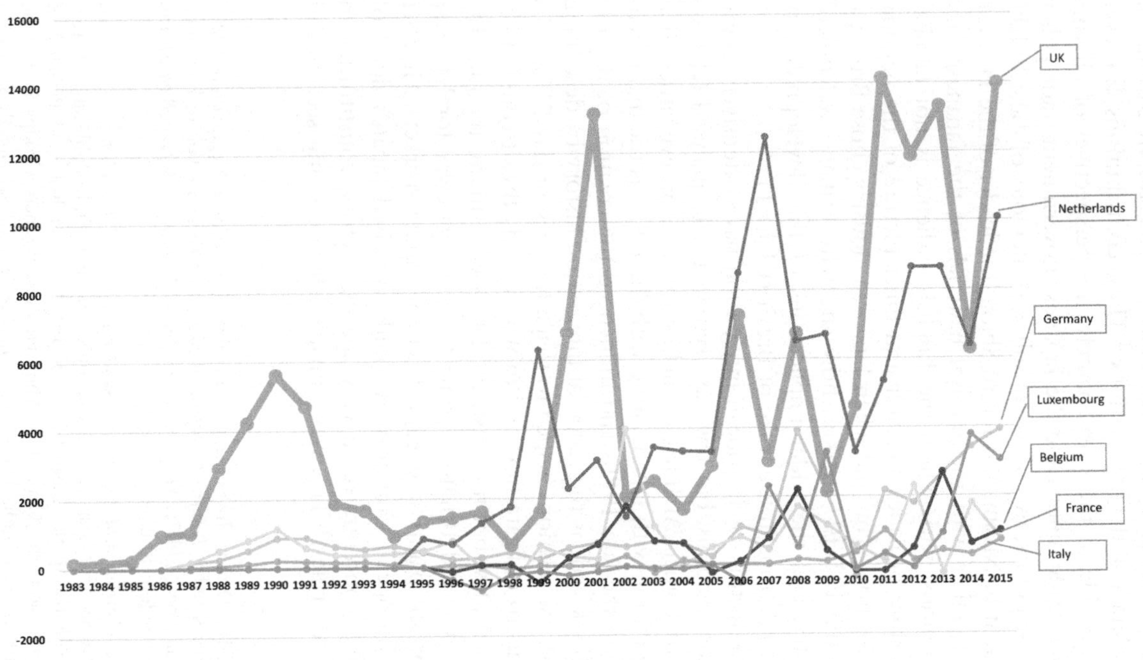

Chart 1 Japan's outward FDI by Country/Region (Balance of Payments Basis, Net and Flow) Unit: US$ million (*Source* https://www.jetro.go.jp/ext_images/en/reports/statistics/data/country1_e_17cy.xls. Accessed on 4 May 2014 and modified by the authour)

local employment. Member states and the European Commission were, however, not firmly unified regarding how to accommodate Japanese investments in the EC due to the controversy. New Japanese plants would create employment in stagnating areas but at the same time could lead to over-capacity in the sector and the closing of European plants. Why and how was Margaret Thatcher's "brave" decision to welcome Japanese investments made, and who took it to Brussels?

One of the main focuses of the Single European Act (SEA), although not written in the text of the act, was to make Europe competitive with the US and Japan.[5] The person who prepared the content of the SEA was Lord Cockfield, then Thatcher's trusted advisor. This book focuses on how the Confederation of British Industry (CBI) formed its Japan policy, when and how that policy was shared with Tory MPs, and how it found its way into the draft of the SEA. Britain chose to accommodate Japanese industry for three reasons. The first was Thatcher's firm decision that British industry needed rationalisation; for that purpose, she aimed to introduce Japanese production automation and Japanese trade unionism into British plants.[6] The second was the CBI's desire to learn from the Japanese approach to competitive production and to collaborate with Japan rather than criticising its aggressive exports. These views were based on recommendations from British firms, such as Rolls-Royce (RR) in aero engines and Triumph and Rover in the car sector, that had collaborated with the Japanese. Finally, the third reason was Japan's insistence on launching its European plants in Britain on the basis of a joint consensus among the Japanese government, industry, and, to a lesser extent, trade unions.

The Nissan deal bore fruit, regardless of the harsh criticism emanating from British public opinion and other EC member states. The Nissan Sunderland case has been described as an "exceptional" case where

seiji), Tokyo: Iwanami-shoten, 1998; Albrecht Rothacher, *Economic Diplomacy Between the European Community and Japan 1959–1981*, Aldershot: Gower, 1983.

[5] Laurent Warlouzet, *Governing Europe in a Globalizing World; Neoliberalism and Its Alternatives Following the 1973 Oil Crisis*, Abingdon: Routledge, 2018, p. 193; Francis Arthur Cockfield, José María Cuevas, Hans-Dietrich Genscher, Tuulikki Kannisto, Mario Monti, Lubomír Soudek, Sir Iain Vallance, and Karl von Wogau, *Is the Single Market Working?*, Philip Morris Institute for Public Policy Research, 1996, p. 19.

[6] Suzuki, 2015a, pp. 43–45.

domestic manufacturers failed to survive,[7] but it soon became clear that the Nissan deal was actually an orthodox path defined under the EU's industrial and foreign trade policy.[8] The absence of parliamentary debate helped to secure the Nissan deal by bypassing opposition and doubts. This approach was not entirely successful in speeding up the negotiations. Crucial debate regarding whether the deal was adequate and necessary for advancing technological standards and improving production efficiency[9] or was merely a redundancy that was doomed to end in the over-capacity and closure of other European plants was lacking. Trade unions in both countries played a role in successfully launching the plant but caused a serious split and eventual decline of trade unionism.

The second chapter summarises Japan's and Nissan's post-war reconstruction. Nissan played a central role in internationalising Japan's car industry and trade unionism. Nissan President Katsuji Kawamata launched the Japan Automobile Manufacturers Association (JAMA) in April 1967. Nissan was also at the forefront of internationalising Japanese unions in the car sector. Ichiro Shioji formed the Japan Automobile Workers' Unions (JAW) in October 1972. Nissan's overseas projects were launched under both leaders with American (trade union) pressures in mind.

The third chapter briefly reviews the post-war British car industry and introduces the queen's first visit to Japan in 1975 as a turning point in Anglo-Japanese relations, in terms not only of formal diplomacy but also of changing the climate for Japanese investments in Britain. British membership in the EC and Nissan's European strategy are examined, with an emphasis on Nissan's contradictory behaviour in targeting the British/EC market, which resulted in both accepting the Anglo-Japanese voluntary self-restriction of car exports (VER) on one hand and choosing to launch a green-field plant in Britain on the other. The Labour government's reaction to the Japanese challenge and the CBI's Japan policy in response are also reviewed.

[7] Pardi, 2017.

[8] Christopher Lord, "Industrial Policy and the European Union," in David Coates (ed.), *Industrial Policy in Britain*, Basingstoke: Macmillan, 1996, pp. 221–233.

[9] Christophe Bouneau, David Burigana and Antonio Varsori (eds.), *Trends in Technological Innovation and the European Construction: The Emerging of Enduring Dynamics?*, Brussels: P.I.E. Peter Lang, 2010; Coates 1996.

The fourth chapter illustrates the negotiations between the Thatcher administration and Nissan. In basic terms, the Society of Motor Manufacturers and Traders (SMMT) and the Trade Union Congress (TUC) accepted Nissan's announcement that it was launching a feasibility study in Britain. The CBI held to its policy to welcome Japanese investments in Britain and lobbied Tory MPs, MEPs, and Eurocrats in Brussels in support of such views. When the Thatcher administration hesitated to provide "generous" subsidies—a regional development grant (RDG) and selective financial assistance (SFA)—Nissan responded by showing reduced versions of its plant project. Negotiations over British local content and governmental subsidies heated up. The Falkland crisis in the spring of 1982 and the G7 Williamsburg summit in May 1983 marked turning points in the negotiations, almost forcing the reluctant opponent, Kawamata—Nissan's Chairman—to retreat. Thatcher herself visited Japan in September 1982 and met with Kawamata in private.

The fifth chapter describes how the negotiations on subsidies and local content were concluded. Kawamata—as a typically careful former Japanese banker—proposed a two-stage plan to allow Nissan's possible retreat in case the pilot plant failed to perform. To seal the deal, Thatcher decided to provide increased SFA to Nissan, but this decision led to disagreement with chancellor Nigel Lawson. A gentleman's agreement stipulating 80% British local content and subsidies was signed on 1 February 1984 between the Department of Trade and Industry (DTI) and Nissan.[10]

However, the plant location was not yet decided. It was solely up to Nissan to choose a profitable site. Regarding this issue, Nissan focused mostly on which trade union(s) was its best partner, as described in the sixth chapter. It was a question of how the Japanese typical single union agreement allowed only one union in the plant to organise the workers and employees. Nissan Motor Manufacturing (UK) Ltd. (NMUK) announced in March 1984 that the plant would be located at the former Sunderland airfield. NMUK and the Amalgamated Union of Engineering Workers (AUEW) signed an agreement in April 1985 that contained a contested non-strike agreement. The first Bluebird was assembled in July 1986 and was exported to the continent in September

[10] Robin, Mountfield, "Course of the Nissan Negotiation 1980–84," in Hugh Cortazzi (ed.), *Britain & Japan: Biographical Portraits* Vol. 6, Honolulu: University of Hawaii Press, 2007b, p. 350.

1988. NMUK gained British manufacturer status from the SMMT in April 1991. Upon seeing Nissan's success, Toyota and Honda immediately took their chances and launched plants in Burnaston and Swindon in 1992. The British government argued against retaliation from the continent, which intended to control the exports of made-in-Britain Japanese cars, and export monitoring ceased in 1999.

Finally, the seventh chapter examines Sunderland's performance during the 1990s. The plant was successfully launched and proved profitable but failed to reach its maximum annual output. The local sourcing of the Primera and the Micra never failed reaching 80%, but was reduced to a level that was barely high enough to be defined as made in the EU immediately after Carlos Ghosn arrived in Tokyo as Nissan's COO in 1999. Ironically, the annual output of 300 thousand units was achieved the next year. The capacity rose to 500 thousand, but with sacrifices.British local content decreased to half, seriously damaging the British components sector. The Japan-EU Economic Partnership Agreement (EPA) signed in July 2018 worked as a pressure in the post-Brexit debates, encouraging Japanese assemblers to decide whether to reduce assembly in Britain, transfer plants (and jobs) to the continent, or once more export from Japan, this time without tariffs. The future of Japanese plants in Britain remains to be known and is heavily dependent on the exact terms of Brexit.

CHAPTER 2

Japan's Post-War Reconstruction, the Car Industry, and Nissan/Datsun

Abstract The outbreak of the Korean War resulted in American (and British) occupation powers to lift Allied restrictions on Japanese industry. The Japanese car industry revived under MITI's guide and its market protection. Although ranking second next to Toyota in domestic shares, Nissan superseded in exports and overseas assembling. Nissan's leadership was essential in both launching JAMA and internationalising Japanese trade unions. Facing competition from the aggressively rising Honda, Nissan gave full gas to its plant projects in the US and Europe. The queen's visit to Japan in May 1975 marked a turning point for improving Anglo-Japanese relations, encouraging the Japanese to invest in Britain. Britain was targeted as one of the most suitable location in Europe, but not without rivals.

Keywords Japanese car industry · Reconstruction · Export drive · Ministry of International Trade and Industry · *Keidanren* · Japan Automobile Manufacturers Association · Japan Automobile Workers' Unions

H. Suzuki, *Japanese Investment and British Trade Unionism*, New Directions in East Asian History, https://doi.org/10.1007/978-981-15-9058-0_2

1 Introduction

Reconstruction after the Second World War started only after the Korean War broke out in 1950. Allied restrictions on the Japanese industry were loosened, allowing Japanese car assemblers to fully return to business. The Ministry of International Trade and Industry (MITI) played a central role in protecting the Japanese car market, guiding the industry to technological advances and promoting exports. Nissan's post-war reconstruction started with its collaboration with the British manufacturer Austin in 1952. Based on its improved competitiveness, Nissan advanced into Europe, starting in 1959 with Norway, a member country of the European Free Trade Association (EFTA), and then found a gateway to Britain in 1968 with clear hope in Britain's future EC membership. It was Nissan under President Katsuji Kawamata, who was later promoted to chairman, that took the lead in liberalising car imports and capital movement, launching the Japan Automobile Manufacturers Association (JAMA) lobby group in April 1967. Kawamata's leadership was made possible not only because Nissan was more aggressive in exports than the "careful" Toyota but also because Nissan's trade unions under the JAW were at the forefront of Japanese unions' internationalisation. JAW president Ichiro Shioji, who also remained an active leader until the mid-1980s, organised his fellow workers in Japan and across other Asian countries, constructing a reliable and cooperative labour–management relationship with Kawamata. Among Japanese manufacturers, Nissan was at the forefront and was ready for a full commitment in Britain. These aspects are overlooked in the current English literature, which describes Kawamata and Shioji as opponents of the Nissan deal.[1]

2 Reconstruction and Nissan

On 15 August 1945, the Japanese heard a radio announcement from the Showa emperor announcing "his" decision to agree to a cease-fire and accept the Potsdam Declaration. It was the first time that most Japanese people had directly hear the emperor (*arahitogami*) speaking in his own voice directly to the people. On 2 September, the Japanese government signed the "unconditional" surrender on the battleship USS Missouri.

[1] Mountfield, 2007a, pp. 111, 114; Cortazzi, 2002.

As the emperor announced, to "bear the unbearable," Japan was reconstructed from ruins. Colonised countries won independence, and the Japanese economy had to restart without relying on foreign resources. Under American—and British—occupation,[2] the new constitution was unveiled in November 1946, making Japan a country, at least in legal terms, with democracy, rule of law, human rights, gender equality, and a free economy.

However, the economy had hardly been reconstructed before the outbreak of the Korean War in June 1950. Starting with repairing American military equipment, Japanese industry swiftly recovered and experienced a lift-off due to loosened restrictions on the economy and industry. Thereafter, Japan enjoyed nearly 10% economic growth each year. In 1956, the phrase "the post-war period is away (*mohaya sengo dewa nai*)" appeared in the *Annual Report on the Japanese Economy* (Keizai hakusyo) issued by the Economic Planning Agency (*Keizai kikakuchou*). One of the largest engines of the Japanese economy was the automobile sector.

Before the war, Japanese manufacturers had been ordered to assemble trucks, tanks, and components for both military land vehicles and aircraft. In 1936, car assembly was limited to Toyota and Nissan under governmental restrictions, and foreign manufacturers—Ford and GM—were pushed out of Japan.[3] The assembling of civilian cars had to be relaunched after the war. The outbreak of the Korean War in 1950 brought the Japanese car industry to a resurgence, with the US placing purchase orders for more than seven thousand trucks.[4] To reconstruct, MITI targeted three sectors—steel, petroleum chemical, and car—and, while protecting the Japanese market, concentrated capital, promoted exports, and guided the industry to technological advancement.[5] Car production surpassed pre-war levels in 1953. MITI preferred technological transfer to arrive

[2] HughCortazzi, *Japan and Back and Places Elsewhere; A Memoir*, Folkestone: Global Oriental, 1998, pp. 34–47.

[3] Chalmers Johnson, *MITI and the Japanese Miracle; The Growth of Industrial Policy, 1925–1975*, Stanford University Press, 1982, pp. 132–133. Nobusuke Kishi—later the Japanese prime minister—was in charge of this policy before accepting a post in Manchuria. Kishi and Nissan's founder, Yoshisuke Ayukawa, worked closely together.

[4] Ibid., p. 200.

[5] Ibid., pp. 9, 237, 258.

through collaboration with foreign manufacturers. Jeeps driven by American GIs gave hints to Toyota and Mitsubishi on how to build four-wheel drive vehicles, later realised as the Land Cruiser and the Pajero. British brands were also one of the benchmarks of civilian cars. The pre-war level of car exports was recovered in 1959.[6]

One of MITI's beloved Japanese car manufacturers was Nissan. Nissan's headquarters was called in Japan the "MITI of Ginza."[7] The nickname came from Nissan's then headquarters in Ginza,[8] the wealthy heart of Tokyo, and captured the firm's character as an almost exact copy of MITI's export policies. Another characteristic of Nissan was its *zaibatsu* connection with the electronics multinational firm Hitachi and the Industrial Bank of Japan (*Nihon Kogyou Ginkou*, from 2002 Mizuho Bank). Nissan purchased electronic components primarily from Hitachi, and the latter in turn purchased Nissan cars for corporate use. The close relationship originated during the intra-war period and continued until the US broke up such "pre-modern" and protectionist connections during the late 1980s and early 1990s in order to open opportunities for foreign capital. The Industrial Bank of Japan had long been the main financer of Nissan, and the latter depended heavily on loans provided by the former.[9]

[6] Johnson, Werner, and Noguchi pointed out Japanese continuity from the pre-war to the post-war economy. Johnson and Noguchi emphasised the role of MITI and bureaucrats in the economy, while Werner emphasised the Bank of Japan. Noguchi downplayed the role of Japanese dependence on exports for post-war growth; Yukio Noguchi, *Post-War Economic History; Where Have We Failed* (Sengo keizai-shi; watashitachi wa dokode machigaetanoka), Tokyo: Nikkei, 2019; Richard Werner, *Princes of the Yen; Japan's Central Bankers and the Transformation of the Economy* (2nd ed.), Carnforth: Quantum Publishers, 2018.

[7] Masaaki Sato, *Nissan; Glory and Disgrace* (Nissan, eikou to kutsujyoku), Tokyo: Bungei-shunjyu, 2012, p. 22; Jiro Uesugi, *Nissan's Fall and Come-back; Why Japanese Failed to Revive* (Nissan-jidousha no shippai to saisei), Tokyo: KK Bestsellers, 2001, pp. 46, 134, 157. Former *Nihon-keizai-shinbun (Nikkei)* journalist Sato wrote three Japanese books on Toyota, Honda and Nissan, among which the last one—and the most contested—has not been translated into English. Masaaki Sato, *The Toyota Leaders; An Executive Guide*, Vertical, 2008; Masaaki Sato, *The Honda Myth; The Genius and His Wake*, Vertical, 2006.

[8] Nissan's headquarters moved to its hometown, Yokohama, in August 2009 to celebrate the harbour's centennial.

[9] Based on the Japanese abbreviation "*Kogin*" of *Nihon Kogyou Ginkou*, Nissan was also nicknamed *Kogin*-motors; Uesugi, 2001, p. 149.

As the following chapters show, Nissan's overseas operations risked financial shortages. To provide Nissan with leadership in financial matters, Katsuji Kawamata was sent from the Industrial Bank of Japan to Nissan in 1947. Kawamata was born in 1905 and graduated from Tokyo University of Commerce (which became Hitotsubashi University in 1949) in 1929 before joining the bank. After solving one of Nissan's (and Japan's) worst labour disputes in 1953, he was named Nissan's president in 1957.[10] Kawamata's mediation was made possible because Ichiro Shioji and "his" unions sided with Kawamata by launching a second union and weakening the leftist unions under the *Souhyou*.[11]

Nissan has also been characterised in Japan as a British-oriented assembler. Nissan's post-war reconstruction started with its collaboration with the British manufacturer Austin in 1952.[12] Nissan was founded by Yoshisuke Ayukawa in Yokohama in 1933, and its first model, the Datsun 13, was unveiled the next year. However, the firm suffered from the negative rumour that its pre-war Datsun Type 11 model "resembled" the Austin Seven—or the French Rosengart LR2—without a patent licence. Its reputation was restored by its official partnership with Austin in 1952. Nissan annually imported two thousand kits of the Austin A40 Somerset, which were assembled in the Tsurumi plant and sold under the Austin brand in Japan.[13] Based on its agreement with Austin, Nissan gradually replaced the British-made components with Japanese and was also

[10] Ishihara was more than ambitious to become president and intended to talk down Kawamata. Former *Nikkei* journalist Sato described Ishihara's attitude as visiting Kawamata's house without appointment and, lounging on a sofa with his feet on the table, telling Kawamata to leave Nissan and join a subsidiary; this was the "president's decision, confirmed by the main bank *Kogin*." It was a plot, but Ishihara's coup d'état failed. The unions, Nissan-*rouso*, stopped the assembly lines in protest and directly lobbied *Kogin* to express the unions' support of Kawamata's presidency; Sato, 2012, pp. 39–41; Shioji, 2012, pp. 76–78.

[11] See Sect. 4 of this chapter on Shioji. Kawamata owed him for driving the leftist unions out of the plants and thereafter relied on Shioji's leadership; Hisao Inoue, *Nissan vs. Ghosn; Two Decades of Dictatorship and Turmoil* (Shihai to antou no nijyu-nen), Tokyo: Bungei-shunjyu, 2009, pp. 71–73.

[12] Koichi Shimokawa, *The Japanese Automobile Industry; A Business History*, London: Athlone Press, 1994, p. 110; Mountfield, 2007a, p. 117.

[13] Nissan, 1983, pp. 98–99.

permitted to use the same components for its other models.[14] Furthermore, Austin promised to provide Nissan, if necessary, with mechanical tools and machinery to produce the necessary components. The first Somerset rolled out on 4 April 1953. In August 1956, all the Somerset components were replaced with Japanese components a mere three years and nine months after the agreement. The cooperation helped Nissan to develop its first successful saloon, the Bluebird, in 1959,[15] enabling Nissan to proclaim "Nissan as the leader of technology (*gijyutsu no Nissan*)." Exports to the USA started in June 1958, and in March 1960, the collaboration with Austin terminated. Nissan's component supplies and assembly were of British origin.

Based on its improved competitiveness, Nissan was the most active of the Japanese manufacturers in developing plants in Asia and Latin America. Nissan focused on Asian countries that had been significant markets since before the Second World War. The home markets had to be recovered.[16] Exports resumed in 1958, but merely 23% of the assembled cars were exported.[17] Knock-down exports to Taiwan and India were initiated as early as 1957 and 1960, respectively, but exports before 1958 consisted only of small numbers of lorries shipped to South Korea, Thailand, India, Taiwan, and Okinawa.[18] Nevertheless, exports to Asian countries amounted to 42.6% of Nissan's overall exports.[19]

The second-largest destination was Latin American countries, which constituted 28.9% of the overall exports; in sharp contrast to Nissan's current sales and exports (Tables 1 and 2), exports headed to the developed countries of Europe and North America together accounted for merely 21% in 1958. To expand exports to the American continents, Nissan focused on Mexico, where it started knock-down exports in 1961. This was due to Mexico's policy of requiring automobiles to be produced domestically. The Cuernavaca plant was launched in 1966 with the aim

[14] Ibid.

[15] Kawamata as president named the car. He admitted this later on and told PM Margaret Thatcher that the Bluebird's success owed heavily to the British. See Sect. 14 in Chapter 4.

[16] Nissan, 1975, p. 155.

[17] Ibid., p. 154.

[18] Ibid., p. 155. The reversion of Okinawa from the US to Japan took place on 15 May 1972; thereafter, drivers drove on the left side of the road, as on the mainland.

[19] Ibid., p. 154.

Table 1 Nissan sales records by region (million yen)

	2012	*2013*	*2014*	*2015*	*2016*
Japan	1,904,108 (21.8%)	2,077,135 (19.8%)	1,853,000 (16.3%)	1,799,650 (14.8%)	1,827,937 (15.6%)
Overseas total	6,833,212 (78.2%)	8,405,385 (80.2%)	9,522,207 (83.7%)	10,389,869 (85.2%)	9,892,104 (84.4%)
North America	3,313,296 (37.9%)	4,337,127 (41.4%)	5,063,298 (44.5%)	5,861,732 (48.1%)	5,807,622 (49.6%)
Europe	1,372,970 (15.7%)	1,666,307 (15.9%)	1,745,837 (15.3%)	1,748,122 (14.3%)	1,670,283 (14.3%)
Asia	1,027,166 (11.8%)	1,215,769 (11.6%)	1,374,551 (12.1%)	1,443,889 (11.8%)	1,260,964 (10.8%)
Others	1,119,780 (12.8%)	1,186,182 (11.3%)	1,338,521 (11.8%)	1,336,126 (11.0%)	1,153,235 (9.8%)
Total	8,737,320 (100.0%)	10,482,520 (100.0%)	11,375,207 (100.0%)	12,189,519 (100.0%)	11,720,041 (100.0%)

Source Industrial Journal, *Nissan; Group Activity of 2018*, Nagoya: IRC, 2018, p. 12, modified by the authour

Table 2 Nissan exports by region (units)

	2013	*2014*	*2015*	*2016*
North America	354,144 (64.8%)	225,469 (45.0%)	182,587 (37.2%)	307,301 (50.3%)
Europe	26,306 (4.8%)	51,252 (10.2%)	75,419 (15.4%)	90,713 (14.9%)
Others	166,204 (30.4%)	224,786 (44.8%)	232,379 (47.4%)	212,442 (34.8%)
Total	546,654 (100.0%)	501,507 (100.0%)	490,385 (100.0%)	610,456 (100.0%)

Source Industrial Journal, *Nissan; Group Activity of 2018*, Nagoya: IRC, 2018, p. 93, modified by the authour

of exporting to North American markets. It was the first Japanese plant in the region, but the plant operation taught Nissan the hard lessons that laws changed frequently and that local workers and component suppliers were sometimes difficult partners.

Nissan's first steps into Europe started in 1959 with Norway, a member country of the European Free Trade Association (EFTA), as a European country without its own automobile manufacturer. Another crucial aim was to develop sea lanes for exporting cars to Europe at a reduced cost. Shipping to European countries was restricted by the limited quota of ships controlled by the European shipping conference. The cartel made export costs high for Japanese assemblers. Norway later became crucial for Nissan's exports when it left the shipping conference in 1971. It was the first case of a Japanese assembler signing a contract with the Norwegian firm Höegh and Ugland Auto Liners.[20] With the resulting reduction in shipping costs, Nissan radically increased its exports to Europe.

Based on its success in Norway, Nissan started to export to Finland in 1962, and 713 Bluebirds were exported in the first year.[21] Based on a decision made in early 1964,[22] Nissan turned from its success in the Nordic countries to the EC and opened offices in Belgium in July 1964 and in the Netherlands in May 1966. Nissan finally found a gateway to Britain and France in 1968, with clear hope for Britain's future EC membership. Nissan provided Nissan-Datsun UK with an exclusive import licence in June 1968,[23] exporting Sunny and Bluebird. Datsun UK took over Nissan-Datsun UK in December 1970 with 100% British capital and dominated as the largest importer of Japanese brands in Britain. Datsun UK has imported Nissan cars into Teesport since 1972.[24] Datsun UK under president Octav Botnar became one of the driving forces in the first phase of Nissan's negotiation with the British government.[25] Nissan's exports to France also had a British element, as they were managed by a branch of British Leyland (BL) in France. Similar to Renault and Fiat, Nissan attempted to launch a plant in Hungary and export to Western Europe, initiating talks in 1968.[26] A team visited

[20] Ibid., p. 181.

[21] Ibid., p. 395.

[22] Ibid., p. 160.

[23] Ibid., p. 397.

[24] TNA (The National Archives, Kew), FV22/133, Gardiner to Boonham, 21 August 1978.

[25] Mountfield, 2007a, p. 109.

[26] Zoltán Südy, "Memoires on Japanese Investments to Hungary (*Nihon kigyou no tai-Hungary toushi no denkiteki-kousatsu*)," in Shuichi Ikemoto and Hiroshi Tanaka (eds.), *Japanese Multinationals' Entry into the New Developing Markets in Europe; Perspectives from Central Europe and Russia* (Oushu shinkou-shijyou-koku eno Nikkei-kigyou no shinshutsu), Tokyo: Bunshin-dou, 2014, pp. 232–233.

Hungary in December 1969, but the project was abandoned due to the intervention of the USSR.[27]

3 Nissan and JAMA

In the 1960s, Nissan's overseas activities developed considerably, which made the firm the foremost representative of the Japanese automobile sector both domestically and internationally. Japan joined the Organisation for Economic Co-operation and Development (OECD) in 1964. This meant that the Japanese market would be opened to foreign manufacturers. In 1966, under Katsuji Kawamata's leadership, Nissan successfully launched the Sunny, a high-volume car available for Japanese households. Its rival, Toyota, launched the Corolla the same year[28]; thus, 1966 was referred to as Japan's "first year of my car," when each household came to own a car. Kawamata's reputation grew, and he came to be called the founder of Nissan's renaissance.[29] In the same year, Nissan merged with Prince Motor, solidifying its status as the second-largest Japanese assembler.[30] The year 1966 was also a symbolic year for Japan because it surpassed Britain's production volume of automobiles and emerged as the world's third-largest producer after the US and (West) Germany. The car industry became the largest sector in Japan in 1968. In the next year, the number of exported cars surpassed that of cars produced for the domestic market.

The Japanese automobile sector was, however, not unified in supporting liberalisation. MITI was also split. A group of MITI officials plotted to prevent Honda, which had developed as a motorcycle assembler,[31] from entering automobile assembly. MITI feared that adding another assembler would lead to over-capacity and the closing of other assemblers. A strong opponent to this plot was the president of

[27] Ibid.

[28] The launch of the Subaru 1000 also occurred in 1966.

[29] Sato, 2012, p. 11.

[30] In consultation with its owner, Shojiro Ishibashi, also the founder of Bridgestone, Yoshio Sakurauchi as MITI's minister mediated the merger; Inoue, 2019, pp. 74–77.

[31] After its first challenge in the Manx Tourist Trophy in 1959, Honda won the TT in 1961 and then launched its motorcycle plant in Belgium in September 1962. Assembly started in May 1963.

Keidanren—Taizo Ishizaka—who played a strong leadership role in liberalising Japan's trade and capital. Ishizaka was president of Toshiba and solved one of its worst labour disputes in 1949. His fame for reviving Toshiba led to his promotion to the first presidency of the Japan Productivity Center, which was launched in February 1955. Ishizaka was named *Keidanren*'s president in February the following year and remained in that post until May 1968. Ishizaka firmly opposed governmental intervention. Shortly before Japan joined the OECD in 1964, MITI attempted to adopt a policy of targeting specific "strategically important" sectors, including automobiles, and intervening to merge car assemblers. The French mixed economy was the model.[32] Ishizaka opposed such policies and stated,

> The Japanese steel industry surpassed Germany and has become the world's second largest. [...] Now that Japan is developed, reversing liberalisation is similar to an adult sitting in a baby cart, dressed like a baby, and crying that open doors let in cold winds.[33]

The Japanese banking sector supported Ishizaka, and liberalisation became the trend. Thanks to *Keidanren*'s support, Japanese manufacturers assembling motorcycles or three-wheeled cars—Honda, Suzuki, and Mazda—stepped up to car manufacturing. Honda launched its first small four-wheeled truck, the T360, in 1963 and a sports car, the S600, in 1964. In the same year, Honda became the first Japanese manufacturer to mount a Formula One challenge, winning the first Grand Prix in Mexico in October 1965. Honda became an automobile assembler.

The Japanese car industry adopted liberalisation policies. Based on an agreement reached in the GATT Kennedy Round, Japanese import tariffs on automobiles were reduced from 40 to 36%.[34] Former *Nikkei* journalist Masaaki Sato, who had long focused on the Japanese automobile sector, argued that Katsuji Kawamata—Nissan's president and later chairman

[32] Takumi Anzai, *Keidanren; The Fall of Japanese Business's Headquarters* (rakujitsu no zaikai-souhonzan), Shicho-sha, 2014, p. 105. Again in 1968 a high-ranked MITI official stated that Japanese car assemblers should merge under two groups, Toyota and Nissan; Masaaki Sato, *Automobile Industry; The Making and Breakup of Alliances* (Jidousha gasshou-renkou no sekai), Tokyo: Bungei-shunjyu, 2000, pp. 22–23.

[33] Anzai, 2014, p. 104.

[34] Sato, 2000, p. 23.

beginning in November 1973—led the liberalisation of car imports and capital movement.[35] For such purposes, Kawamata launched the JAMA lobby group in April 1967.[36] As a result of the GATT Tokyo Round held between 1973 and 1979, Japanese import tariffs on cars were reduced to 0% in 1978.

4 Japanese Trade Unions

Kawamata's leadership was made possible, not only because Nissan was more ambitious in exports than the "timid" and careful Toyota but also because Nissan's trade unions under the JAW were at the forefront of Japanese unions' internationalisation. JAW president Ichiro Shioji, who also remained an active leader of the Nissan unions and the International Confederation of Free Trade Unions (ICFTU) until the mid-1980s, organised workers across the Asian countries and constructed a reliable and cooperative labour–management relationship with Kawamata.[37]

Shioji was born in downtown Tokyo in 1927. He experienced a difficult life and educated himself at a chemical firm, NOF Corporation (*Nichiyu*), an oil refinery and supplier that was part of the Nissan conglomerate before the war. While working as an employee, Shioji took evening classes and earned a degree from the Law Faculty of Meiji University in Tokyo. He then applied for a job at Nissan, which he barely secured in 1953. Nissan was dominated by employees who had graduated from the University of Tokyo or other national universities, and Shioji's academic record fell short. The strong anti-communist trade unionism he had shown at NOF, however, caught the interest of Nissan executives.[38] Nissan unions were affected by the communist-biased *Souhyou*,[39] and the executives sought to recruit a less militant union leader. Shioji won trust and support from the management as a reliable and cooperative negotiating partner but was condemned by Nissan-*bunkai* members as a renegade and "puppy of management." To counter the influential

[35] Sato, 2012, p. 11.

[36] Ibid.

[37] Suzuki, 2015a, pp. 28–34; Sato, 2012, pp. 10–12.

[38] Sato, 2012, p. 11.

[39] Ichiro Shioji, *The Rise and Fall of Nissan; Testimony by the President of the Jidousha-rouren* (Nissan-jidousha no seisui), Tokyo: Ryokufu Publishing, 2012, pp. 13–14.

leftist *Bunkai* under *Souhyou*, a second union, Nissan-*rouso*, was launched on 30 August 1953.[40] On 23 January 1955, the unions of sales agencies and suppliers were unified with Nissan-*rouso* and jointly launched the *Jidousha-rouren* (which became Nissan-*rouren*, the Federation of All Nissan and General Workers' Unions, on 1 January 1989).[41]

In 1960, Shioji joined the newly launched Trade Union Course of Harvard University.[42] There, he came to know prominent American trade union leaders, including Walter Reuther, president of the United Auto Workers (UAW).[43] Shioji travelled around the US in his Nissan Bluebird, visiting plants, trade union colleagues, and local authorities in order to understand the country. This journey added nearly 30 thousand kilometres to his Bluebird's odometer.[44] His strong connections with UAW leaders were vital for Shioji in becoming one of the most influential union leaders in the Japanese automobile sector. After finishing his course at Harvard in 1961, Shioji returned to Yokohama and was elected president of Nissan-*rouso*. Shioji was also elected as president of *Jidousha-rouren*, a post in which he remained until February 1986. His strong leadership and wealth gave him a controversial reputation as a "labour aristocrat,"[45] and, next to the "emperor" Kawamata, he was nicknamed the "shadow emperor."[46] Critics such as Garrahan and Stewart described Japanese industrial relations as "unhealthy," labelling Nissan's arrival in Britain as "radical changes of Sunderland's local political economy" and

[40] Nissan-*rouren* http://www.ngu.or.jp/soshiki/history/. Accessed on 23 October 2019.

[41] Nissan, 1983, pp. 245–246; Nissan-*rouren* http://www.ngu.or.jp/soshiki/history/. Accessed on 23 October 2019.

[42] Shioji, 2012, pp. 79–90.

[43] Ibid., pp. 80–82; Sato, 2000, p. 106.

[44] Shioji, 2012, pp. 82–87.

[45] Ryo Takasugi, *Labour Aristocrant* (roudou-kizoku), Tokyo: Kodansha, 1986. Shioji was known to own a yacht, drove a Nissan Z, and rarely hesitated to hide his private wealth, questioning why it was wrong for a union leader to sail on a yacht and enjoy (expensive) drinks in Ginza.

[46] A majority of Japanese analysts, biased on the management side, have criticised Shioji's dominant leadership as an abuse of power. Noriaki Kawakatsu, *Nissan's 2300 Secret Files; Seven years' war of a manager against the "absolute power"* (Nissan-jidosha gokuhi file 2300) Tokyo: President, 2018; Uesugi, 2001, pp. 52–56, 137–142.

commenting that Nissan would find Thatcherite anti-union approaches "comfortable,"[47] an issue that is discussed in Chapter 6.

Based on his successful leadership in the Nissan group, Shioji took the lead in internationalising Japanese trade unions in the automobile sector.[48] On 3 October 1972, he launched the Confederation of Japan Automobile Workers' Unions (*Jodousha-souren,* JAW), which unified the unions of major Japanese manufacturers and suppliers.[49] With 500 thousand member workers, the JAW became the third-largest union in Japan after the textile and steel sectors. In July the same year, Shioji was elected as one of the vice presidents of the ICFTU. The JAW joined the ICFTU in November 1979.[50]

5 US Plant Project

Nissan's exports to the US in the post-war period started in June 1958. Nissan Motor Corporation in the USA was launched in Los Angeles in September 1960.[51] The two presidents of Nissan USA were Yutaka Katayama, the legendary chief developer of the Nissan/Datsun Z, and Takashi Ishihara. Ishihara was a rugby player who had graduated from Tohoku University and joined Nissan in 1937. Confident in being Yoshisuke Ayukawa's disciple,[52] Ishihara never hid his ambition to become Nissan's president by his 40s,[53] which he eventually accomplished

[47] Philip Garrahan and Paul Stewart, *The Nissan Enigma: Flexibility at Work in a Local Economy*, London: Mansell Publishing, 1992, pp. 1–5.

[48] Suzuki, 2015a, pp. 29–34.

[49] JAW http://www.jaw.or.jp/intro/intro8.html. Accessed on 23 October 2019.

[50] Ibid.

[51] Nissan, 1975, pp. 156–157.

[52] The name Nissan Motor originated in June 1934. Ayukawa was the owner of a metal casting firm in Tobata, Fukuoka of Kyushu, which later became Hitachi Metals. During the late 1930s, Ayukawa became one of the three influential Japanese officials (the others were Nobusuke Kishi—prime minister after the war—and Yosuke Mastuoka) ruling Manchuria.

[53] Sato, 2012, p. 40.

two decades later and launched the British plant project in 1980.[54] He had long served Nissan in exports and accounting.[55]

For a long period, Japan enjoyed a fixed exchange rate of 360 yen/dollar, which kept export costs low and favoured Japan's export drive. The sudden uncertainty caused by the Nixon shock of August 1971 and the end of the Bretton Woods system made Nissan consider alternative methods. The US plant project soon came to the fore. The American trade unions did not miss their chance and persuaded Nissan's—and Japanese car assemblers'—union leader Shioji that Japanese exports would inevitably lead to a Japan-US automobile conflict and that Nissan must launch a US plant before the conflict flared up. The launch would not only prevent such a problem but also enable Nissan to win respect from American consumers.[56] Shioji sketched out a plan and submitted it to Kawamata, who initially hesitated because the project imposed a heavy financial burden on Nissan.[57] In 1973, Kawamata named Tadahiro Iwakoshi his successor and himself became chairman of Nissan. Iwakoshi gave the go-ahead to the US project, while Kawamata avoided making internal decisions and focused on his new role of externally representing the firm. Kawamata was named vice president of *Keidanren* in 1972. This became the first case of a leader from the automobile sector becoming a leader of *Keidanren* because it had long been ruled by leaders from the steel industry.

For Iwakoshi, the US project was his pragmatic strategy for overcoming the ever-dominant leader, Toyota. Because Toyota's domestic market share was almost insurmountable, Iwakoshi aimed to gain a structural advantage in the world's largest market and then transfer profits back from the US to Japan in order to compete.[58] Although Toyota maintained its top production and sales records in Japan, it was not

[54] See Sect. 6 of the next chapter.

[55] Shioji, 2012, p. 214. PM Thatcher recalled her visit to Japan in September 1982 and pointed out that one clue to Japan's industrial success was its industrialists having had earlier careers in engineering. In contrast, she characterised British management as being limited to administration and accountancy; Margaret Thatcher, *The Downing Street Years*, London: HarperCollins, 1993, p. 496. Ironically, her 'favourite' counterpart, Ishihara, had the latter background.

[56] Sato, 2012, pp. 50–52.

[57] Ibid.

[58] Ibid.; Sato, 2000, p. 107.

a company that was willing to fight above its weight and was overly conscientious in making major decisions. Whereas a Japanese saying describes carefulness as "tapping a stone bridge before crossing (*ishibashi wo tataite wataru*)," Toyota would "tap the bridge *without* crossing."[59] If successful, a Nissan plant in the US would give Nissan an incomparable advantage over Toyota, whose continuously large amount of exports from Japan would face a severe reaction from the American public because compared to Nissan, it refused to make a positive contribution to the American economy. In the spring of 1976, Iwakoshi sent vice president Sadamichi Sasaki and export managing director Masataka Okuma to the US. Okuma was a former banker of the Industrial Bank of Japan who had been sent to Nissan, similar to Kawamata's career path. Soon after their visit, a feasibility study team was secretly launched and sent to the US.[60]

However, Nissan's immediate and "real" rival in the US soon proved to be not Toyota but Honda. The Nissan team encountered a rumour in the US that Honda had employed a consultant and launched a feasibility study in the same year.[61] Owing to its pride as the pioneer of Japanese assemblers' overseas expansion, Nissan could not simply lose face and be overtaken by a mere motorcycle assembler.[62] The Nissan team was somewhat relieved to discover that Honda was seeking a motorcycle plant. Nonetheless, the worries were not dissipated because Honda's pragmatic plan was to start with a small-scale motorcycle plant and then step it up into a full-scale automobile plant in the following years. Honda's reputation in the USA had grown rapidly, thanks to the Honda Civic CVCC engine of 1972. The Civic was the first to comply with the Muskie Law of emission controls.

Nissan could not waste time idling but launch a plant immediately and restore its fame. The oil shock of 1973 added further pressure for Japanese assemblers to reduce exports from Japan. The Nissan team rapidly concluded its study and recommended sites in Missouri, Kansas City, and St. Louis. Iwakoshi himself visited the sites in the spring of 1977.[63] The project was now awaiting the final approval, but it never

[59] Shioji, 2012, p. 207.

[60] Sato, 2012, p. 52.

[61] Sato, 2000, p. 107.

[62] See Sect. 3 of this chapter.

[63] Sato, 2012, p. 52.

came. It came only under Iwakoshi's successor, Ishihara, in 1980. Nissan's strategy started to weave and change lanes. In contrast, Honda swiftly launched its Marysville plant in Ohio and produced motorcycles beginning in September 1979, soon launching a feasibility study for automobile assembly.[64] The first Honda Accord rolled out in Marysville in 1982 as the first Japanese car made in the USA.

[64] Sato, 2000, p. 94.

CHAPTER 3

The British Car Industry and Anglo-Japanese Relations in the Post-War Period

Abstract Britain enjoyed the world's largest car exporter status in the immediate post-war years. But its car manufacturing faced increased competition with French, Italian, German, and, last but not least, Japanese. While exports to the US were sustained, those to the EEC were hampered with high tariff walls. British cars were exported instead to the Commonwealth countries and the EFTA, but again faced competition with the Germans and the Japanese. The oil shock of 1973 hit British assembler the hardest, due to a double kick caused by Britain's EC membership and tariff-free imports from the continent. While limiting Japanese car imports, the idea of inviting Japanese plants into Britain emerged in Whitehall.

Keywords British car industry · Commonwealth · European Free Trade Association · European Economic Community · Customs union · Tariffs · Voluntary export restriction

1 Introduction

This chapter summarises the post-war British car industry and discusses the queen's first visit to Japan in 1975 as a turning point in Anglo-Japanese relations, in terms not only of formal diplomacy but also of

H. Suzuki, *Japanese Investment and British Trade Unionism*,
New Directions in East Asian History,
https://doi.org/10.1007/978-981-15-9058-0_3

changing the climate for Japanese investments in Britain. Owen described the post-war British automobile industry as a history of decline and a shift from empire to Europe.[1] British manufacturers had gradually lost their competitive edge both overseas and domestically during the 1960s and at the same time faced American and French assemblers launching plants in Britain. While avoiding competition in the EEC market, British exports were headed towards the Commonwealth countries. The Labour government urged British assemblers to merge under British Leyland (BL). The oil crisis and Britain's EC membership in 1973 added further challenges. Market demand dropped sharply, but German, French, and Italian rivals uncompromisingly made tariff-free inroads into Britain. To compete with Europeans, Nissan began to seek an assembly plant in the enlarged EC, focusing on Ireland, Belgium, and Britain. The Heath administration and the Wilson/Callaghan governments were reluctant to openly invite Japanese industry into Britain because exports to Japan were hampered by Japanese import tariffs and non-tariff barriers, and Britain therefore had no advantage. Furthermore, British public opinion viewed Japan as a hostile invader that would cause unemployment. The SMMT and JAMA agreed upon voluntary export restriction (VER) in 1975. Conservative Party leader Margaret Thatcher proposed a different solution, deciding to invite Japanese car assemblers into Britain, a process that is not fully covered by the current literature including her own memoirs.

2 British Leyland, the "British Disease," and EC Membership

After the Second World War ended, the British car industry became the world's largest car exporter. The American market was the most favoured outlet until French, Italian, and German rivals increased their sales. British exports to the continent expanded modestly compared to those headed to the US. High tariff barriers prevented British assemblers from exporting to the EEC; thus, they instead targeted Commonwealth countries. However, British exports also suffered there due to competition with American, Japanese, and European rivals. Japanese car exports

[1] Owen, 1999.

to the Commonwealth started to diminish British exports.[2] In other words, Japanese exports urged Britain's shift from the Commonwealth to Europe. The shift was welcomed by Japan for two reasons. The first reason was that Japanese exports to Australia and New Zealand would face less hostility from British rivals. The second reason was Britain's future EC membership and its expected role as a gateway to Europe.

British car assemblers merged under BL during the 1960s in pursuit of a scale advantage. Leyland Motors merged with Standard-Triumph in 1960. Austin, Morris, and MG had already merged under BMC, and Jaguar joined the group in 1966, forming British Motor Holdings (BMH). The next year, Leyland purchased Rover. Under the Labour government's initiative, Leyland-Triumph-Rover and BMH were unified in 1968 to form a national champion, British Leyland Motor Corporation (BLMC), which ranked as the fourth-largest assembler in Europe. However, BLMC failed to improve sales and production. A lack of investment led to the development of less attractive models and further reduced sales, which resulted in further reductions in investment. Trade unions rigidly demanded increased wages and went on strikes when these demands were rejected. Production costs failed to decrease, and assembly halted frequently. The situation came to be known as the "British disease."

The Conservative government under Edward Heath did not make a fundamental change to the Labour government's policies. Rolls-Royce (RR) was nationalised in 1971 due to its financial crisis caused by the costly RB211 jet engine project.[3] In 1972, British automobile assembly reached its peak of 1.8 million units of annual output, but the amount decreased to less than half that number in the following decade.[4] Vickers took over RR's car assembly in 1973. After Britain joined the EC in January 1973, the home market was heavily penetrated by imports from

[2] Increased exports to the Commonwealth gave advantages to Japan, Germany, and the US but not Britain. During the negotiation for accession, PM Harold Wilson stressed that the EEC was enormously more powerful than Britain and that Japan had surpassed Britain in some aspects of the race. Stephen Wall, *The Official History of Britain and the European Community; Vol. II From Rejection to Referendum, 1963–1975*. Abingdon: Routledge, 2012, p. 48; Melissa Pine, *Harold Wilson and Europe; Pursuing Britain's Membership of the European Community*. London: I.B. Tauris, 2012, pp. 55–56.

[3] Keith Hayward, *International Collaboration in Civil Aerospace*, St. Martin's Press, 1986, p. 139.

[4] Mountfield, 2007a, p. 108.

Germany, France, and Italy. Nearly half of the registered cars in Britain became foreign brands.[5] In contrast, BL was not able to take full advantage of the tariff-free EC market, and Britain's trade balance worsened. The first oil shock drove the situation from bad to worse. Even worse, Japanese manufacturers started to expand their exports to the EC because exports to the USA had faced strong criticism and pressure after the first oil crisis. Britain was not far from becoming the worst loser in the automobile sector. BL brands suffered losses in domestic sales and were nationalised in 1975 under the Labour government. The later Tory leader Margaret Thatcher criticised such policies because, in her view, nationalisation further weakened competitiveness. In her memoirs, Thatcher wrote, "[The] state should not be in business. [...] Decisions about investment are made according to criteria quite different from those [...] in the private sector. [...] State-owned businesses can never function as proper businesses. [...] The spur is just not there."[6]

The Japanese stock brokerage firm Daiwa Securities, which had close ties with Nissan, issued a report in 1972 and concluded that Ireland, Belgium, and the Netherlands were the best locations for foreign direct investment in the enlarged EC. This report caused alarm in the DTI. However, the Heath administration still hesitated to actively invite Japanese investment.[7] Heath's decision was not totally wrong because tariffs on Japanese cars would increase owing to Britain's EC membership, and the pound/yen exchange rate added to increases in the prices of imported Japanese cars.[8] However, the DTI's fear soon became a reality. Nissan immediately launched a knock-down plant in Ireland, importing Nissan Sunny component kits from Japan and assembling them effortlessly.[9] In April 1973, the first Sunny rolled out in Ireland.

Britain suddenly faced a risk that similar plants in any other member state would export Japanese cars to the British market without import tariffs. This would further reduce BL's market share. Even worse, such

[5] TNA, FV22/133, Brocklebank-Fowler to Joseph, 12 February 1980; TNA, BT 177/2813, Cammell to Mountfield, Annex A "Inward investment: Nissan," 14 July 1980.

[6] Thatcher, 1993, p. 677.

[7] TNA, FV22/15, McKenzie to Moody, 8 June 1972.

[8] Nissan, 1975, p. 398.

[9] Suzuki, 2015a, p. 23; Nissan, 1975, p. 162.

plants would not be bound by rules to purchase British-made components, further damaging national interests. Nissan reinforced its exports to the EC by launching a branch in Germany with 100% Nissan capital and coordinated Nissan's overall operations in Europe.[10] Japanese plants in the EC had to be settled in Britain before other member states would take their chances.[11] However, British public opinion viewed Japan as a hostile invader that caused unemployment. The negative image was coupled with memories of British prisoners of war receiving inhumane treatment during the war.[12] Any contact with the Japanese had to be highly confidential and avoid public attention. This mood was changed by the queen's visit to Japan in 1975.

3 The Queen's Visit to Japan

The queen's first visit to Japan in May 1975 marked a turning point in Anglo-Japanese relations. The Showa emperor had been deprived of the Order of the Garter because of the outbreak of the Second World War. Shortly before the Pearl Harbor attack on 8 December 1941, Japanese forces launched an attack against the British in Kota Bharu, Malaysia. Two days later, Japanese navy fighters and bombers sank HMS Prince of Wales and HMS Repulse. The inhumane treatment of surrendering British soldiers and civilians was reported back to Britain and resulted in a negative image of Japan in the post-war period.[13]

In such a hostile atmosphere, prince Akihito, who would later become emperor from 1989 to 2019, visited Britain in June 1953. Prince Akihito participated in the queen's coronation ceremony. His visit was the first occasion for the Japanese royal family to reconcile with the new queen and opened a new era for improved Anglo-Japanese relations. The prince

[10] Nissan, 1975, p. 162.

[11] TNA, FV22/15, McKenzie to Moody, 8 June 1972.

[12] Hitoshi, Suzuki, Yu Suzuki, and Yoshimi Igawa, "Japan and the European Union," in Finn Laursen (ed.), *Oxford Encyclopedia of European Union Politics*, Oxford: Oxford University Press, 2019; Naoko Kumagai, "Japan's Reconciliation in the Issue of Comfort Women with the Netherlands and South Korea: Pragmatic and Reflective Reconciliation," *Journal of European Integration History*, 25(1), 2019; Suzuki, 2015a, pp. 38–42; John Dower, *War Without Mercy: Race and Power in the Pacific War*, New York: Pantheon Books, 1986, pp. 33–73.

[13] As a former DoI/DTI official Mountfield pointed out that the question of wartime memory was already not a significant factor in the 1980s. Mountfield, 2007a, p. 110.

visited the North East to pay tribute to Lord Armstrong, who had contributed to Japan's industrialisation and modernisation before the war.[14] However, the Japanese shipbuilding industry had rapidly expanded and exported ships to the US and Europe, causing serious damage to its rivals and increasing unemployment in the North East throughout the 1960s and 1970s.[15] It was only in the 1970s that Anglo-Japanese relations entered into a period of rapprochement.

In April 1970, prince Charles visited Japan. The prince visited the Japan World Exposition in Osaka. In turn, the Showa emperor visited Britain in October the next year. The visit was part of the emperor's visit to seven European countries within eighteen days, led directly by foreign minister Takeo Fukuda—later PM from 1976 to 1978—as the head of protocol. The emperor visited Denmark on 27 and 28 September and then spent the next four days in Belgium, 2–4 October in France, 5–7 October in Britain, the next two days in the Netherlands, one day in Switzerland, and finally 11 to 13 October in Germany. The intense visits were described by Fukuda as "the emperor crowning Japan's rapprochement with European countries which had been distant due to the war."[16] The queen's visit to Japan was prepared as a courtesy return call.

The queen and the duke of Edinburgh paid their first visit to Japan in May 1975. Arriving on 7 May, the queen and the duke of Edinburgh received an audience with the Showa emperor. During parades and short visits, the queen took time to speak with the crowd, leaving a strong impression that the royal family was open to the public. The decade-long experience of trade conflicts had made the Japanese feel that they were sometimes treated unfairly by Western countries, but the queen appeared to oppose such images.[17] The queen was welcomed by enthusiastic crowds during her six-day visit, with the numbers of those

[14] Conte-Helm, 1989, pp. 128–135.

[15] Ibid., p. 128.

[16] Hitoshi Suzuki, "Japan's Relations with the FRG and the GDR, 1966–1981 (*Tou-zai-doitsu to nihon 1966–1981-nen*)," in Yuichi Hosoya (ed.), *The History of Post-War Asian-European Relations* (Sengo Asia-Europe kankei-shi), Tokyo: Keio University Press, 2015c, p. 204.

[17] Christopher Soames—the vice president of the commission from Britain and in charge of external relations—was an exception who was aware of the necessity of not treating the Japanese unfairly; Hitoshi Suzuki, "Negotiating the Japan-EC Trade Conflict: The Role and Presence of the European Commission, the Council of Ministers, and Business Groups in Europe and Japan, 1970–1982," in Claudia Hiepel (ed.), *Europe in a Globalising World:*

assembled to see her estimated at 342,400 in Tokyo, 248,000 in Kyoto, and 776,000 total.[18] Shortly before the queen's visit, department stores in Tokyo launched British exhibitions, and 300 million yen worth of goods were imported from Britain. British "soft power" in Japan was restored, giving an impression that Britain was the friendliest to Japan among the European countries.

The impression that the queen made on Japanese businessmen was concrete and focused. On 8 May, the queen gave a speech to three hundred top Japanese business leaders.[19] Most of them were prominent executives of Japanese multinational corporations affiliated with *Keidanren*. Referring to King James I and Tokugawa *shogun*, the queen praised the legacies of the history of Anglo-Japanese relations and referred to the latest state of bilateral trade. Although Britain was Japan's tenth-largest trade partner, and although bilateral trade had grown 6.5 times more than its level a decade earlier, Japanese exports amounted to 1,529 million dollars, while those of Britain (solely) amounted to 878 million. The queen referred to made-in-Japan products and their popularity in Britain, emphasising that in addition to academics, artists, and diplomats, businessmen had contributed the most to Anglo-Japanese relations. It was a surprise, and a welcome one, to Japanese businessmen that the queen's message was concrete but not hostile to Japan and its pride in its exported products. Her message was interpreted to mean that Britain welcomed Japanese investments.

There was hardly any disagreement on welcoming the queen except for a minor railway delay and a religious arrangement to visit the Ise shrine (*Ise-jinjya*). The Japan National Railway (JNR) failed to escort the queen on the bullet train *shinkansen* from Tokyo to Kyoto due to a strike by the railway workers but barely saved face by securing the trip back. The *shinkansen* heading back to Tokyo unusually braked at the bridge over the *Fujikawa* River so that the queen and the duke of Edinburgh could admire the view of Mount Fuji from the best vantage point.[20] Japanese lawyers intervened in the queen's visit to western Japan by making the

Global Challenges and European Responses in the "long" 1970s, Baden-Baden: Nomos, 2014a, p. 218.

[18] *Asahi-shinbun*, 13 May 1975.

[19] *Asahi-shinbun*, 9 May 1975.

[20] *Asahi-shinbun*, 13 May 1975.

point that the queen could not officially "worship" at the *shinto* shrine because of the religious neutrality defined in the constitution.[21] The queen "visited" the shrine on 11 May.

The two incidents turned out to be a mere storm in a teacup. The Japanese public felt that Anglo-Japanese relations had been restored and strengthened by the visit. However, the British media viewed the situation from a different perspective. The *Daily Telegraph* reported that the only British car hitting the Japanese streets was the queen's RR, in sharp contrast to the number of Japanese cars in Britain.[22] However, the queen had also referred to the automobile sector during the visit, emphasising that the British and Japanese cherished shared habits of gardening and driving cars on the left side.[23] The lights were green, at least in Japanese eyes, for Japanese assemblers to fully commit themselves in Britain.

4 The Labour Government's Response to the Japanese Challenge

While Japanese car exports to Britain and the EC steadily increased after the first oil shock, provoking further hostility, the Labour governments of Harold Wilson and James Callaghan were determined not to directly intervene and restrict car imports. In their view, the British components industry was performing well in exports.[24] Although Britain's foreign trade balance of assembled cars had fallen into deficit, direct and official restrictions on imports would violate EC laws.[25] Retaliation from Japan and other EC member states had to be avoided. Therefore, the Labour government welcomed the voluntary agreement between the British and Japanese motor car industries to restrict Japanese exports. The SMMT and JAMA reached the VER agreement, which stipulated that the Japanese market share in Britain was "not to exceed the level

[21] *Asahi-shinbun*, 27 March, 30 March, 12 May 1975.

[22] *The Daily Telegraph*, 9 May 1975.

[23] *Asahi-shinbun*, 12 May 1975.

[24] TNA, PREM 16/2272, Dell to Varley, 28 November 1977.

[25] TNA, BT241/2479, Daniels to Harris, 7 October 1975.

of the previous year," in September 1975.[26] As a result, the Japanese share was capped at 11%. The prices of Japanese cars soared due to the ensuing shortage, and although Japanese exports were capped, Japanese assemblers profited from the agreement.[27]

In 1975—the same year the queen visited Japan—the Labour government issued a report on the British automobile industry. The Central Policy Staff pointed out five conclusions.[28] The first was a forecast that the European automobile market would continuously experience intensified competition until the mid-1980s. The second was an analysis of British manufacturers. The British had failed to make the right management decisions, resulting in decreased competitiveness and production over-capacity. The third was lack of quality, worsened labour–management relations, low productivity, and over-staffed plants. The production output per person had fallen to nearly half that of plants on the continent. The fourth was a concrete forecast of the sector. If productivity did not improve rapidly, the sector's trade balance would worsen by 1 billion pounds by 1985. This would result in 275 thousand jobs lost in Britain, including jobs in the assembly, components, and related sectors. Finally, the reasons for this grave and discouraging reality were attributable to both British labour and management and the government, as the BL stockholder, must actively propose reform of the sector.

The report further investigated details of the British automobile sector and targeted industrial relations as the major problem. Wage bargaining and disputes among the unions were identified as causes of halting production. Disputes in the automobile sector occurred ten times more frequently than in other sectors, and nearly 60% of production losses were due to labour disputes. The content of the report soon proved correct. Contrary to its constituents' expectations, the Labour government failed to improve labour–management relations. The winter of discontent

[26] TNA, BT 241/2478, 9 August 1975; TNA, PREM 16/2272, Owen to Secretary of State for Trade, 22 December 1977. As former ambassador, Sir Hugh criticised the British assemblers not making efforts during this time to rationalise; Cortazzi, 1998, p. 163.

[27] Ibid.

[28] MRCW (Modern Records Centre, University of Warwick Library), MSS 292D 617 1, Report by the Central Policy Staff, The Future of the British Car Industry, November 1975. In the same year, the Ryder report also pointed out lack of investment and negative labour practices as reasons for BL's slump.

occurred in late 1978, opening the way for Thatcher's "radical" neoliberal claims to win popularity.

5 The CBI's Japan policy and Margaret Thatcher

When the SMMT and JAMA agreed upon Japan's VER on car exports in 1975,[29] the other sectors in Britain accepted this agreement with mixed reactions. The majority of CBI members criticised Japanese exports as aggressive and damaging to British manufacturers. However, such views were not reflected in the CBI's Japan policy. The CBI adopted policies based on the experience of British firms that jointly collaborated with the Japanese. It was not until 1982 that the CBI openly debated whether Japanese exports were a threat at its annual conference. The CBI's Japan policy closely echoed the policies of the Conservative Party and especially its new leader, Margaret Thatcher.

The CBI policies were prepared by issue-based committees under the confederation president. Policies were then taken to the Council, where decisions were made by the president and the heads of the Commissions. The Overseas Commission was in charge of policies concerning Japan and its industry. This decision-making structure allowed greater respect for the voices of British firms that launched collaborations with Japanese counterparts,[30] with RR and Kawasaki in aero and marine engines[31] and Rover-Triumph and Honda in the car sector at the forefront. These firms, having experienced Japanese competition elsewhere, chose to collaborate rather than trying to drive Japanese firms out of Britain. The CBI's Japan policy was to welcome investments in Britain and to learn Japanese competitiveness through collaboration.[32] Protectionist methods were rejected.[33] In turn, the CBI requested liberalisation of the Japanese market, not only in manufactured goods but also in the banking

[29] See the previous section.

[30] Hitoshi Suzuki, "Post-Brexit Britain, the EU, and Japan: The Car Industry, the Aero Sector, and Military Cooperation," forthcoming.

[31] Ibid.

[32] MRCW, WOO 996, "CBI Publications; International Trade Policy for the 1980s" May 1980; MRCW, MSS.200/C/2014 Box343, meeting of 18 May 1983.

[33] MRCW, MSS.200/C/2014 Box343, meeting of 18 May 1982.

and insurance sectors.[34] It was crucial for the CBI to avoid protectionism in fear of retaliation from Japan or other EC member states.[35]

Margaret Thatcher, who became the Conservative Party leader in 1975, positioned herself in close alignment with CBI policies. Upon an invitation from the Liberal Democratic Party (LDP), Thatcher flew to Tokyo in April 1977. She visited Canon's Shimomaruko plant, Meiji-McVitie Biscuits in Odawara, and Nissan Zama. Kawamata, as Nissan's president, showed Thatcher around the Zama plant himself without the slightest sense that she would take advantage of this invitation five years later as a bargaining chip.[36] Zama was one of Nissan's most advanced plants, with the highest ratio of automation achieved by reducing the number of workers and installing robots. Nissan's trade unions became one of the first Japanese unions to debate robotisation and challenged such changes.[37] However, Nissan executives, represented by Ishihara as the prominent anti-union man, stated in front of Nissan employees that they aimed to realise plants without workers to the greatest extent possible.[38] Ishihara went further, emphasising that this solution would reduce costs such as holiday and overtime pay.[39] Zama had become a test bench of robotisation and was visited by numerous heads of state and prominent politicians. Thatcher was satisfied with her observation that "clamorous" workers and union members were being replaced by mute robots, and Nissan became her favourite example.[40] She was convinced that Japanese production automation and less militant trade unionism should be copied in Britain.[41]

[34] MRCW, MSS.200/C/3/INT/1/6, 10 September 1980.

[35] It was only at the Annual Conference of 1982 that aggressive Japanese exports were openly criticised by CBI members. MRCW, MSS.200/C/2014 Box343, meeting of 26 May 1982.

[36] See Sect. 14 of the next chapter.

[37] See the Sect. 9 of the next chapter.

[38] Sato, 2012, p. 132.

[39] Ibid.

[40] Garrahan and Stewart, 1992, pp. 5–6.

[41] Suzuki, 2015a, p. 45; Sato, 2012, pp. 305–306; Cortazzi, 1998, p. 228.

6 Power Change in Nissan

Shortly after Thatcher visited Japan, the president of Nissan changed. At the stockholder meeting held on 29 June 1977, Takashi Ishihara was announced as the new president, succeeding Tadahiro Iwakoshi. Katsuji Kawamata remained as the chairman. Ishihara had challenged Kawamata, but in vain, when the latter had been a candidate for the presidency in 1957.[42] The rivalry between the two never faded because Ishihara was sent from Ginza to the US shortly thereafter.[43] Whether Kawamata had intended to name Ishihara as his successor was not made clear, but it was known that he had considered Sadamichi Sasaki as an alternative up to the final moment.[44] Sasaki left Nissan shortly thereafter and became president of Subaru in October 1978, which enjoyed a sales boost with its successful four-wheel-drive vehicles under his presidency. Kawamata underestimated Ishihara's possible desire for revenge and the latter's stubborn anti-union attitude, which could threaten Shioji's leadership. Shioji, as union leader, had cooperated with Kawamata throughout his presidency, and together they had created the foundation for Nissan's success in the post-war era.[45] In contrast, Ishihara was as hostile to the unions as Margaret Thatcher was.[46]

As the new president, Ishihara announced his aim as "global 10," targeting a 10% global share for Nissan. In August 1977, Ishihara became vice president of JAMA. He was then responsible for negotiating bilateral VERs for Japanese car exports. Nearly ignoring the US—Nissan's largest overseas market—Ishihara chose instead to visit Europe. In May 1979, he visited Italy to meet Giovanni Agnelli, owner of the Fiat group. Ishihara

[42] See the Sect. 2 in Chapter 2.

[43] Ishihara lived in Tokyo during his presidency of Nissan-USA and sometimes visited the US; Mountfield, 2007a, p. 115. It was a leadership in opposition to that of the other president, Katayama, who had moved to the US, thoroughly studied the market, and won fans around the country as "Mr. K," the father of the Datsun Z. Ishihara argued for locating Nissan-USA's headquarters in New York, but Katayama opposed this suggestion and located it in Los Angeles for the sake of importing facilities from Japan. Owing to Katayama's efforts, Nissan surpassed Volkswagen in 1975 and became the largest importer in the US. When Ishihara became president of Nissan in 1977, Katayama resigned his post; Inoue, 2019, pp. 81–84.

[44] Kawakatsu, 2018, p. 61; Sato, 2012, p. 54.

[45] See the Sects. 2–4 in Chapter 2.

[46] Suzuki, 2015a, p. 165.

had intended to approach Alfa Romeo, then suffering a financial crisis. The deal was first favoured by the Italian government but was soon toned down due to pressure from the French government.[47]

Such a negative reaction in Europe never distracted Ishihara from his focus on the EC market. In the same year, Ishihara had also approached the French national manufacturer Renault but was carefully declined.[48] Ishihara recalled in his memoirs that his emphasis on the EC market came partly from his experience during the 1960s, when he had to concentrate on the American market and missed the chance to offer a challenge in Europe.[49] Kawamata came to regret that he had named Ishihara, questioning why Ishihara had learned few lessons during his career in the US. Ishihara's aggressive overseas strategy could be understood as his decision not solely as Nissan's president but also as president of JAMA as of May 1980. He was urged to show a model case for other Japanese assemblers and was in a hurry for achievements. Ishihara chose to abandon the brand name Datsun and unified it with that of Nissan, also fuelling controversy over Nissan's overseas strategy.[50]

Nissan's executive board soon became divided between those who wanted to prioritise the US plant project and those who wished to focus on Britain and the EC. The former group was led by Kawamata, firmly supported by his trade union counterpart, Ichiro Shioji. Shioji had been persuaded by the leaders of the UAW to become a supporter of Nissan's US plant project.[51] Opposing Kawamata and Shioji was the group focusing on Britain and the EC, led by Ishihara. Ishihara concentrated his efforts on weakening the trade unions, phrasing this goal as "correcting and normalising labour–management relations."[52] In 1978, a thirty-seven-year-old man with strong anti-union sentiment was

[47] TNA, BT177/2813, Discussion Paper, Cammell to Mountfield, 14 July 1980.

[48] Shioji, 2012, p. 7. Ironically, Nissan was later saved by Renault, and therefore by the French government, from its financial crisis in 1999.

[49] Kawakatsu, 2018, p. 60.

[50] This decision was criticised by analysts because the change in brand caused confusion among consumers. The name Datsun—owing to president Katayama's efforts in the US—was better known than Nissan. Katayama left Nissan shortly after Ishihara became president.

[51] Shioji, 2012, pp. 177–181; Sato, 2012, p. 50.

[52] Takashi Ishihara, *My Career and Nissan* (Watashi to Nissan-jidousha), Tokyo: Nikkei, 2002, pp. 162–169, 202. Ishihara's career was reviewed in a *Nikkei* newspaper article,

named the manager of the section in charge of external affairs—liaising between Nissan, government ministries, and LDP politicians—in Nissan's Public Relations Division.[53] Noriaki Kawakatsu joined Nissan in 1967 and moved from the production division to public relations in 1975. In 1979, under Ishihara's presidency, he launched a secret task group of eight men to collect scandals on Shioji and, eventually, force his resignation.[54] Whether Nissan would launch a plant in the US or Europe/Britain became a subject of uncompromising battle among the executives and the unions.

Rather than taking over an old and less competitive BL plant, Ishihara sought a green-field plant. This decision was based on advice from Datsun UK.[55] It was a costly option, and the risks were high. Nissan's aggressive overseas strategy was based on its ambition to overtake its impeccable rival, Toyota. Toyota dominated the Japanese market as the largest manufacturer, but in terms of exports, Nissan had advanced earlier and was more successful.[56] MITI and MOFA wished to see Japanese manufacturers operate plants in overseas markets instead of flooding those markets with exports from Japan so that trade conflicts could be eased and Japan's leverage in trade negotiations could increase.

"My Career (*watashi no rirekisho*)," and the contents were later published as his memoirs. He added a chapter on trade unions and emphasised their negative role.

[53] Kawakatsu, 2018, pp. 20, 70–73. In his memoirs, published in 2018, well after Shoiji's death in 2013, Kawakatsu recalled his team's 'voluntary' war against Shioji as a "group of ants hunting down an elephant"; Ibid., p. 11. Recruited personally by him, the team members came from the production and public relations divisions and were all solidly anti-Shioji; Ibid., pp. 71–72. He claimed that, similar to Kawakatsu's own team, Shioji and his unions operated an "owl troop" in Nissan plants and activated a "Gestapo"—in Kawakatsu's term—among the executives to sniff out any scandal among anti-union executives and occasionally to violently sabotage them; Ibid., pp. 38–43, 88–101. To counter such people Kawakatsu "had to choose more or less similar methods"; Ibid., p. 101. His memoirs are based on the files that his team collected, which were information gained through informal contacts with Nissan workers and executives.

[54] Ibid., pp. 70–73. Information centred around Shioji's money and girlfriends. Ibid., pp. 75–85. Kawakatsu claimed that his team and its secret mission were based on his own decision owing to his sense of justice and wrath and *not* on president Ishihara's orders. Kawakatsu's exchanges with Miyuki Furukawa, former president of Nissan Australia but purged by Shioji, were decisive in Kawakatsu's judgement that Shioji should be purged; Ibid., pp. 92–101.

[55] TNA, BT177/2813, Discussion Paper, Cammell to Mountfield, 14 July 1980.

[56] Sato, 2012, p. 22; Shimokawa, 1994, pp. 111–113.

CHAPTER 4

Negotiations over Financial Assistance and Local Content

Abstract The Labour governments were reluctant to openly welcome the Japanese and providing a gateway into the EC market. Margaret Thatcher arrived as a game-changer, who had visited Japan as the Tory leader and was convinced with Japanese production management and trade unionism. The DTI put priority on high British local content requirements when negotiating with Nissan, using governmental aids as a bargaining chip. The SMMT insisted on the highest possible local contents and required Nissan to equip its plant with engine assembling and R&D centre. The TUC leaders expected new jobs created by Nissan, while member unions and local workers feared further redundancy in BL plants. The largest obstacle was Nissan's internal conflict, not between management and the unions but within management and among the unions.

Keywords Thatcher administration · Department of Trade and Industry · Nissan · Society of Motor Manufacturers and Traders · Trade unions · Local contents · Regional development grant

H. Suzuki, *Japanese Investment and British Trade Unionism*, New Directions in East Asian History,
https://doi.org/10.1007/978-981-15-9058-0_4

1 Introduction

After Thatcher became British PM, the Department of Industry (DoI, from 1983 Department of Trade and Industry, DTI) took charge of arranging local content for assembled motor cars and negotiating financial assistance—the regional development grant (RDG) and selective financial assistance (SFA)—for Nissan. It was solely up to Nissan to decide on the plant location, which will be discussed in the next chapter. Thatcher insisted that Nissan use a very high proportion of British components (up to 80%) because she rightly understood that a high ratio was necessary to persuade the SMMT, the TUC, British public opinion, and, last but not least, the governments of other EC member states that a British-made Nissan vehicle would be a "genuine" homemade product. Nissan's president, Takashi Ishihara, agreed to the 80% goal owing to the DoI/DTI's 'generous' offer of financial support. In February 1984, the DTI and Nissan signed an agreement on local content and financial support. What is relatively unknown is that the negotiations were supported by simultaneous efforts made by British MEPs and civil servants in Brussels, who criticised other member states' protectionism and wished to welcome Japanese foreign direct investment. Such efforts calmed Nissan's fears and made its executives confident in placing a stake in Britain.

2 Thatcher Comes to Power

On 4 May 1979, Margaret Thatcher became PM. By the time her premiership ended, Thatcher had come to be known around the world as the Iron Lady, so named by Mikhail Gorbachev, the woman who confronted the Falkland crisis and led Britain until the Cold War ended. However, in 1979, her main focus was not on foreign policy. Thatcher concentrated on fiscal reforms, monetarism, and the revival of the British economy. Contrary to her image as a firm Euro-sceptic, Thatcher was dedicated to driving forward European integration in her own way, especially through the single market.[1] Along with her neoliberal colleagues, Thatcher looked upon Japanese investment as a source of new jobs, a stimulus to innovation, and, last but not least, an example of modern

[1] Stephen Wall, *The Official History of Britain and the European Community. Vol. III, The Tiger Unleashed, 1975–1985*, Abingdon: Routledge, 2019, pp. 332, 336.

production techniques and labour practices.[2] She maintained her tough line on Japanese exports,[3] which put pressure on the Japanese to invest in Britain instead. As the following chapters describe, more than half of the Japanese plants' outputs—whether in electronics or cars—were exported to the continent. The tiger was unleashed.[4]

Shortly after becoming PM, Thatcher once more visited Japan in June 1979 to participate in the G7 Tokyo summit.[5] She used the occasion to invite Japanese industry to launch plants in Britain or to collaborate with the British. In December the same year, RR and the three Japanese aero firms—Ishikawajima-Harima (after a merger with Nissan's aero section in the millennium year as IHI Aerospace), Kawasaki,[6] and Mitsubishi—signed an agreement to co-develop a jet engine, which later developed into the successful V2500, which equipped the Airbus A320.[7] The Japanese electronics industry launched plants in Wales during the late 1970s.[8] However, still to come was a Japanese car plant in Britain.

In response to Thatcher's invitation, Nissan showed its renewed commitment in Britain, donating 1.5 million pounds (734 million yen) in June to the University of Oxford, from which Thatcher had graduated. The purpose was to launch the Nissan Institute for Japanese Studies with the aim of cultivating knowledge on Japan.[9] The institute became one of the most advanced centres of Japan studies. Nissan also donated one million dollars (267 million yen) to Harvard University for its project of launching a Japanese research centre.[10] Ishihara's emphasis was clearly more on Britain (and Thatcher) than on America, as the donation to Oxford was more than double that to Harvard. Ishihara himself was

[2] Mountfield, 2007a, p. 109.

[3] Laurent Warlouzet, *Governing Europe in a Globalizing World; Neoliberalism and Its Alternatives Following the 1973 Oil Crisis*, Abingdon: Routledge, 2018, p. 80.

[4] Wall, 2019, p. 155.

[5] On her last visit in April 1977; see Sect. 5 of the previous chapter.

[6] Cortazzi, 1998, p. 164.

[7] Hitoshi Suzuki, "Post-Brexit Britain, the EU, and Japan: The Car Industry, the Aero Sector, and Military Cooperation," forthcoming.

[8] See Sect. 9 of this chapter and Sect. 9 in Chapter 6.

[9] Nissan, 1985, p. 377; Nissan, 1983, p. 238.

[10] Nissan, 1985, p. 377.

present at the opening ceremony in Oxford, and lecture courses started in October 1981.[11]

3 The Fraser Tornado and Nissan's US Plant Project

Takashi Ishihara as Nissan's president announced in 1980 his plan to launch plants in the USA and Britain. The year 1980 was symbolic for Japan because it surpassed America's annual production volume of automobiles and became the world's largest producer.[12] In May the same year, Ishihara was promoted to president of JAMA. There was not a moment to lose in reducing exports from Japan and easing foreign pressure. The response from the USA was cold and harsh. Japanese analysts have described the year as the beginning of the end of Nissan's golden era.[13] In his memoirs, trade union leader Shioji described that the choice of Britain instead of the US was the fatal mistake and worsened labour–management relations within Nissan under Ishihara's presidency to "a point of no return."[14] For Shioji, the US was a market of two million Japanese cars per annum, while the British market reached merely 100 thousand.[15] The true priority was crystal clear to Shioji, making him think, "What is bloody wrong with our management?"[16]

On 8 January 1980, Ishihara announced his intention to launch a plant in the USA. The plant would produce Datsun pickup trucks. The announcement ran counter to former president Iwakoshi's carefully prepared plan to assemble passenger cars. Ishihara refused to carry out a plan prepared by Iwakoshi and Shioji and tried instead to rapidly develop his own original idea. The *slight* change was criticised as an inadequate decision of "serving *sushi* for a customer wanting hamburgers" by *Nikkei*

[11] Ibid.

[12] RIETI, vol. 2, 2013, p. 110. Japan's number-one status lasted until 1991, when the US once more surpassed it. In 1990, when the bubble economy was about to die down, Japanese domestic car assembly reached its peak at 13,486,796 units per annum and thereafter decreased.

[13] Uesugi, 2001, p. 155.

[14] Shioji, 2012, p. 236.

[15] Ibid., p. 239.

[16] Ibid.

journalist Sato.[17] The American response to Ishihara's announcement arrived without delay, leaving little ambiguity.

On 28 January 1980, American ambassador Michael Mansfield announced in a press conference that the fuse had been lit in the Japan–US automobile crisis. He openly stated that Toyota and Nissan must follow Honda and immediately launch plants in the USA.[18] In the following February, UAW president Douglas Fraser flew to Tokyo. He had only one issue to pursue: Japanese assemblers should build plants in the US or restrict exports from Japan. Japan welcomed Fraser by arranging talks with PM Masayoshi Ohira, foreign minister Saburo Ooki, MITI minister Yoshitake Sasaki, and minister of labour Takao Fujinami as well as executives of Japanese automobile manufacturers. Shortly after Fraser left Tokyo, MITI asked Toyota and Nissan to launch plants in the US, but executives of those companies carefully declined by saying that "it was taken under consideration."[19]

It was Nissan's trade union leader, Shioji, who invited Fraser to Japan through the connection between the UAW and JAW.[20] Before Fraser's arrival, Shioji advised Ishihara to reject his announcement of manufacturing pickup trucks and return to the "original" plan.[21] Ishihara ignored this advice and told Fraser that he refused to make decisions under political pressure.[22] Ishihara had told the press that American workers required high wages, while their skills were doubtful.[23] Similar negative reports would reach him from the feasibility study team that he sent to Britain in the following years, but Ishihara targeted the Americans. Fraser and Shioji were deeply disappointed by his stubbornness.[24] However, Fraser was satisfied to hear from Honda that it would expand its motorcycle plant in Marysville in May and enter into car assembly.

[17] Sato, 2012, pp. 17, 59.

[18] Ibid., p. 68; Shioji, 2012, p. 196.

[19] Shioji, 2012, p. 198.

[20] Suzuki, 2015, p. 53; Sato, 2012, p. 69; Shioji, 2012, p. 193.

[21] Sato, 2012, pp. 70–71.

[22] Ibid.

[23] Ibid., pp. 56–57.

[24] Shioji recalled one of Ishihara's motives for his stubborn refusal as his sense of racial inferiority against "white" people. Shioji also pointed out this factor as one side of the coin of Ishihara's flattering compliance with Margaret Thatcher. Shioji, 2012, p. 214.

On 17 April, one month before acquiring the post of JAMA president, Ishihara again announced his intention to launch a pickup truck plant in the US. Fraser had warned him that the US would increase import tariffs on pickup trucks should Nissan not return to its plan to produce cars. In May, the US announced that it was increasing the 8% tariff on pickup trucks to 25%. Ishihara showed little interest in the announcement and launched Nissan Motor Manufacturing Corporation in July. In October, Nissan announced the plant location in Smyrna, Tennessee,[25] and in the following February, construction of the plant started. At the launch ceremony, the Smyrna plant was unexpectedly interrupted by members of the UAW.[26] In January 1981, Ronald Reagan became the US president and launched a new reform plan to reinvigorate the American automobile industry. MITI promised that Japanese assemblers would self-restrict exports (VER) to 1.68 million units from April 1981 to March 1982.[27] The first Datsun truck rolled out in June 1983. The VER would last for the first three years, but in 1984, JAMA extended the agreement, capping exports at 1.85 million units annually. From 1985 to 1991, the numbers were extended to 2.3 million units.[28] The VER continued until MITI announced its termination in March 1994.[29]

4 The First Encounter

In the 1970s, as the president of Datsun UK, Octav Botnar had lobbied both the DoI and Nissan headquarters for a Nissan plant in Britain. While seeking possibilities for Nissan to take over the BL plant in Seneffe, Belgium,[30] Botnar wished Nissan to launch its plant in Teesside, where

[25] Nissan, 1985, p. 197. The first truck rolled out in June 1983. Immediately afterward, the US government announced a reduction on tariffs on pickup trucks from 25% back down to 8%. This damaged the Kyushu plant's exports of pickup trucks.

[26] *Nikkei Business Daily* (Nikkei Sangyo Shimbun), 9 February 1981.

[27] RIETI, vol. 2, 2013, pp. 111–113.

[28] Ibid.

[29] Suzuki, 2015a, p. 55.

[30] Mountfield, 2007a, p. 109; Mountfield, 2007b, p. 344.

he pooled Nissan cars imported from Japan.[31] He was keen to circumvent or lift the Anglo-Japanese VER so that his firm could profit.[32] Nissan vice president Masataka Okuma was in charge of Nissan's overseas operations under Ishihara's presidency. Okuma had been in charge of exports as managing director and was involved in the US plant project.[33] He had criticised the EC member states for their protectionist barriers and pointed to Britain for excluding Japanese cars while hopelessly injecting financial help into BL.[34] In 1977, he had denied the possibility of investing in Britain.[35] Due to Okuma's hostility, the DoI was doubtful when Datsun UK lobbied Whitehall in January 1980.[36] The DoI suspected that the Japanese were attempting to circumvent the bilateral VER by ambivalent proposals that could be postponed or withdrawn at any time.[37] Seeing the DoI's reluctance, Datsun UK employed an advisor who had formerly worked for Chrysler and had close connections with DoI officials. This time, the lobby worked, and the DoI called on Datsun UK in Worthing, West Sussex. Soon afterward, the DoI found that Nissan was more serious about the British project than it had initially estimated.

After Honda had carefully declined a full commitment to Rover/BL,[38] the DoI turned to Nissan in April 1980. It was feared that Nissan, considerably larger than Honda, would "gobble BL up."[39] Nonetheless, the DoI asked Nissan via Datsun UK for equity participation in BL.[40] Nissan refused this proposal and instead counter-proposed the launch of a green-field plant.[41] The reason was that Datsun UK had warned

[31] TNA, FV22/15, Dearing to Homan, 18 May 1972; Mountfield, 2007b, p. 343.

[32] Mountfield, 2007a, p. 110.

[33] See Sect. 5 in Chapter 2.

[34] TNA, FV22/133, Note for the record by Binning, 14 November 1977; Mountfield, 2007b, p. 344.

[35] Mountfield, 2007a, p. 108.

[36] Mountfield recalled that contacts were made as early as late 1976; Mountfield, 2007b, p. 343.

[37] TNA, BT177/2813, Mills to Mountfield, 24 July 1980.

[38] Mountfield, 2007b, p. 345.

[39] TNA, FV22/134, Mountfield to Secretary, 28 March 1983.

[40] Shioji, 2012, p. 237.

[41] Ibid.

Nissan headquarters in Ginza that by sharing a stake in an existing BL plant, Nissan would risk becoming embroiled in worsening management–labour relations, low productivity, and poor quality.[42] Up to this point, the DoI had understood that Toyota and Nissan were reluctant to fully commit themselves in Britain and that Nissan was more "naive" than the small but aggressively expanding Honda.[43] Via Mitsui Bussan, Toyota and Aston Martin sought collaboration.[44] Was Nissan brave enough to act on its own? Nonetheless, Nissan's counterproposal was worth attention. Thatcher welcomed the idea because she expected that Japanese industrial relations (and trade unionism) could be introduced to Britain by Nissan's arrival.[45]

The first contact between the DoI and Nissan took place on 24 June 1980 in Tokyo. Upon the approval of the DoI, the Invest in Britain Bureau (IBB) sent Robin Hope and Graham Fry for a visit to Nissan in Tokyo. To their surprise, the visitors were directly welcomed by Okuma and managing director Yutaka Kume,[46] both at the highest level in charge of Nissan's overseas operations.[47] Okuma did not waste time in expressing his concerns about the British project.[48] Was it not controversial for the British government to aid BL while at the same time welcoming Nissan's launch of a new plant in Britain? Would British public opinion react as in the case of Hitachi?[49] Another concern was the harsh reaction of other EC member states against Nissan cars made

[42] TNA, BT177/2813, Discussion Paper, Cammell to Mountfield, 14 July 1980.

[43] TNA, BT177/2813, Mills to Mountfield, 24 July 1980; Mountfield, 2007b, p. 346.

[44] Mountfield, 2007b, p. 347.

[45] PM Thatcher expressed this opinion to foreign minister Sakurauchi in London in the spring of 1982, as Sakurauchi told Shioji in Tokyo; Sato, 2012, pp. 121, 305–306.

[46] Mountfield, 2007a, p. 109.

[47] Kume became Nissan's president shortly before the Sunderland plant celebrated its opening in September 1986.

[48] TNA, BT 177/2813, Cammell to Mountfield, Annex A "Inward investment: Nissan," 14 July 1980; TNA, BT177/2813, Mills to Mountfield, 24 July 1980; Mountfield, 2007a, p. 109.

[49] Hitachi, an electronics firm, had close links with Nissan. Hitachi announced the launch of a colour television plant in Wales with GEC but faced a strong negative reaction from British trade unions and the public.

in Britain. Nissan's greatest concern was British trade unions.[50] Nissan wished to operate the new plant being based on a Japanese-style single union agreement.[51] In Nissan's view, industrial relations were the core of successful high productivity. Kume intervened in Okuma's argument and specifically asked whether British law required worker participation in management boards, similar to German codetermination laws.[52] Would a future Labour government attempt to nationalise Nissan's plant when the economy slumped? If all these issues could be sorted out, Nissan wished to receive a considerable amount of financial aid from the British government. Nissan leaders hoped that if Nissan launched a green-field plant in Britain, as other Japanese multinational corporations had done in electronics,[53] there would be a possibility of facing only one union.

With the Hitachi case in mind, but without any specific schedule, Okuma strongly requested that the British government officially support Nissan's project. The British Embassy in Tokyo had warned the DoI via the FCO to avoid "another Hitachi case,"[54] which would discourage Japanese investment. British ambassador Sir Hugh Cortazzi estimated that the Nissan deal, if successful, would have a spillover effect and promote further Japanese investment in Britain.[55] If it failed, the Thatcher administration anticipated worsening Anglo-Japanese relations.[56]

Nevertheless, officials of the Treasury and the DoI feared that Nissan's entry could further damage BL's domestic market share. Supplying Nissan with BL components would partially compensate for such losses, but insisting that Nissan make these purchases could threaten the deal itself.

[50] As the head of the Vehicles Division of the DoI, Mountfield testified that those who opposed the British project within Nissan did so with particular reference to "the English disease." Mountfield, 2007a, p. 111. Memoirs by Ishihara (2002) and Shioji (2012), however, do not mention this.

[51] See Chapter 6.

[52] Hitoshi Suzuki, *Digging for European Unity; The Role Played by the Trade Unions in the Schuman Plan and the European Coal and Steel Community from a German Perspective 1950–1955*, Ph.D. dissertation (History and Civilization), European University Institute, December 2007; Bo Stråth, *The Organisation of Labour Markets: Modernity, Culture and Governance in Germany, Sweden, Britain and Japan*, Routledge, 1996.

[53] NSK, YKK, and Sony were earlier examples.

[54] Cortazzi, 1998, pp. 168–169.

[55] Ibid., p. 170.

[56] TNA, PREM19/821, Report by Officials, "Proposed Investment in the UK by Nissan," 8 December 1980.

If Nissan took advantage of the vague proposal to circumvent the VER, the DoI would be criticised not only by the SMMT but also by British trade unions, the public and, last but not least, other EC member states. However, if the Thatcher administration hesitated to support Nissan, as the Heath administration had done,[57] other member states would take their chances. This scenario had to be avoided because German, French, and Italian cars had heavily penetrated the British market after Britain joined the EC. Because Okuma himself welcomed the IBB members with the red-carpet treatment,[58] the DoI felt that Nissan's project could lead to a hard sell.[59]

The DoI estimated the pros and cons of the proposal. A Nissan plant in Britain with an output of 100 thousand units per annum would improve the trade balance by 110 million pounds compared to imports of 60 thousand units from Japan.[60] The plant would employ four thousand workers and would reduce unemployment payments by 17.3 thousand pounds. If other member states retaliated against British steel or lamb exports, it would not seriously diminish the merits of a Nissan plant and its exports to the continent. The steel industry in Wales had declined because supplies of steel sheets to BL had diminished sharply.[61] Ford in Britain purchased steel sheets outside Britain and, even worse, imported cars from its German plant when production was halted by strikes in Britain.[62] The Nissan deal could avoid such cases by negotiating a high ratio of local content requirements and finding the "right" trade union partner(s). The British components industry could benefit by improved productivity and quality by supplying Nissan, which would also indirectly help improve BL.[63] Should Nissan prove successful, Toyota and Honda would try to compete.[64] The DoI and the Treasury found little disagreement in "calculating national interests, making decisions, and crossing the bridge." Once closed, the window would not be left open for a long

[57] See Section 2 in Chapter 3.

[58] Mountfield, 2007a, p. 109.

[59] TNA, BT177/2813, Bell to Pirie, 14 April 1980.

[60] Of the 100 thousand units, 40 thousand would be exported to the continent.

[61] TNA, BT177/2813, Bridges to Carey, 3 July 1980.

[62] TNA, PREM19/821, Transcript of Press Conference held on 29 January 1981.

[63] TNA, BT177/2813, Bridges to Carey, 3 July 1980.

[64] TNA, BT177/2813, Owen to Mountfield, 25 July 1980.

time.[65] The Nissan project was named "quicksilver,"[66] and the circulation of documents was restricted to Thatcher's secretaries, the secretary of state for industry, the chancellor of the exchequer, and officials directly working for them. Nissan vice President Okuma visited London on 31 July and promised to return within three months with a detailed plan.[67]

5 Nissan-Alfa Romeo, Volkswagen, and Motor-Iberica

Nissan deserved the name quicksilver. The firm sought alliances elsewhere with European partners outside Britain. Ishihara targeted Italian, Spanish, and German manufacturers for collaboration. The DoI was puzzled and irritated by Nissan's unclear manoeuvres. Whether Nissan was serious about its British project was still doubtful.

In October 1980, Nissan announced a collaboration with the Italian manufacturer Alfa Romeo. Alfa Romeo suffered financial difficulty and sought a partner with cash. The alliance launched a plant in southern Italy with the intention of producing small cars based on the Nissan Pulsar. In March 1983, assembly resumed, but Nissan suffered long afterward because the financial burden was too heavy.[68] It happily handed over the plant to Fiat in January 1987.

In December 1980, Nissan turned to the Germans and announced that it would assemble the Volkswagen Santana at the Nissan Zama plant. The agreement was signed in September 1981. Ishihara claimed that this was the first step in cooperation for European manufacturers to expand their business in Japan.[69] Few others understood the deal in such a way.[70] If the alliance proved successful, there was a possibility of Nissan cars being assembled in Volkswagen's plant in Germany. The German government would be obliged to openly counter the bilateral VERs and safeguards

[65] TNA, BT177/2813, Day to Mountfield, 29 July 1980; TNA, BT177/2813, Wilford to Carey, 3 July 1980.

[66] TNA, PREM19/821, To Prior, 16 January 1981.

[67] Shioji, 2012, p. 237.

[68] Sato, 2012, pp. 64–66.

[69] Nissan, 1985, pp. 204–205.

[70] Shioji, 2012, p. 230.

on Japanese cars of other EC member states.[71] Furthermore, exports to Britain from other German plants would be a nightmare when Ford, Vauxhall, and Talbot imported cars from the continent.[72] Fortunately for Britain, the Nissan-Volkswagen deal never advanced to a fruitful alliance. Nissan sold a mere 70 thousand units of the Santana in Japan over the following seven years before the alliance was abandoned.[73]

Last but not least, Nissan merged with the Spanish tractor manufacturer Motor-Iberica in January 1980. This was Nissan's second step in launching an overseas plant after its Australian case in March 1976.[74] The rapid increase in the Japanese trade surplus and the risky exchange rates drove Nissan to assemble cars in the markets where they would be sold.[75] Motor-Iberica had suffered financial difficulty and was sold to Massey-Ferguson but never improved. The pro for Nissan to operate in Spain was the low labour costs for assembling lorries (Vanette) and SUVs (Safari/Patrol), but the cons were the financial problems, lack of quality, and low productivity.[76] Shioji used his trade union connections and found that the plant was unprofitable and therefore asked Ishihara how he would handle the forecast five-billion-yen debt after the merger.[77] Ishihara responded, with a smile, that he would resign if the project failed.[78] The Spanish project cost Nissan heavily. Sato criticised Ishihara's

[71] Ibid.

[72] See the previous section and Sect. 5 of the next chapter.

[73] Sato wrote that there were 50 thousand units; Sato, 2012, p. 87; Uesugi, 2001, p. 145.

[74] Industrial Journal (*Sangyou journal*) (ed.) *Nissan; Group Activity of 1992* (Nissan-jidousha group no jittai 1992), Nagoya: IRC, 1992, p. 7. Nissan's plant in Australia assembled cars beginning in September 1977 but ceased production in September 1992.

[75] Industrial Journal (*sangyou journal*) (ed.) *Nissan; Group Activity of 1996* (Nissan-jidousha group no jittai 1996), Nagoya: IRC, 1996, p. 305.

[76] On the comparison of Britain and Spain, see Yasutaka Takahashi, "Nissan's European Strategy: NMISA (*Nissan-jidousha no Europe senryaku* - NMISA)," in Yasutaka Takahashi, Shigemitsu Ashizawa (eds.), *The Strategy of the Car Manufacturer of Europe* (EU jidousha-mekaa no senryaku), Tokyo: Gakubunsha, 2009, pp. 244–253.

[77] Sato, 2012, pp. 62–64; Shioji, 2012, pp. 218–219. Shioji had also asked trade union colleagues in Brussels and determined that Spain would not soon be able to join the EC; ibid.

[78] Sato, 2012, pp. 62–64; Shioji, 2012, pp. 222–223.

"rubbish" decisions based on his motive of hiding the losses of domestic sales in Japan.[79]

One motive behind Ishihara's hasty and ill-prepared decisions was his eagerness and ambition to achieve results as president not only of Nissan but also of JAMA.[80] In contrast to his careful and pragmatic predecessors—Kawamata and Iwakoshi—Ishihara failed to understand Nissan's limits and was in too much a rush to overtake Toyota. Toyota, as Japan's largest manufacturer, held an advantage in its financial self-dependence—unlike Nissan—and its solidity in decision-making of never fighting over its weight. Ishihara's career had been built solely in Nissan, while Kawamata, as a former banker, had realistically understood Nissan's capacities and limits as "merely" the second-largest car manufacturer. At best, Ishihara's rapid decisions put pressure on Thatcher, the DoI, and British trade unions that Nissan could choose any other European partner(s) should it be dissatisfied with the British deal[81] in terms of subsidy, local content requirements, or labour–management relations. Robin Mountfield, who led the Vehicles Division of the DoI, misunderstood Ishihara's priority as being the US rather than Britain,[82] but the problem was the lack of clear priorities among his various overseas projects. Ishihara attempted to push all of them through.

6 The Announcement

What was crucial for Thatcher was the prospect that a new Nissan plant would reduce unemployment and boost the British local economy. The Japanese electronics industry had launched plants in Wales under the Labour governments. An automobile plant would employ at least ten times more workers and many more in the related component sectors of steel, rubber, textile, glass, and electronics. Eight sites were listed by Nissan: Sunderland, Eaglescliffe, Ingleby Barwick, North Killingholme, Stallingborough, Shotton, Llanwern, and Wentloog.[83] Thatcher preferred

[79] Sato, 2012, pp. 15–16, 60.

[80] Suzuki, 2015, pp. 76–77.

[81] Suzuki, 2015a, p. 77.

[82] Mountfield, 2007a, p. 111.

[83] *The Financial Times*, 8 April 1981.

the North East.[84] A remarkable reduction in unemployment was desired because the numbers had steadily increased since Thatcher had come to power. The DoI negotiated local content requirements and financial aid, while the location of the plant was left to negotiations between local authorities and Nissan.[85] Furthermore, Nissan would negotiate with British trade unions and "choose" its favoured partner. This was the core of Nissan's decision.[86] Nissan would decide on a plant location where the local unions agreed to Nissan's request that only one union would organise the workers. At this point, the overall investment cost to launch a plant with an annual output of 100 thousand units was estimated at 200 million pounds.[87]

The DoI had sent its deputy secretary to Tokyo shortly after the IBB visit to Nissan in June and suggested a feasibility study for plant with an annual output of 200 thousand and with 80% local content.[88] This was understood by Nissan's executives as an invitation to Britain. Okuma was told that 60% local content would allow Nissan to freely export to EFTA countries in addition to the EC.[89] Ishihara gathered a small team and sketched out a plan to launch a plant with an annual output of 200 thousand Nissan Violets. Construction began in 1982, and production commenced in 1984, with local content reaching 60% at this point.[90] The full output of 200 thousand units was reached in 1986, when 80% local content was achieved. The overall investment was estimated at 175 million pounds. The plan was submitted to the DoI on 17 November 1980.[91] Ishihara refused to consult his trade union counterpart, Shioji,

[84] Lord Jenkin of Roding, "Foreword," in Conte-Helm, 1989, p. xvi.

[85] TNA, CAB130/1198, Cabinet Official Group on British Policy Towards Japan, 2 February 1982.

[86] See Chapter 6.

[87] TNA, FV22/133, Department of Trade to Cammell, 12 August 1980.

[88] Mountfield, 2007a, pp. 109–110; 2007b, p. 347.

[89] TNA, FV22/133, Cammel to Okuma, 22 August 1980.

[90] TNA, CAB19/821, Joseph to PM, 9 December 1980. Sato wrote that the investment was 142 billion yen; Sato, 2012, p. 95. Shioji testified that the investment cost was 141 billion yen; Shioji, 2012, p. 237.

[91] Shioji, 2012, p. 237.

until the very last moment before the plan was finalised.[92] This merely worsened the mistrust between Ishihara and Shioji.

The DoI was surprised by Nissan's unexpectedly ambitious plan. The British plant would be larger than any of Nissan's plants in Japan.[93] Ishihara's plan was submitted to a cabinet meeting on 11 December and received the go-ahead on 17 December.[94] Thatcher's administration and Nissan reached agreement on four basic points. The first was that the output would start at 100 thousand units. The second was the final goal of local content, starting at 60% and ultimately reaching 80%. The third was for Nissan to solely decide on the plant location. Finally, there was an agreement that the two parties should negotiate the necessary financial aid to be provided for Nissan. On 5 January 1981, Sir Hugh in Tokyo notified Ishihara that the British government fully supported Nissan's "full commitment in Britain."[95] The ambassador sounded as if Nissan's plan was not merely a proposal to launch a feasibility study but rather that there was a consensus on launching a plant. Sir Hugh proposed jointly organising a press conference at the House of Commons to publicly announce the plan.[96] The conference was scheduled for 29 January.

On 26 January, Ishihara briefly notified Shioji about his plan, merely three days before the announcement in London.[97] While struggling to unify the voices of his Japanese unions on overseas projects, Shioji sought to contact his British colleagues.[98] It was not only Shioji who learned the details of the plan on such short notice. Kawamata went into a rage when he learned of it at a management board meeting merely a week before

[92] For trade unions' responses, see Sect. 9 of this chapter.

[93] TNA, PREM19/821, Joseph to PM, 9 December 1980.

[94] TNA, PREM19/821, Joseph to PM, 22 December 1980.

[95] Sato, 2012, p. 96.

[96] Ibid., p. 96; Shioji, 2012, p. 237.

[97] Shioji, 2012, p. 236. In contrast, Kawakatsu claimed that the unions were not pre-notified about the British project and that Shioji irrationally opposed it with "illegal" strikes; Kawakatsu, 2018, pp. 110–111. Injury incidents, which Kawakatsu described as "slight injury," in plants in Oppama—a worker killed—Yokohama, and Yoshihara were followed by strikes or line stops; ibid., pp. 104–109. Kawakatsu blamed Shioji for these union actions, attributing them to Shioji's desire for power and international status, which led him to oppose Ishihara; ibid., pp. 104, 108, 114, 131. However, it is doubtful whether Shioji, who had been vice president of the ICFTU since 1972, sought international status and fame through the British project.

[98] See Sect. 9 of this chapter.

the press conference. He had decided to trust Ishihara's leadership and avoided intervening in internal corporate decisions up to this point, even if the latter's US pickup truck plant project seemed unfeasible.[99] This time, he had to intervene, not only because he had not been consulted but also because the British plan was overwhelmingly costly for Nissan.[100] He scolded Ishihara and his supporters[101]:

> Our private entity is not a charity. We do business. Why does a (British) minister have to announce a project of a mere private firm in the Parliament? Do you assume we could still say "No" if the feasibility study fails to reach our standards? An announcement in the Parliament is equal to promising our full commitment in Britain. It should not be too late to call off the thoughtless press conference organised by their government. (additions by the authour)

Kawamata's tone was furious, and the executives froze. A long silence took place. Ishihara did not say anything but closed his eyes and folded his arms with a displeased expression.[102] No one dared to speak out. Seeing the executives keeping silence, trying to avoid siding with either Ishihara or him, Kawamata reluctantly approved the announcement in London. Kawamata's first intervention had failed, leaving a deep division among the executives.

A few days before the scheduled press conference, the FCO advised Thatcher of its diplomatic routine to notify the French and other member state governments.[103] The DoI intervened and denied the necessity of such notification because an advance briefing would do little to ease negative reactions,[104] especially those of rival manufacturers and public opinion. Britain would have to bear the same level of pressure and criticism that Japanese had been receiving. Thatcher did not waste time siding with the DoI. The announcement would take place without previous notice. At an Anglo-French bilateral meeting, French president Valéry Giscard d'Estaing had warned her against allowing Japanese investments

[99] See Sect. 3 of this chapter.

[100] Sato, 2012, p. 93.

[101] Shioji, 2012, pp. 244, 258; Sato, 2012, p. 97.

[102] Sato, 2012, p. 97.

[103] TNA, PREM19/821, By Private Secretary, 11 December 1980.

[104] TNA, PREM19/821, Joseph to Carrington, 24 November 1980.

into Britain.[105] However, Thatcher felt that whether Japanese investment came to Britain was none of his business. Thatcher had felt similarly ever since the Franco–British conflict over EC budget refunding.[106] Two days before the press conference, the DoI and Nissan examined the wording of the announcement together and held a briefing to prepare for questions.[107] A day before the press conference, the *Daily Mail* leaked Nissan's project, resulting in anger from MITI and MOFA that Nissan had not notified them beforehand.[108]

The press conference announcing Nissan's launch of the feasibility study was held late in the afternoon of 29 January 1981 at the House of Commons. It was organised in the late afternoon to avoid making the announcement before aid plans for BL were announced.[109] Norman Tebbit, as minister of state for industry, chaired the conference, and Masataka Okuma and Yutaka Kume participating on behalf of Nissan. Tebbit had explained to the House of Commons that Nissan intended to launch a feasibility study and planned by 1986 to launch an assembly plant with an annual output of 200 thousand units on 800 acres of land. Local content would reach 80% by 1986, and a considerable amount of exports was expected.[110] The plant would create approximately four to five thousand jobs, with an estimated investment cost of 100 billion yen. Tebbit did not forget to add that Nissan's greatest concern was labour–management relations and the quality of locally purchased components and that the British government warmly welcomed the proposal.[111] Pleased with the announcement, Thatcher caught Robin Mountfield by his elbow as he was about to escape from the Chamber and told him in a low and vibrant tone, "That went splendidly."[112]

[105] TNA, PREM19/821, Carrington to Secretary of State of Industry, 10 November 1980.

[106] Thatcher, 1992, pp. 61–71.

[107] TNA, PREM19/821, Mason to Lankester, 27 January 1981.

[108] Sato, 2012, pp. 89, 97.

[109] TNA, PREM19/821, by Private Secretary, 11 December 1980; TNA, T466/200, Worman (Industry Development Advisory Board), 22 January 1982.

[110] TNA, PREM19/821, Mason to Lankester, 27 January 1981; TNA, T466/200, DOI, 2 July 1981.

[111] TNA, PREM19/821, Transcript of Press Conference held on 29 January 1981.

[112] Mountfield, 2007a, p. 107.

At the press conference, questions centred on the plant location and the estimated amount of financial aid. Tebbit refrained from giving any hints but briefly answered that the location was solely up to Nissan to decide and that the government would not intervene. As a result, Nissan might choose an unprofitable site.[113] Okuma (unnecessarily) added that Nissan was considering a few developing areas and would negotiate suitable aid provided by the British government for such areas. A storm of questions and requests for hints about the possible sites arose from Scottish, Welsh, and Northern Irish media representatives. Tebbit interrupted, asking them to speak more clearly without accents so that Okuma could comprehend.[114] Okuma and Kume never gave any hint of the plant location or a concrete schedule but discussed possible exports from the British plant. Referring to the high level of local content, Okuma emphasised that Nissan should be viewed as a British firm and asked for support from the public.

The conference attracted the attention of the media, but the main point of Nissan's announcement was *merely* a launch of a feasibility study,[115] with a vague blueprint for a possible assembly plant. Thatcher stated immediately after the press conference that she "welcomed the initiative." Just as Kawamata feared, the wide public attention immediately made it difficult for Nissan to show hesitation, postponement or, worse still, retreat from Britain.[116] Governmental "quicksilver" documents were declassified and circulated widely to officials, and the codename was no longer used.[117] Except for France, other EC member states did not openly react negatively, and the European Commission welcomed Nissan's announcement in general terms.[118]

However, Nissan's announcement caused a shock back in Japan. Nissan's stock price dropped due to worries about its worsened balance sheet.[119] The firm was already heavily in debt to its main financer, the Industrial Bank of Japan. Rumour soon reached Whitehall that Nissan

[113] TNA, PREM19/821, Transcript of Press Conference held on 29 January 1981.

[114] Ibid.

[115] Mountfield, 2007a, p. 108.

[116] Shioji, 2012, p. 258; Sato, 2012, p. 117.

[117] TNA, PREM19/821, Morris to Walden, 3 February 1981.

[118] TNA, T466/200, Tebbit to Joseph, 3 April 1981.

[119] Sato, 2012, p. 97.

was viewed as having "gone crazy."[120] The announcement also coincided with UAW President Fraser's visit to Japan,[121] leaving him upset and disappointed that Nissan was ignoring the voices of American workers.

British trade union leaders of the TUC were, however, not as negative as the DoI had estimated. The TUC issued a short statement after the press conference that it welcomed Nissan's proposal.[122] The Department of Employment contacted TUC general secretary Len (Lionel) Murray to ensure that the unions would respond positively to the announcement.[123] The Stockton TUC opposed Nissan's plan as possibly causing further unemployment and protested against the overall atmosphere that doubts about Nissan were "not allowed," phrasing it as "(being) steamrolled by high unemployment into a position where unions having to promise there be no trouble."[124] However, the TUC leaders understood that similar Japanese investments could contribute to creating new jobs and improving productivity[125] and had to find a way to mediate disagreements among their members. Britain's car assembly had fallen to 924 thousand units in 1980, merely half the amount of 1972.[126]

7 The First Feasibility Study

Nissan launched its feasibility study team in March 1981. The team consisted of ten men led by managing director Isamu Kawai. Kawai was chairman Kawamata's trusted man[127] and was one of the best negotiators of financial aid. Ishihara's confirmation of Kawai showed his willingness to convince Kawamata that Nissan could bear the heavy financial burden. Kawai's team was tasked with investigating the issues of available subsidies, plant location, quality and cost of British-made components,

[120] Mountfield, 2007a, p. 111; 2007b, p. 348.

[121] See Sect. 3 of this chapter.

[122] MRCW, MSS, 292D/617/3, from the TUC for the Press, Nissan, 29 January 1981; Mountfield, 2007b, p. 348.

[123] TNA, PREM19/821, Secretary of State for Employment to Joseph, 19 January 1981.

[124] Conte-Helm, 1989, pp. 144–145.

[125] On the TUC's report on the British car industry, see Sect. 5 in Chapter 5.

[126] Mountfield, 2007b, p. 348.

[127] Shioji, 2012, p. 238.

possibilities of exporting to the EC market, and labour–management relations in Britain.[128] The team arrived in Britain in late March 1981 and visited nearly eighty British component suppliers and the eight possible plant sites.[129]

While clarifying its own position, the DoI observed the Nissan team, tense and anxious. Should Nissan choose a development area, an RDG would be automatically provided for the launch. The question was SFA. The DoI decided that SFA would be offered only when Nissan agreed to, or was very close to agreeing to, the 80% local content requirement.[130] Such aids were unthinkable back in Japan.[131] The European Commission had been discussing banning subsidies for the automobile sector because the market was saturated, and overcapacity of production was foreseen.[132] Thatcher was inconsistent in her neoliberal policies, and the DoI doubted such policies[133] willing to provide funding in two areas. The first was regions where manufacturing was in decline, and the other was the high-tech sector.[134] Nissan's assembly plant fulfilled the former criterion, while the second criterion could be applied to specific component suppliers in electronics.

Another issue was whether to measure local content by the price/value of the components or by their weight. The latter would disadvantage Nissan because expensive but lightweight electronic components would be measured as equal to nuts and bolts with heavyweight but low value. The agreement would make it difficult for Nissan to import components from Japan. This solution was demanded by the British component sectors, which requested a 90% requirement that was rejected by the DoI.[135] Forcing a requirement that was too high could threaten the whole deal.[136] How far the DoI could push Nissan depended on the

[128] Nissan, 1985, p. 205.

[129] TNA, T466/200, Tebbit to Joseph, 3 April 1981; Shioji, 2012, p. 238; Mountfield, 2007a, p. 111.

[130] TNA, T466/200, Tebbit to Joseph, 3 April 1981.

[131] Sato, 2012, p. 92.

[132] TNA, BT177/2813, Pulvermacher to Owen, 29 July 1980.

[133] Warlouzet, 2018, pp. 141–142.

[134] Ibid., pp. 129–130.

[135] TNA, FV22/133, Bullock to Cammell, 26 September 1980.

[136] Ibid.

results of the feasibility study.[137] The DoI was still confident in the competitiveness of the British components industry.[138]

In Nissan's first feasibility study, the reliability of British-made components was seriously questioned in terms of both their quality and the pound exchange rate, which would hamper the export competitiveness of the assembled cars.[139] A confidential report sent to Nissan headquarters stated that the project would suffer debt for seven years after assembly started in 1984 and would not gain its first profits until the eighth year, 1991. In 1994, 30 billion yen of debt would remain.[140] Upon seeing the report, Ishihara went into a rage and ordered not that the plan be rethought from scratch but that a way be found to keep the debt as small as possible.[141] Nissan struggled to develop a better calculation and postponed its next proposal until the Falkland crisis was over.

Rumour soon reached the DoI and No. 10 Downing.[142] The cons were so overwhelming that Nissan could rescind its proposal. Okuma had questioned the IBB officials during their first contact in June 1980 about the possibility of purchasing components from the continent.[143] The German, French, and Italian components industries were tough rivals in terms of quality, price competitiveness, and reliability of delivery. Nissan had incentives to purchase components from other member states in order to promote sales of Nissan cars in the suppliers' countries.[144] Okuma notified the DoI that he foresaw difficulty in expecting profit from exports due to the costs of British-made components.[145] Okuma told the British media that there was a potential problem in maintaining Japanese quality standards if components were purchased in Britain.[146]

[137] TNA, T466/200, Tebbit to Joseph, 3 April 1981.

[138] TNA, BT177/2813, Mills to Mountfield, 24 July 1980.

[139] TNA, PREM19/821, RNE to Prime Minister, May 1981; TNA, PREM19/821, Tebbit to Lankester, 1 June 1981; Sato, 2012, p. 134.

[140] Shioji, 2012, pp. 238–239; Sato, 2012, pp. 98–99.

[141] Shioji, 2012, p. 239.

[142] TNA, PREM19/822, Butler to Spencer, 5 October 1982.

[143] TNA, FV22/133, Bullock to Okuma, 11 August 1980.

[144] TNA, T466/200, Lambirth to Chivers, Lovell and Chancellor, 26 November 1981.

[145] TNA, T466/200, Tebbit to Lankester, 1 June 1981.

[146] *The Financial Times*, 29 May 1981; Conte-Helm, 1989, p. 145.

Nevertheless, Thatcher insisted that Nissan use a very high proportion of British local content, up to 80%.[147] One intention behind this was to save the British components industry[148] rather than saving the "budget-wasting" BL brands. Thatcher successfully gave Nissan the idea that the 80% requirement was the government's pre-condition for defining Nissan cars not as "made in Japan" but as "made in Britain." EC law defined 45% as sufficient to claim that a car was locally manufactured in the EC.[149] Thatcher correctly understood, however, that an 80% achievement was necessary to persuade the SMMT,[150] the TUC,[151] British public opinion, and, last but not least, the governments of other member states that a British-made Nissan was a "genuine" homemade vehicle.[152] She assumed that if pros for Britain existed in the long term, they would also exist for Nissan.[153] Fortunately, the Fraser tornado and bilateral VERs had put strong pressure on Ishihara to compromise with the British.[154] If Nissan accepted the 80% requirement, Thatcher would exclude British-made Nissan cars from the Anglo-Japanese VER,[155] and Nissan's plant in Britain would freely export to the continent without restrictions.

8 The SMMT and the TUC

In May 1981, observing Nissan's feasibility study, the SMMT submitted a report on Nissan to the DoI. The SMMT had made a brief comment to welcome Nissan's announcement in late January 1981. However, for SMMT members, Nissan was nothing less than a Trojan horse for

147 TNA, PREM19/821, Private Secretary to Hampson, 26 August 1980.

148 Pardi, 2015, 2017; Mountfield, 2007a, pp. 119–120.

149 TNA, FV22/133, European Communities Regulation (EEC) No. 2632/70, 23 December 1970.

150 TNA, T466/200, SMMT, "A Study on the Effect of the Nissan Assembly Plant in the UK on the British Motor Industry," 15 May 1981.

151 MRCW, MSS, 292D/617/3, Motor Industry Study, Economic Committee, TUC, 13 January 1982.

152 TNA, PREM19/821, Private Secretary to Hampson, 26 August 1980.

153 TNA, PREM19/821, PJ to Prime Minister, 12 November 1981.

154 TNA, T466/200, Tebbit to Lankester, 1 June 1981.

155 Whether British-made Nissans were defined as made in the EC/EU or in Japan became a problem after the Sunderland plant was launched. See Section 10 in Chapter 6.

Japan.[156] The SMMT report stated its aim to propose ways to make Nissan's entry positive for the British economy.[157] However, in detail, the SMMT was thoroughly and concretely critical of Nissan and the DoI.

The most significant issue was local content and the way to measure it. Following voices from the components industry, the SMMT proposed measuring it by the weight of each component instead of ex-work value.[158] This would force Nissan to accept higher requirements for local sourcing, well above the level of the DoI's definition. The SMMT also suspected that Nissan would purchase components from the continent and, worse still, could allow Japanese suppliers to join its entry into Britain. Should this occur, not only Nissan but also British assemblers would purchase Japanese components made in Britain,[159] which, in the SMMT's view, would seriously damage British national interests.

Furthermore, the SMMT suspected that Nissan had a hidden intention of circumventing the bilateral VER, which capped the market share in Britain at 11%.[160] Nissan proposed assembling the Violet (formerly Bluebird), which was a larger car than those exported so far to Britain. The SMMT was furious because it was responsible for negotiating the VER and monitoring Japanese exports, together with its Japanese counterpart, JAMA. Forecasts stated that Nissan's market share alone would rise to 14% in Britain, and the total Japanese share would increase by up to 20%. If the exchange rate of the pound worsened, Nissan cars made in Britain would fail to reach the continent and be sold in Britain instead. This would further diminish BL's market share, and more workers would accordingly be unemployed. Therefore, the SMMT insisted that Nissan be required to equip its plant with engine assembly facilities.[161] An engine requires the largest number of and most expensive components in a car and therefore would have to be assembled in Britain rather than coming from Japan as completed kits.

[156] TNA, T466/200, Tebbit to Joseph, 3 April 1981.

[157] TNA, T466/200, SMMT, "A Study on the Effect of the Nissan Assembly Plant in the UK on the British Motor Industry," 15 May 1981.

[158] See the previous section.

[159] TNA, T466/200, Tebbit to Joseph, 3 April 1981.

[160] See Sect. 4 in Chapter 3.

[161] TNA, T466/200, SMMT, "A Study on the Effect of the Nissan Assembly Plant in the UK on the British Motor Industry," 15 May 1981.

The SMMT insisted on requiring very high local content for Nissan, defining favourable measures for counting those components, assuring a considerable amount of exports from the new plant, and, last but not least, reducing the imports of both assembled cars and component kits from Japan. Still not satisfied, Ford in Britain separately lobbied Thatcher's administration because, in contrast to the SMMT, it was not willing to welcome Nissan.[162] Along with Ford, Lucas—a British component supplier—was most hostile to Nissan's project.[163] The SMMT's proposal hit the DoI like a stream of cold water because the latter welcomed Nissan's ambitiously large project. The Treasury started to raise doubts about the DoI's statistics and forecasts.[164] The DoI had estimated that Nissan's launch would create twenty- to twenty-five thousand jobs, including in the components sector. However, this number was larger than BL's employment and thus had been criticised because rationalisation was necessary to justify it. While welcoming Nissan, the Treasury started to show caution about providing an unnecessarily large amount of aid(s). The SMMT estimated the number of new jobs at fifteen thousand.[165]

In June, Norman Tebbit met the leaders of the SMMT. Tebbit agreed to SMMT's claims about the significance of high local content.[166] However, he disagreed with the SMMT's lack of awareness, whether intended or not, of the risk of other EC member states inviting Nissan to launch its first green-field plant.[167] Ishihara had sought as many possible alliances on the continent as possible.[168] The SMMT represented not only BL but also the American multinational Ford, the French Peugeot-Talbot and the American General Motors subsidiary Vauxhall (from March 2017 under the French Peugeot-Citroën, PSA, together with the German Opel). The multinationals showed little hesitation in closing down plants in Britain should they not operate profitably. The SMMT estimated that

[162] TNA, T466/200, DoI, 2 July 1981.

[163] Mountfield, 2007a, p. 110; Mountfield, 2007b, p. 349.

[164] See Sect. 11 of this chapter and Sect. 4 of the next chapter.

[165] TNA, T466/200, Kosmin to Lambirth, 25 November 1981.

[166] TNA, T466/200, DoI, 2 July 1981.

[167] Ibid.

[168] See Sect. 5 of this chapter.

if 150 thousand units of British-made Nissans were assembled annually, SMMT members would lose forty-five to seventy thousand units of market share.[169] Tebbit had proposed a more optimistic forecast and was determined that British-made Nissans would not be included in the counts of the Anglo-Japanese VER.[170] Tebbit did not hesitate to criticise the German assemblers who condemned Britain as the "Trojan horse of Japan,"[171] counterarguing,

> Surely it is better for the British people to buy Japanese cars made by British workers than to buy German cars assembled by Turks.[172]

On another occasion he stated,

> What is the difference between purchasing in Britain a Volkswagen assembled by Turkish workers in Germany, and exporting to Germany a Nissan assembled in Britain by British workers? Both are absolutely normal competition. The Germans who adore fair and legal competition should know this without ambiguity.[173]

Tebbit was a hard-line Tory and was far from gaining support from the unions. Len Murray—the TUC general secretary—described him as "a rough sod but very able."[174] Murray added,

> [Tebbit] would put his knee in your stomach just to attract your attention with a smile on his face. But he was the sort of fellow you could do a deal with. He would drive a hard bargain but you knew he would deliver.[175]

In the case of the 1982 Employment Act, Tebbit gave a body blow to the unions,[176] but in Nissan's case, he delivered a "favourable" deal. Unlike

[169] TNA, T466/200, Lambirth to Chivers, Lovell and Chancellor, 26 November 1981.

[170] TNA, T466/200, DoI, 2 July 1981.

[171] See Sect. 10 of this chapter.

[172] *The Financial Times*, 21 April 1981; Conte-Helm, 1989, p. 144.

[173] TNA, PREM19/821, Transcript of Press Conference held on 29 January 1981.

[174] *Observer*, 2 September 1984; Robert Taylor, *The TUC: From the General Strike to New Unionism*, Basingstoke: Palgrave, 2000, p. 247.

[175] Ibid.

[176] Ibid.

Thatcher, the DoI officials and ministers avoided insisting on ideological differences with the unions, at least in the Nissan case, and focused on British national interests so that the deal would be made in the right terms.

Murray made a statement after Nissan's announcement in January 1981 and emphasised that[177]

> Japanese investment up to now has been positive in the sense that it created jobs for British workers. This was due to clear agreement among the parties about local contents, export competitiveness and labour-management relations. The significance of all these aspects apply especially for the automobile industry.

Considering the earlier cases of Japanese plants in Britain, Murry had to avoid conflicts among the member unions about which union(s) would organise the workers in the Nissan plant. The TUC leaders saw a green-field plant as more difficult than a joint venture between BL and the Japanese.[178] There was no guarantee that its familiar tactics could be carried out in a purely Japanese plant, which would make it difficult for the British union(s) to put pressure on the Japanese regarding a high level of local content.[179] On the other hand, the TUC leaders were also aware of the risk that should they insist on British ways of trade unionism or too much local content, Nissan would abandon the project and seek a plant in Belgium.[180] Nevertheless, they had to insist on a high level of local content because the TUC leaders were well aware of the competitiveness of the European and Japanese components industries.[181] New jobs must be created in Britain.

To clarify its view on Japanese entry, the TUC's Economic Committee took the lead in issuing a report on the British automobile industry. This was the first case in which the TUC focused on the theme and reported on it. The Labour Party had invited the TUC to participate

[177] MRCW, MSS, 292D/617/4, from the TUC for the Press, "Nissan," 29 January 1981.

[178] MRCW, MSS, 292D/617/3, "Motor Industry Study," Economic Committee, TUC, 13 January 1982.

[179] Ibid.

[180] MRCW, MSS, 292D/617/4, Aide Memoire of meeting on 13 April 1981.

[181] Ibid.

on a similar occasion led by George Park, MP.[182] However, the TUC declined and decided to join Party's research after concluding its own.[183] The Economic Committee launched the research project in July 1981.[184]

9 Trade Unions and Plant Location

Keeping in line with the British government, the TUC refrained from intervening in Nissan's plant location. If the TUC recommended a certain location, each local union would claim that its home was most appropriate, which would cause further conflict among the unions. One exception was the unions of North Wales, which requested that the TUC leaders resolve to recommend Wales.[185] With the Welsh steel industry in decline, union leaders in Shotton thought it ideal that unemployed workers would be employed by Nissan.[186] This would help steel suppliers to recover as well. BL's decline had hit the local economy hard. However, the TUC leaders did not side with the Shotton union and remained neutral. Shotton and two sites in England were designated special development areas where the highest subsidies for plant construction and mechanical equipment would be provided for the assembler.[187] Therefore, Sunderland, Teesside, and Shotton were the most promising candidates among the eight sites.[188]

The Nissan team visited the eight sites during its first visit in early April 1981. The team visited the NSK Europe plant in Peterlee. NSK, a Japanese firm producing ball bearings, had launched NSK Bearing Europe in April 1974 in London under the Labour government. After examining possible locations in Germany, the Netherlands, Belgium, France,

[182] MRCW, MSS.259/AEU/1/1/247, Executive Council meeting, 18 May 1982.

[183] MRCW, MSS, 292D/617/3, Carter to Lea, 14 September 1982.

[184] The TUC refined its draft three times while consulting member unions and internal committees. The final report was concluded in November 1983 and was submitted to Robin Mountfield, the DTI. See Sect. 5 of the next chapter.

[185] MRCW, MSS, 292D/617/3, Callaghan to Cooper, 10 March 1981.

[186] MRCW, MSS, 292D/617/3, The Iron and Steel Trades Confederation to Okuma, 5 March 1981.

[187] TNA, T466/200, DOI, 2 July 1981; Conte-Helm, 1989, p. 143.

[188] These were Sunderland, Eaglescliffe, Ingleby Barwick, North Killingholme, Stallingborough, Shotton, Llanwern and Wentloog. See also Sect. 6 of this chapter.

and Ireland,[189] Peterlee was chosen not only for its hardworking local employees but also for the enthusiastic and continuous welcome by Dennis Stevenson,[190] later Baron Stevenson of Coddenham, who was chairman of the Newton Aycliffe and Peterlee New Town Development Corporation. The plant was launched in 1976 with 54 local and 9 Japanese staff members,[191] and it employed nearly two hundred workers by 1981.[192] Japan had faced pressure from the German government and had been accused of price dumping on Japanese-made bearings but had barely been able to avoid the penalty claimed by the European Commission. Ball bearings and taper roller bearings are highly crucial components for engines, axles, and suspensions. Nearly 80% of Peterlee's products were exported to the continent by the late 1970s,[193] and it had achieved nearly 60% of local sourcing.[194]

The Nissan team visited Peterlee with the aim of observing how the Japanese-style single union agreement was operating. Bearings were one of the items most closely related to assembling cars. The visit was organised by Shioji and his Nissan union, *Jidosha-rouren*.[195] Nissan officials' fears of British trade unions were somewhat eased, but they were not fully convinced that Nissan's assembly plant could operate as successfully as the NSK plant. An assembly plant would have to employ ten times as many workers as the NSK plant. Nissan employed a specialist on labour issues shortly after the visit. The DoI understood that Nissan had taken one step forward.[196]

The Nissan team was also relieved to find that Japanese plants in Britain were facing less hostility from the public. Japanese electronics plants in Wales became successful in exports, changing public criticism to silent approval or praise. The Sony colour TV plant in Bridgend was

[189] NSK, *Towards Tomorrow, Towards the World: NSK's 75th Anniversary Commemorative Publication*, 1991, p. 29.

[190] Ibid., pp. 29–30. NSK was also supported by Margaret Thatcher as Tory leader.

[191] Ibid.

[192] By 1991, employment had expanded to 800 in Peterlee. Ibid., p. 28.

[193] TNA, T466/200, Japanese Inward Investment to the UK, without date; NSK, 1991, pp. 30–31.

[194] Ibid.

[195] Conte-Helm, 1989, p. 144.

[196] TNA, T466/200, Mason to Tebbit, 13 July 1981.

honoured by receiving the Queen's Award for Enterprise (International Trade/Export) in April 1980. Nissan could expect to face less harsh reactions.[197]

As the president of both JAW and Nissan's union, *Jidosha-rouren*, Shioji also visited Britain in April 1981. Although Ishihara had not sufficiently consulted him before announcing the project, Shioji would be blamed by the unions and his colleagues should the new plant fail to realise cooperative labour–management relations. An unsuccessful launch would have a negative effect on workers in both countries.[198] Shioji held meetings with leaders of the Transport and General Workers' Union (TGWU) and the AUEW in London, Moss Evans and Terry (Terrence) Duffy.[199] Shioji asked the leaders whether a single union agreement in a new Nissan plant was possible. Duffy answered that it was not, but the creation of a single wage bargaining system in the plant was.[200] This was not the answer Shioji expected. The term "single bargaining" did not guarantee a "single union" in the plant. Shioji remained reluctant to approve the British project, similar to Nissan's chairman Kawamata. He did not push for further options at this point. Shioji exchanged a memorandum with the British unions that they would cooperate closely on the issue.[201]

However, Duffy as the general secretary of the AUEW was more positive than Evans in response to Shioji's argument. The AUEW was the single union organising workers of the NSK plant in Peterlee and the Japanese electronics industry in Britain. With its "modest militant" self-image,[202] the AUEW was willing to accept the deal with Nissan. Duffy refrained from actively persuading Shioji in London. Evans was with Duffy, and the TGWU was one of the most influential unions in the British automobile sector and was firmly leftist.[203] Immediately after

[197] Mountfield, 2007b, p. 345.

[198] Sato, 2012, p. 99.

[199] MRCW, MSS, 292D/617/3, Terry Duffy to Ichiro Shioji, 28 July 1982.

[200] MRCW, MSS, 292D/617/3, General Secretary to David Basnett (GMWU), 8 April 1981; TNA, T466/200, Tebbit to Joseph, 3 April 1981.

[201] Sato, 2012, p. 99.

[202] MRCW, MSS.259/AEU/1/1/254, Executive Meeting, 12 April 1983.

[203] Peter Wickens, *The Road to Nissan: Flexibility, Quality, Teamwork*, Basingstoke: Macmillan, 1987, pp. 135–137. He recalls that the most powerful union in the North

the meeting, Duffy wrote to Shioji and expressed his union's welcome, stating that a Nissan plant in Britain was in the interest of both countries' workers.[204]

Knowing that Shioji was not enthusiastic about the project, Duffy took the initiative and persuaded Nissan's feasibility study team to speak with local British trade union leaders.[205] The AUEW called on NSK-Peterlee managing director Kawasaki for help in contacting the Nissan team.[206] Duffy was not fully aware, however, that Shioji did not oppose overseas operations but was cautious about the heavy financial burden of the British project. In fact, he was one of the few Japanese union leaders who were active in pushing overseas projects forward[207] while also paying attention to the losses of Japanese employment caused by such projects. Shioji had concentrated his unions' efforts on questioning the effects of the automation and robotisation of car assembly on workers' employment.[208] It was the first case in the world of unions addressing this problem.[209]

The local unions were quick to respond to Nissan's announcement, notably in the North East. The Northern Region Council (NRC) of the TUC held an executive meeting on 30 April, one month after Nissan had launched its feasibility study. At the meeting, the NRC decided that Nissan's plant must be established in the North East and that this was of the utmost priority.[210] The union leaders made certain that they would not greet the Nissan team with dozens of union leaders in a queue but

East was the GMB. Regional Secretary Tom Burlison was also chairman of the Northern TUC. The TGWU was strong in transport and docks, while the AUEW/AEU was strong in the engineering sector, shipbuilding, and mechanical crafts.

[204] MRCW, MSS, 292D/617/3, Terry Duffy to Ichiro Shioji, 28 July 1982.

[205] MRCW, MSS, 292D/617/3, General Secretary to David Basnett (GMWU), 8 April 1981; TNA, T466/200, Tebbit to Joseph, 3 April 1981.

[206] MRCW, 807/Box 19, vol. 2, AUEW Executive Council, 21 May 1985.

[207] On Nissan's plant project in the US, see Sect. 5 in Chapter 2 and Sect. 3 of this chapter.

[208] TNA, FO972/117, Foreign Policy Document No. 116, Labour Unions in Japan: Recent Developments and Future Prospects, 26 June 1984.

[209] Ibid.

[210] MRCW, MSS, 292D/77/36, Minutes of a meeting of the Executive Committee, 30 April 1981.

would limit their representatives to a maximum of five.[211] This was to avoid giving Nissan the image that the trade unions in the region were in conflict with each other. It was a wise choice based on the DoI's advice, which was brought to the unions in the North East by Labour MPs.[212] Losing the deal to Wales, Scotland, or Northern Ireland was not different from losing Nissan to other EC member states.

The NRC resolved on the day that the local member unions unanimously agreed to accept Nissan's single union agreement that it would pursue the same deal in sectors other than car assembly.[213] The NRC had component suppliers in mind and aimed to accommodate Nissan's request as widely as possible. It was decided on the matter because unemployment was very high due to the industrial decile, but the decile had also provided a chance. Labour–management relations were relatively cooperative compared to other parts of Britain where the steel and automobile sectors were still in business.[214] The resolution would later play a decisive role when Nissan decided on its plant location in March 1984.[215]

10 Lobbying Brussels

Now that Nissan had launched its feasibility study, the Thatcher administration, while showing hesitation to provide SFA, began to channel Britain's Japan policies to Brussels.[216] There was a risk that the European Commission would prohibit subsidies to sectors such as automobiles where overcapacity was suspected.[217] Commissioner Étienne Davignon

[211] Ibid.

[212] MRCW, MSS 292D 77/36, TUC Northern Region Council, Appendix 2 to Secretary's Report to be Presentation to the TUC Northern Regional Council Executive Committee, 26 March 1981.

[213] MRCW, MSS, 292D/77/36, Minutes of a meeting of the Executive Committee, 30 April 1981.

[214] Ibid.

[215] See Sect. 5 in Chapter 6.

[216] Hitoshi Suzuki, "How British Corporate Interests and Their Views on Japan Were Transferred to Brussels. The Case of Nissan Sunderland Plant and the Single European Act," in Christine Bouneau and David Burigana (eds.), *Experts et expertise en science et technologie en europe des années 1960 à nos jours. Société civile organisée, démocratie et prise de décision politique*, Brussels: P.I.E. Peter-Lang, 2017b, pp. 75–79. See also Sect. 5 of the previous chapter on the CBI's Japan policy.

[217] TNA, BT177/2813, Pulvermacher to Owen, 29 July 1980.

criticised Japanese plants launched in the EC for causing market distortion.[218] Britain had to confront such arguments.

The CBI lobbied Tory MPs through the Brighton Conservative Club[219] so that the CBI's policy of promoting collaboration with Japanese firms and welcoming their investments in Britain would be reflected at the EC level.[220] The CBI did not rely on its European umbrella organisation—the Union of Industrial and Employer Confederations of Europe (UNICE)—because it understood that the latter experienced sector-to-sector differences. Such conflicts frequently became member state-versus-member state confrontations. Thus, the CBI understood that the UNICE could not unify its voice effectively.[221] The CBI chose to lobby the Tories, who would take its concerns more efficiently to the heart of Brussels.

Among the Tory MPs, Julian Amery of the East Sussex constituency shared the CBI's views on Japan. From the same constituency, Sir John (Jack) Stewart-Clark was elected MEP. Sir John had regular contact with Amery and took the issue to Brussels. His report on Japan was issued in June 1981 for the External Economic Relations Committee of the European Parliament (EP) and clearly reflected the CBI's views on the Japanese.[222] Britain had surpassed the "free trade country" Germany in terms of openness to Japanese industry and was condemned not only by France and Italy but also by Germany as a "Trojan horse of Japan."[223] Sir John resisted such claims and criticised the EC for living the 1950s rather than facing the challenges of the 1980s and for creating a patchwork of protectionist methods.[224] While emphasising the European Commission's role in criticising Japan's trade surplus, his report proposed the necessity of the Commission and the Japanese government jointly launching an

[218] TNA, FV22/133, Cortazzi to McLaren, 11 July 1980.

[219] CACC (Churchill Archives Centre, Churchill College, Cambridge University), AMEJ 2/1/111, 30 April 1982.

[220] MRCW, MSS.200/C/3/INT/1/5A, meeting of 13 October 1980.

[221] MRCW, MSS.200/C/2014 Box 333, meeting of 5 February 1982, 7 June 1982.

[222] ACEU (Archive of the Council of the European Union) CM2, temporarily LR21360, European Parliament, "Working Documents 1980–1981, Trade Relations Between the EEC and Japan," 3 June 1981.

[223] TNA, FV22/133, Cortazzi to McLaren, 11 July 1980; Mountfield, 2007b, p. 346.

[224] ACEU, CM2, temporarily LR21360, European Parliament, "Working Documents 1980–1981, Trade Relations Between the EEC and Japan," 3 June 1981.

investment office to accommodate Japanese investments in Europe and to provide information on the Japanese market to small and medium-sized firms and trade unions to expand exports.[225] The EP did not adopt Sir John's report but instead chose a report that was more critical of aggressive Japanese exports, which was more reflective of the French and Italian claims. Sir John's arguments did not win a majority at this point. However, his suggestion that the EC should list protectionist methods hampering imports and investments would become the basic policy of the later Internal Market White Paper and the SEA prepared by Lord Cockfield.[226] The Thatcher administration became a forerunner of EC common policies owing to, although not solely depending on, Anglo-Japanese relations.

11 Negotiating Financial Aid

At the beginning of the negotiations, the DoI intended to provide Nissan with RDG but no SFA. The talks soon reached a deadlock[227] due to Nissan's retreat from its initial plan after the first feasibility study.[228] Robin Mountfield refused to give any promise on SFA until Nissan accepted the 80% requirement for local content.[229] Sir Keith Joseph, secretary of state for industry, envisaged that Britain should provide Nissan with its requested amount to seal the deal,[230] but he did not win majority support among the cabinet members at this point.[231] The extent to which the DoI should accommodate Nissan's requests became a key factor.

The Nissan team returned to London on 17 July 1981. To the DoI's disappointment, the team submitted a plan falling far short of its announcement in January.[232] There were five new points.[233] First, the

[225] Ibid.

[226] See Sect. 3 in Chapter 6.

[227] Suzuki, 2015a, pp. 87–90; Mountfield, 2007, p. 111.

[228] TNA, T466/200, DOI to PM, 30 July 1981.

[229] TNA, T466/200, Chivers to Chief Secretary, 13 November 1981.

[230] Ibid.

[231] For further arguments on aid, see Sect. 8 of the next chapter.

[232] TNA, T466/200, DOI to PM, 30 July 1981.

[233] Ibid; TNA, T466/200, NT, DOI to PM, 30 July 1981; Mountfield, 2007a, p. 111.

launch of production would take place in 1984 as knock-down exports with 30% local content. Second, Nissan would export an additional 100 thousand units from Japan *outside* the Anglo-Japanese VER. Third, a new model would undergo assembly with 61% local content in 1986, but exports to the continent would be postponed to 1987. Fourth, the achievement of 200 thousand units of annual output would be postponed to 1989, and 45 thousand of those units would be exported; at this point, local content could *possibly* reach 80%. Finally, Nissan wished to receive 52 million pounds of SFA in addition to the automatically provided RDG of 75 million. This would help Nissan earn its first profit in 1988.

Thatcher was deeply disappointed with the retreat. With her approval, the DoI immediately refused the proposal.[234] Almost all the original aspects had been scaled down or delayed. The project was not worth 127 million pounds of the taxpayers' money. It was obvious that the DoI suspected that Nissan was trying to abandon the project without saying so.[235] The DoI replied to Nissan that 30% local content was too low and that the VER amount was up to the SMMT and JAMA; therefore, the DoI could not intervene.[236] The DoI prioritised Nissan's achievement of local content over the deadline for realising it. The Thatcher administration notified Nissan that it would not negotiate financial aid.

It was Nissan's turn to be surprised by the unexpectedly negative reaction. Nissan immediately withdrew the second point on exports outside the VER count and requested that this point not be reported in the cabinet meeting. However, the DoI, deeply disappointed, did report to the cabinet, although it refrained from using this incident as a bargaining chip.[237] The DoI's anger immediately attracted the attention of FCO officials who were specialised in Asian affairs, and they warned the DoI to be careful not to give Nissan the slightest impression that the British government's welcome was being withdrawn.[238] The Thatcher administration was extremely cautious not to allow the media to hear the phrase "30% local content," which would inevitably spark fury among British

[234] TNA, T466/200, NT, DOI to PM, 30 July 1981.

[235] Ibid; Mountfield, 2007a, p. 111.

[236] TNA, T466/200, NT, DOI to PM, 30 July 1981.

[237] TNA, T466/200, Private Secretary to Mason, 5 August 1981; TNA, T466/200, NT, DOI to PM, 30 July 1981.

[238] TNA, T466/200, Gowrie to Tebbit, 6 August 1981.

trade unions and the public.[239] It would have an impact not only on the Nissan deal but on all Japanese investments should negative public opinion flare-up.

Reconciliation and rapprochement came from the Nissan side after the summer. Nissan invited ministers and DoI officials to Japan.[240] A follow-up negotiation began on 16 September in Tokyo.[241] More crucial was Nissan's invitation to Mountfield and his staff to visit Nissan's R&D section, which was closely restricted to Nissan's own people and Japanese component suppliers.[242] Observing Nissan's courtesy, Mountfield felt that Nissan would not withdraw from the British project and was somewhat relieved.[243] He advised Nissan that the achievement of 80% local content could be postponed to 1985 or 1986 if Nissan adhered strictly to the 80% level and submitted an exact list of components imported from Japan.[244] The deadline for Nissan to decide was 1982.[245] Nissan in turn asked Mountfield why SFA was not offered, but in vain. Mountfield and his staff estimated that twenty to thirty million pounds of aid was sufficient.[246] The Treasury sided with Mountfield and was reluctant to pay SFA as well.[247] There was a risk that the European Commission would intervene in "unnecessary" subsidies.[248]

To convince the British guests of the necessity of Japanese-style labour–management relations, Nissan took Mountfield and his staff to three Japanese component suppliers: one of Nissan's own, one of Toyota, and one of *Toyo Kogyo* (Mazda).[249] This tour was unusual because it was still the time when Japanese assemblers purchased components primarily from

239 Ibid.

240 Contrary to the contents of archival files, Mountfield testified that the DoI had request a visit to Japan; Mountfield, 2007a, p. 111.

241 TNA, T466/200, Mountfield to Secretary of State, 1 October 1981.

242 Mountfield, 2007b, p. 351.

243 TNA, T466/200, Mountfield to Secretary of State, 1 October 1981.

244 Ibid.

245 Ibid.

246 TNA, T466/200, Chivers to Chief Secretary, 13 November 1981.

247 TNA, T466/200, Brittan to PM, without date.

248 TNA, T466/200, Chivers to Chief Secretary, 13 November 1981. See also the next section.

249 Mountfield, 2007b, p. 351.

their own *keiretsu* suppliers.[250] Shioji and his JAW connection organised this trip to show the visitors that single union agreements were not a phenomenon limited to Nissan but were the best practice shared among Japanese manufacturers. Stocks of components in plants were kept to a minimum[251] in the so-called just-in-time "lean" production approach, which decreased assembly costs. Purchasing contracts for components in Japan covered long periods in order to reduce the costs, and the *keiretsu* connection was vital to ensure that the contract was not unilaterally abandoned by either side. Single union agreements were at the core of sustaining this system by diminishing strikes that would delay the supplies.[252] It was the core of the Toyota (and Japanese) just-in-time production system.

Mountfield replied to Nissan merely in general terms, stating that labour–management relations in Britain had improved compared to the past. Quite the opposite would become true in British coal mines in the following years, but it was significant that Mountfield and the DoI officials took note of the trade union dimension as crucial for Nissan's final decision. The DoI provided necessary information on the Nissan negotiation to the TUC leaders and local member unions. This became an indispensable element for Sunderland in the North East being selected.[253]

Ishihara and Sir Keith Joseph held a meeting in Tokyo. They were joined by Sir Hugh from the embassy and Mountfield with his team. Sir Keith, who was willing to provide Nissan with the extended amount of financial aid it had requested, was tougher on Nissan in his demands. He told Ishihara that Nissan's decision should be made before long owing to the possible tightening of EC regulations on Japanese cars and member states' additional exclusions.[254] Costs and "mere details" were not significant.[255] Sir Keith was crystal clear about the 80% local content

[250] See Sect. 2 in Chapter 2.

[251] Mountfield, 2007a, p. 111.

[252] TNA, T466/200, Mountfield to Secretary of State, 1 October 1981.

[253] See Sect. 5 in Chapter 6.

[254] TNA, T466/200, Allan to Chancellor, 7 October 1981; TNA, T466/200, Mountfield to Secretary of State, 1 October 1981.

[255] TNA, T466/200, Mountfield to Secretary of State, 1 October 1981.

requirement, of which Thatcher had repeatedly emphasised the indispensable importance.[256] Seeing Sir Keith's decisiveness, Nissan withdrew its retreating proposal and returned to its original announcement of January. Thatcher was relieved.[257] If the Nissan deal failed, it would not go down alone but would affect Japanese investments in Britain as a whole.[258] She and the DoI were certain in their offer that Nissan would be provided primary access to the EC market, which in the long term would benefit Nissan more than other Japanese assemblers.[259] In contrast, Nissan felt that its project, if successful, would cause a spillover effect and attract further Japanese investment and that it was therefore entitled to generous financial aid.[260] While both sides were firmly in consensus on the European dimension of the project, negotiations on RDG and SFA were doomed to face difficulty.

The DoI's concerns were not merely directed at Nissan. Although confirming the merits of Nissan's plant in Britain and its future exports, the Treasury carefully questioned the actual scale of Nissan's contribution to the British economy. High local content was at the core. The Treasury attempted to use every opportunity to reduce the amount of financial aid. The DoI counterargued that the effect generated by Nissan would not be limited to export profits and new jobs but would spill over widely to learning good management, production, and quality control practices.[261] However, the Treasury also raised an important point that the DoI underestimated the risk of other member states—France and Italy—continuing to maintain protectionist methods to hamper British exports of Nissan cars by "ignoring" EC laws.[262] The Treasury's fear later proved to be correct.[263]

[256] TNA, T466/200, Private Secretary to Ellison, 16 November 1981.

[257] TNA, T466/200, Ellison to Scholar, 6 January 1982.

[258] TNA, T466/200, Lovell to Mountfield, 5 January 1982.

[259] TNA, T466/200, PJ (DOI) to PM, 12 November 1981.

[260] TNA, T466/200, Nissan Motor Co. Ltd., The Proposed Project of Inward Investment: Government Financial Assistance Required, February 1982.

[261] TNA, T466/200, Lovell to Chivers, 18 November 1981; TNA, T466/200, Bruce-Gardyne to Chief Secretary, 13 November 1981.

[262] Ibid.

[263] See Sect. 10 in Chapter 6.

12 The Second Round of Talks

At the end of 1981, Ishihara announced that Nissan would pursue the British project. He insisted on not sufficiently consulting the unions before his decision. Nissan had already incurred a debt of 500 billion yen at this point, but Ishihara was willing to accelerate the 1000-billion-yen project.[264] As much financial aid as possible would have to be secured from the British government. RDG covering 15% of the total investment costs would be increased to 22% if Nissan chose a special development area. The DoI and Nissan held the next negotiation on 18 February 1982.[265]

To secure the necessary amount of RDG, Nissan asked Thatcher's administration whether the RDG would be affected by future financial reforms. The latter did not answer specifically but replied that the government would amicably consider future losses should Nissan face them.[266] As the secretary of state for industry, Patrick Jenkin issued a memorandum to Nissan on this issue to accommodate its concerns. The DoI started to consider the possibility of providing Nissan with SFA covering 8% of Nissan's overall investment, which would cover nearly 30% of the overall costs if combined with RDG.[267] At this point, Thatcher was determined not to provide SFA.

Facing a vague reply, Nissan made a bold request that the British government cover half the total investment costs. This meant RDG of 122.1 million pounds, covering 22% of the costs, and SFA of another 184.5 pounds.[268] Nissan wished to obtain compensation for the reduced 15% coverage of RDG by receiving SFA should it choose a location other than a special development area. The firm believed that a project employing 4,676 workers in the plant alone, with an additional eleven

[264] Sato, 2012, pp. 98–100.

[265] Mountfield recalled these talks taking place in November 1981 in London; Mountfield, 2007a, p. 111.

[266] TNA, PREM19/1073, DTI, "Nissan Project and Regional Assistance Changes," 2 September 1983.

[267] TNA, T466/200, PJ (DOI) to PM, 15 December 1981.

[268] TNA, T466/200, Nissan Motor Co. Ltd., The Proposed Project of Inward Investment: Government Financial Assistance Required, February 1982.

thousand in the component sectors and another 1,500 in plant construction, was entitled to generous aid.[269] Nissan calculated the risks of future inflation, production losses caused by labour disputes, and, furthermore, the possibility of a future Labour government leaving the EC.[270]

The DoI was surprised and appalled by Nissan's "rude" claims.[271] In July the previous year, the latter had retreated from its original announcement, causing disappointment in the DoI[272] by yet again returning to the table and asking for more. The DoI had briefly replied that SFA could be provided up to 10%, and Nissan could receive 12% as a special deal,[273] but this was strictly the upper limit.[274] At the same time, the DoI started to negotiate with the Treasury to convince it that Nissan was entitled to SFA based on the seventh clause of the Industry Act.[275] Nissan was correct in assuming that Thatcher's administration was planning to reduce the government budget and therefore asked for SFA to secure as much aid as possible. The DoI would have to compensate for Nissan's future losses to seal the deal.[276] The huge amount of governmental expenditure could be split over separate budget years so as not to empty the DoI's regional support budget.[277]

Thatcher decided to wait until Nissan proposed a more moderate plan. Nissan's decision would not depend solely on the amount of RDG and SFA.[278] Should Nissan decide to withdraw its project altogether, the public, when hearing Nissan's suggestion of "30% local content,"[279] would not condemn the government but would point at Nissan instead.[280] Tebbit rightly estimated this result and was confident

[269] Ibid.

[270] Ibid.

[271] TNA, T466/200, Chivers to Allan, 22 February 1982.

[272] See the previous section.

[273] Mountfield, 2007a, p. 118. Mountfield mentioned the largest SFA coverage of 15%; Mountfield, 2007b, p. 351.

[274] Sato, 2012, pp. 104–105.

[275] TNA, T466/200, Thornton to Allan, 15 February 1982.

[276] TNA, T466/200, Brittan to PM, 18 December 1981.

[277] TNA, T466/200, Chivers to Cheif Secretary, 12 December 1981.

[278] TNA, T466/200, PJ (DOI) to PM, 15 December 1981.

[279] See the previous section.

[280] TNA, T466/200, Tebbit to PM, 22 December 1981.

that if Nissan abandoned the British project, it would merely worsen the Anglo-Japanese VER. This would damage not only Nissan's exports but also the Japanese assemblers as a whole. Ishihara, as JAMA's president, would receive criticism not only from the British government but even more from his Japanese colleagues. The ball was back in Nissan's court. In early 1982, the two parties started to discuss the actual text of what would later become the Memorandum of Understandings of 1984.[281] It was referred to as a "gentlemen's agreement" that was not legally binding.[282]

The Treasury noted Nissan's bold requests and downgraded the pros of the project. Encouraged by British industry, Treasury officials commented that "two new jobs in a Nissan plant would lead to three unemployment in other British firms."[283] However, Thatcher took Nissan's request seriously. Was the British government demanding more than Nissan had expected?[284] With RDG and SFA combined, the 30% coverage of total investment costs was the definite limit.[285] Should she provide other methods to lighten Nissan's financial burden? Thatcher wrote personally to Nissan's chairman Kawamata and proposed a new idea. The Bank of England could lease plant equipment for Nissan under amicable conditions.[286] For months, no answer came from Tokyo. Then, the Falkland crisis broke out and enabled Nissan to postpone its decision.

13 The Falkland Crisis

The Falkland crisis broke out in March 1982 when Argentines landed on South Georgia Island. The crisis, which took place nearly 12,000 km away from London, had an impact on the Nissan negotiations. In April, combat between British and Argentinian forces started. Because the US attempted to persuade the British not to send troops, Thatcher faced the risk of isolation among Western countries. Japan followed Ronald Reagan's lead,

[281] Mountfield, 2007a, p. 112.

[282] Ibid.

[283] TNA, T466/200, Jenkins to Chivers, 17 Novembe 1981.

[284] TNA, T466/200, Scholar to Ellison, 21 December 1981.

[285] TNA, T466/200, PJ (DOI) to PM, 15 December 1981; TNA, T466/200, Allan to Chief Secretary, 19 January 1982.

[286] TNA, PREM19/1073, PM to Kawamata, 18 March 1981; TNA, PREM19/1073, DTI, "Nissan Project and Regional Assistance Changes," 2 September 1983.

and Anglo-Japanese relations soured. However, Japan had also ignored the American and EC request to join the ban on Argentina based on the hope that Argentina would support Japan in its territorial problems with the USSR on the northern islands.[287] Thatcher was urged to redefine relations with Japan to prevent isolation but without showing economic weakness.

In May 1982, the Treasury, the DoI, the Ministry of Defence and the FCO issued a joint report on Anglo-Japanese relations.[288] Thatcher named the group the Cabinet Official Group on British Policy Towards Japan. She aimed to clarify relations with Japan while maintaining pressure on economic issues. This was necessary not only to continue the Anglo-Japanese VER on automobile exports but also, more concretely, to urge the Nissan negotiations forward. The DoI was in charge of the economic and trade aspects of the report.[289] The Japan policies shared by the CBI and Tory MPs/MEPs, which were transferred to Brussels by Sir John,[290] were once more clarified and consolidated by Whitehall.

The joint report made it clear that Britain should welcome Japanese investment so that the "first" Japanese plants in Europe would be launched in Britain but that it should assure a very high ratio of local content. Japanese screw-driver operations, typically kit imports and knock-down assembly, were not acceptable.[291] For diplomatic pressure, Britain would leave it to the French and Italian governments to criticise Japan's highly protected domestic market and aggressive exports.[292] Sir John, MEP, had criticised France for its strong Trojan horse mentality, but it was still of use for imposing "European" pressure on Japan. The DoI took a dual track on the VER, criticising it as undesirable and a drawback of free trade on the one hand but recommending to maintain

[287] Cortazzi, 1998, p. 158.

[288] TNA, CAB130/1198, Cabinet Official Group on British Policy Towards Japan, 2 February 1982.

[289] Ibid.

[290] See Sect. 10 of this chapter.

[291] See Sect. 2 in Chapter 3 on the Nissan-Ireland case.

[292] TNA, CAB130/1198, Cabinet Official Group on British Policy Towards Japan, 2 February 1982.

the current Anglo-Japanese agreement on the other.[293] The VER would add additional pressure on Nissan to make a decision, as it had successfully urged not only Nissan but also other Japanese assemblers to consider investments in Britain.[294]

In accommodating Japanese investments, the DoI calculated three points of Britain's advantage: favourable corporate taxation, low wages,[295] and the English language. The report emphasised that Japanese plants must be established in Britain and contribute to local employment. Local content requirements were crucial not only for reviving the British component sectors but also for creating jobs. Financial aid was the bargaining chip to make Japanese firms maintain high ratios of local sourcing. Japan's trade conflicts with the EC and member states gave Britain a chance to attract Japanese investment.[296]

The report showed a change in Britain's view towards Japan. Harsh criticism of aggressive Japanese exports had vanished and was replaced with sympathetic understanding of Japan's international circumstances. During the period of Japan–EC trade conflicts, it was rare for a European country to state that "unemployment in Europe was not possibly and solely caused by Japanese exports" and that "Japanese exports were fully legal."[297] Thatcher went so far as to state that "much of the criticism of the Japanese was unfair" and that the Japanese "were everybody's scapegoat."[298] Like the queen in Tokyo seven years before,[299] Thatcher praised made in Japan products and stressed that the Japanese should not be "blamed for producing first-class cars, cheaper video recorders and advanced cameras, bought eagerly by western consumers."[300] In terms of either economics or security, Japan-bashing was not fair in her belief.

[293] The US reached a bilateral agreement with Japan, and Japanese self-restriction under the MITI monitor started in May 1981. VER functioned as an export cartel and was a violation of GATT rules.

[294] Mountfield, 2007a, p. 116.

[295] Wages in Britain had fallen slightly below those in Japan. This was helped by the pound/yen exchange rate.

[296] TNA, CAB130/1198, Cabinet Official Group on British Policy Towards Japan, 2 February 1982.

[297] Ibid.

[298] Thatcher, 1993, pp. 495–496.

[299] See Sect. 3 of the previous chapter.

[300] Thatcher, 1993, pp. 495–496.

Thatcher was willing to defend Japan's position at a time when Japanese multinationals were becoming stakeholders in the British (and the EC) economy. Her fame grew rapidly in Japan.

After the Falkland conflict had ceased, Nissan Vice President Okuma once more visited London in August.[301] He told the DoI that Nissan desired more time for its decision.[302] The reasons were the economic recession caused by the second oil crisis in 1979 and the Iranian revolution.[303] Seeing that Nissan was attempting further postponement, Thatcher accepted the delay but in turn persuaded Nissan to accept the 80% rule for local content as a definite goal,[304] no matter when the deadline of achieving it would be. Her administration had now solidified its approach to dealing with the Japanese on trade and investments. Bit by bit, Nissan was cut off from its retreating option.

Unable to convince Kawamata and Shioji about the British project, Ishihara chose the tactic of cutting the two leaders off from each other and separately imposing pressure on them. He compelled Thatcher to persuade Kawamata and himself opened fire against Shioji and his unions. He named Taiji Hosokawa head of personnel issues. Hosokawa had graduated from the University of Tokyo with a degree in metallurgy in 1945 and joined Nissan the next year. He was an engineer and had no experience in personnel but was firmly anti-union.[305] Kawakatsu intensified his secret team's propaganda and leaked negative information on the unions to prominent media, namely, *Nikkei*, *Asahi*, Diamond, *Toyo-keizai*, *Bunshun (Bungei-shunjyu)*, and *Keizaikai*.[306] Kawakatsu uncompromisingly cut the unions into pieces based on hints from the privatisation reforms of the Japanese National Railways (JNR, from April 1987 the six

[301] Mountfield testified that this was in July; Mountfield, 2007a, p. 112.

[302] Sato, 2012, pp. 117–118.

[303] Mountfield, 2007a, p. 112.

[304] TNA, PREM19/1073, Cortazzi to FCO, 22 January 1983.

[305] Kawakatsu, 2018, pp. 124–127; Hosokawa was named director in the following year. See Sect. 6 of the next chapter.

[306] Kawakatsu, 2018, pp. 134–139. He claimed that it was he who inspired Takasugi's (anti-union) novel on Nissan via the publisher Diamond; ibid., pp. 138–139. Also see Ryo Takasugi, *Full Gas to Hegemony; A Documental Novel on Nissan* (Haken eno shissou), Tokyo: Kodansha, 1984. Kawakatsu and his team delivered fliers with negative information on Shioji and the unions by obtaining names and addresses, violating, in today's terms, privacy information; ibid., pp. 148–150.

Japan Railway(s) Company (JR) and JR Freight).[307] One of the highlights of the reform was that it broke the resisting leftist unions.

14 Thatcher Visits Japan

Thatcher had visited Japan in April 1977 as Tory leader and a second time in June 1979, shortly after becoming PM. Her third visit in September 1982 was scheduled before her flight to Hong Kong and China. Thatcher had wished to arrive in Tokyo after her heavy responsibilities in Hong Kong were completed and she could relax, but this itinerary was opposed by the FCO for preparation reasons. An invitation from South Korea had to be declined due to the tight schedule. The official purpose of her visit was to prepare for the G7 Williamsburg summit and meet Japanese PM Zenko Suzuki,[308] but a call on Nissan was scheduled from the beginning.[309] Ishihara, together with Okuma, proposed that Thatcher meet Kawamata in private[310] so that he would agree to the project. Thatcher was determined to push the Nissan deal forward. In March, former PM Edward Heath visited Nissan's Oppama plant. Nissan executives would understand the meaning of Thatcher's call without ambiguity.

The invitation was a bolt from the blue for Kawamata and Shioji. Thatcher wrote to Kawamata that she wished to invite him to tea as a

[307] Kawakatsu, 2018, pp. 139–147. Kawakatsu met Yoshiyuki Kasai, who was in charge of personnel issues for the JNR, to learn how to 'negotiate' with the unions. Kasai had studied at the University of Tokyo (BA) and Wisconsin Madison (MA) and became president of JR Tokai in 1995 and then chairman in 2004.

[308] TNA, CAB130/1198, Minutes of meeting, 15 February 1982.

[309] Thatcher's 'invitation' to speak with Nissan's chairman Kawamata has until recently been understood as a sudden announcement that was made merely a month before her visit. Mountfield did not mention a specific name; Mountfield, 2007b, p. 356.

[310] Shioji, 2012, p. 243; *Nikkei*, 12 September 1982. In an interview six years later, Ishihara testified that Sir Hugh as ambassador first opposed this idea because there had been no previous cases of a British PM meeting a corporate official in private and that he as the ambassador must at least join the meeting; Ibid. Kawakatsu, as manager of Nissan's External Affairs Section, claimed that it was he who proposed to MOFA that Thatcher meet Kawamata in person and that MOFA promised him it would contact Sir Hugh; Kawakatsu, 2018, pp. 118–119. This testimony requires examination through third-party sources. Why MOFA trusted a Nissan manager is doubtful given that his proposal was made, according to Kawakatsu's testimony, "without Ishihara's official approval," and therefore, there was no guarantee that Kawamata would oblige.

courtesy for escorting her at the Zama plant in April 1977.[311] Kawamata and Shioji were puzzled by such short notice and doubted her intentions, which were not stated in the letter. Worse still, Thatcher publicly announced on 14 September that she would meet Kawamata in Tokyo. Kawamata could not simply (and rudely) decline the invitation, but once sitting face to face with the PM, he would have to comment on the British project. Thatcher would be the last person to speak negatively about it, making her lose face in public. Thatcher's administration was informed that Kawamata and Shioji were cautious about the financial burden,[312] and the two men were aware that she knew of their caution. A week before Thatcher's visit, Kawamata and Shioji held a meeting and discussed how to face the Iron Lady.[313]

Kawamata: Among our lined-up models in Japan, only Cedric and Gloria are profitable, and all the rest add to our debt. It is surprising that we still survive. That is why I am opposing the British project. Take a look at our debt. But [Ishihara] relocates our profits gained from our exports to overseas investment. I am at a loss.

Shioji: I think [Ishihara] assumes we could borrow money without limit.

Kawamata: We are now able to, but we must repay. [Ishihara] should consider more whether an investment is safe or not. We invested in the US, then Spain, then Italy. […] Another project in Britain will add further burden. I am still not confident that Nissan could bear it.

Shioji: […] I think we should have concentrated in the US.

Kawamata: Toyota […] collaborated with GM (in the US) and fended off the debt risk […]. They will further compete with us in Japan, which is one of the reasons we have reduced our domestic share. […] On the contrary, we wander all over overseas. Flamboyant… […] My personal activity would produce little news in headlines, but she is prime minister of the British Empire. The Iron Lady who won the Falkland crisis. How would she respond if I greeted her coldly? But I dare not respond in her ways.

Shioji: That is her intention, is it?

Kawamata: I expect our government to warn her not to risk losing face (additions by the authour).

[311] Sato, 2012, pp. 118–119. On the Zama plant visit, see Sect. 5 in Chapter 3.

[312] TNA, PREM19/822, Spencer to Butler, 15 October 1982.

[313] Shioji, 2012, pp. 240–241.

At Kawamata's request, Shioji immediately contacted LDP politicians. He asked Yasuhiro Nakasone, then minister of the Administrative Management Agency, who would become PM in a month's time, to inform MOFA of Nissan's (and both men's own) concern about facing Thatcher in person and her hidden intention.[314] MOFA replied that Thatcher merely had to show an effort in the public eye.[315] Foreign minister Yoshio Sakurauchi, MITI's minister during the mid-1960s who had therefore known Shioji ever since,[316] "encouraged" him and Kawamata to make the best of their head-to-head match with the Iron Lady,[317] responding that the government "could not intervene in (mere) corporate matters," and in any case, it was "too late for him to intervene."[318] Kawamata and Shioji felt far from eased because Thatcher could bring with her a bombshell proposal, making it impossible for Nissan to withdraw.

On 17 September 1982, Thatcher arrived at Tokyo-Haneda airport. The last official visit of a British PM dated back to Edward Heath's visit in 1972. Thatcher was greeted by an enthusiastic Japanese crowd who had seen the Falkland crisis on television. The wide media coverage would put further pressure on Nissan to decide about the British project. Thatcher visited a robot plant of Fanuc (Fujitsu) where robots automatically assembled robots for automatic mass production. She was pleased and impressed by the silent, human-free shop floor, which seemed not to be an industrial plant and "was exciting."[319] In a good temper, Thatcher said she would buy lunch for anyone who launched such a plant in Britain.[320] Thatcher held a meeting with PM Suzuki on 19 September, which lasted (merely) half an hour. She stressed that Japan should import as many British industrial products as possible.

Late in the afternoon of 19 September, Thatcher received Kawamata at *Geihinkan*—the State Guest House, Akasaka Palace—where she was

[314] Sato, 2012, pp. 119–121.

[315] Ibid.

[316] See also Sect. 3 in Chapter 2.

[317] Shioji, 2012, pp. 242–243.

[318] Ibid.

[319] *Asahi-shinbun*, 20 September 1982.

[320] Ibid.

staying as the official guest of the Japanese government. Ishihara was travelling in Mexico (or the US) and was unable to attend "as planned."[321] Thatcher started the conversation with a general topic and asked Kawamata about the current state of the automobile sector. Kawamata replied that the market of the developed countries had become saturated and that the sector was now dependent on the rise of developing countries. Uninterested in such side stories, Thatcher immediately came to the point. She did not mean, of course, to force Kawamata into a decision and wished Nissan to freely decide on its project.[322] However, without leaving a breathing space for Kawamata, Thatcher continued by describing Britain as the best suitable location for investment because British labour was highly skilled, and taxes were low. She recounted the British Empire's history of sustaining free trade worldwide and creating employment elsewhere.[323] It was now up to American, European, and Japanese firms to do the same in Britain. Unable to bear the Oxford-style lecture, Kawamata interrupted to ask whether a Nissan plant could be operated with a single union agreement. Slightly disappointed, Thatcher bluntly answered that she knew of several successful Japanese plants, of which two had signed no-strike agreements. There were more than a thousand American firms in Britain and nearly 180 German firms; why were there only 24 Japanese firms?[324] Thatcher resumed her lecture.

After the lengthy talk, Kawamata tried to bring the issue back on track. He carefully pointed out that British-made components were expensive, and furthermore, labour–management relations in Britain were still a serious concern.[325] Kawamata had not yet received a positive report from Shioji on this issue. Seeing that Thatcher was paying close attention, Kawamata asked whether the British government could build the plant at its own expense, purchase all the necessary equipment, and lease it to

[321] There are different sources that explain where Ishihara was during the talks, but the destination is insignificant. Ishihara's absence was most significant for him and Thatcher so that Kawamata would face her in person.

[322] Sato, 2012, p. 124.

[323] TNA, PREM19/822, Record of a conversation between PM and Chairman of Nissan Motor Company, 19 September 1982.

[324] TNA, PREM19/1073, The FCO counted these as 1,500, 200, and 24, respectively. Cortazzi to FCO, 20 January 1983.

[325] TNA, PREM19/822, Record of a conversation between PM and Chairman of Nissan Motor Company, 19 September 1982; Sato, 2012, pp. 124–125.

Nissan.[326] It was the first time Kawamata had spoken about this plan, even to Nissan's executive board. Thatcher responded that the construction was possible, but the lease would have to be confirmed back in London. The meeting had lasted an hour and a half. At the end of their conversation, Kawamata told Thatcher that Nissan owed a great debt to the British manufacturer Austin from the post-war period[327] and that he as president had named Nissan's Cedric saloon based on that experience.[328] Thatcher understood that Kawamata was now speaking from his heart. From this conversation onwards, she personally wrote to Kawamata about financial aid and the lease issue.[329] After bidding farewell to Kawamata at nine o'clock, Thatcher joined an embassy dinner with embassy staff and British businessmen in Tokyo.

On 20 September, Thatcher met MITI's minister Shintaro Abe—former PM Shinzo Abe's father—and emphasised that she wished to see Nissan make a positive decision soon.[330] Assisted by Sir Hugh, Thatcher was desperate to sell BAe146 jets and Harrier jump jets, which had dominated the Falkland combat. Thatcher had lobbied Washington in late 1979 to put pressure on Japan for its increased responsibility for sustaining Western alliances by expanding its defence budget. She had attempted to use American pressure to sell British aircraft to Japan [331] and tried this tactic again with Abe, but in vain. Japanese purchases of aircraft—both military and civilian—were "preserved" for American manufacturers.

At lunch on the same day, Thatcher gave a speech to Japanese businessmen from *Keidanren* and other business groups about how she had been making tremendous efforts to reduce the workforce and rationalise the nationalised industry. Her planned ten-minute talk lasted more than

[326] Ibid.

[327] Mountfield, 2007a, p. 117. See also Sect. 2 in Chapter 2.

[328] TNA, PREM19/822, Record of a conversation between PM and Chairman of Nissan Motor Company, 19 September 1982.

[329] Mountfield, 2007b, p. 357.

[330] *Nikkei*, 21 September 1982; *Asahi-shinbun*, 21 September 1982.

[331] Suzuki, "Post-Brexit Britain, the EU, and Japan: The Car Industry, the Aero Sector, and Military Cooperation," forthcoming.

four times longer.[332] She found more friends in Japan than back home.[333] As Sir Hugh recalled, Thatcher was not in a good mood throughout her stay,[334] possibly because Japanese food was not to her taste, because she had failed to get the go-ahead from Kawamata, or because of the heavy burden awaiting her in Hong Kong. Thatcher left Haneda Airport on 21 September, relieving Sir Hugh and the embassy staff and,[335] to a lesser extent, Kawamata.

15 Ishihara's Call at No. 10 Downing

Despite imposing pressure on Nissan's chairman Kawamata, Thatcher was not fully able to convince Ishihara, with his greatest concern about frequent labour disputes in Britain. Ishihara wanted the new plant to be operated with only one union organising the workers—the single union agreement. This was atypical in British industrial relations and provoked wide debate over Japanisation,[336] especially among the TGWU and the General, Municipal, Boilermakers, and Allied Trade Union (GMB) members, who have traditionally been influential in the British automobile sector. Thatcher invited Ishihara to No. 10 Downing on 19 October 1982. She was joined by her secretary and Sir Patrick Jenkin, secretary of state for industry.[337]

Thatcher started by telling Ishihara that she had no intention of forcing Nissan into a decision, but she emphasised that Britain was the best location for investment in the EC. She referred to the split among Nissan executives and questioned whether she was "of any help for him."[338] Ishihara understood what she meant. Thatcher had risked herself in the public eye by meeting Kawamata in Tokyo a month before. Nissan

[332] *Asahi-shinbun*, 22 September 1982.

[333] See Sect. 13 of this chapter on the privatisation of JNR.

[334] Coratzzi, 1998, pp. 186–187.

[335] Ibid.

[336] See, for example, Dave Beale, *Driven by Nissan?: A Critical Guide to the New Management Techniques*, London: Lawrence & Wishart, 1994; Garrahan & Stewart, 1992, p. 3; Wickens, 1987.

[337] The Department of Industry (DoI) and the Department of Trade (DoT) merged in 1983 and became the Department of Trade and Industry (DTI).

[338] TNA, PREM19/822, Note for the record, PM's Meeting with the President of Nissan, 19 October 1982.

could not further postpone its decision or, even worse, retreat from Britain. She would lose face but would not go down alone. Nissan's reputation in Britain would be seriously damaged. Thatcher resumed the history lecture she had given to Kawamata and stressed that the British Empire had made foreign investments worldwide to counter protectionism and that it was the turn of Japan and its industry to do the same. Thatcher also referred to Nissan's difficulties at its plants in Mexico and the US. Ishihara responded by confirming her view that Britain was the best place for investment and that protectionism damaged industrial competitiveness.[339] They were in harmony on these points.

Thatcher then went into the details of the project and once more stressed the agreement in August that local content would start at 60% and reach 80% at the earliest point possible.[340] Ishihara concurred but requested as much leeway as possible regarding the deadline for reaching the goal. For Thatcher and the DoI, the requirement had been fundamental from the beginning of the negotiations, but she agreed with Ishihara's request, to his relief. The agreement would be reflected in the two parties' agreement signed in February 1984.[341] Thatcher and the DoI refrained from putting pressure on the ambitious export goals so as not to make Nissan retreat in local content requirements. If Nissan cars made in Britain were not exported to the continent, they would be sold in Britain instead, further damaging BL's market share, but Thatcher and the DoI prioritised high local content and, accordingly, saved the British components industry.[342] Thatcher emphasised that Japanese investments were welcomed as long as they created jobs in Britain.

Ishihara had some words about this. Was it possible to face only one union in wage bargaining, as was the case in Japan? Thatcher advised Ishihara to make the single union agreement a pre-condition for Nissan's final decision.[343] Her idea was swiftly supported by Sir Patrick, who raised examples of Japanese multinationals in Britain that had succeed in that

[339] Ibid.

[340] See Sect. 13 of this chapter on the Falkland crisis.

[341] See Sect. 8 of the next chapter.

[342] TNA, PREM19/822, Note for the record, PM's Meeting with the President of Nissan, 19 October 1982. For the same argument see also Pardi, 2014.

[343] Ibid.

way.[344] Ishihara was convinced by this "good idea" and soon adopted it. In addition to his call at No. 10 Downing, Ishihara had sent a team to the North East to meet local union leaders of the TUC's Northern Council and the Advisory, Conciliation and Arbitration Service (ACAS).[345] The Nissan team had asked the ACAS in early October to arrange its visit to NewCastle and Cardiff.[346] Seeing this move, the Executive Council of the AUEW designated G. Arnold to be in charge of the Nissan deal.[347] The AUEW was prepared to welcome Nissan to the North East. Contrary to Nissan's fears, the British unions had gradually reduced their hostility to Japanese investment, partly because requirements for a high proportion of locally produced components could secure employment in Britain[348] and partly because competition from Spanish and Central and Eastern European manufacturers had entered the picture.[349]

At the end of their conversation, Ishihara requested that Thatcher persuade Kawamata to overcome his anxiety about Nissan's financial burden. According to Ishihara, the chairman had not informed him of his plan.[350] However, for Thatcher, persuasion of the executives seemed to be Ishihara's responsibility more than hers. Nonetheless, Thatcher assured Ishihara that it was her intention to do so. Sir Patrick later recalled that Kawamata and Shioji had prioritised the Japanese domestic market more than the overseas market,[351] as had Mountfield.[352] This was not totally untrue but was also not the whole picture. Ishihara's (and Kawakatsu's) propaganda was successful and helped spread his spin in Whitehall.[353]

[344] Ibid.

[345] MRCW, MSS, 292D 77/40, TUC Northern Region Council, Secretary's Report for Presentation to the Executive Committee Meeting, 28 March 1984.

[346] MRCW, MSS.259/AEU/1/1/249, Executive Council meeting, 5 October 1982.

[347] MRCW, MSS.259/AEU/1/1/249, Executive Council meeting, 12 October 1982.

[348] MRCW, MSS 292D/617/3, TUC, Economic Committee, Motor Industry Study, 13 January 1982. On the TUC's report on British automobile sector see Sect. 5 of the next chapter.

[349] Ibid.

[350] TNA, PREM19/822, Note for the record, PM's Meeting with the President of Nissan, 19 October 1982.

[351] Lord Jenkin, in Conte-Helm, 1989, pp. xv–xvi.

[352] Mountfield, 2007a, p. 111.

[353] It was not only officials in Whitehall who were affected by Ishihara's propaganda. Later, Nissan Director Peter Wickens commented that Shioji "vigorously opposed the

Criticism by the British media of Kawamata and Shioji would work as pressure against them. As we shall see in the following sections, both men were concerned about the debt they foresaw from the British project. Furthermore, Ishihara and Kawamata were not totally in conflict in using overseas operations to give Nissan an advantage in countering the dominant leader, Toyota. Profits gained overseas could be used to recover chances back in Japan. In late 1982, Nissan employed former Labour Cabinet Minister Richard Marsh as an advisor to facilitate the government gaining an accurate image of Nissan's internal atmosphere.[354]

16 The Poitier Incident

In November 1982, Japanese PM Zenko Suzuki resigned. Yasuhiro Nakasone was named his successor. Seeing the power change, the French government took advantage and put pressure on Japan's ever aggressively expanding trade surplus. In October, the French government unilaterally announced that Japanese video recorders exported to France would be stocked solely in one of the smallest customs services of Poitier. Nearly sixty thousand recorders were stocked during the next month to await customs clearance. Although it was a breach of EC laws, this treatment lasted until April the next year.

The Japanese government was outraged by this discriminatory tactic, which targeted solely the Japanese. The media heated up on the "battle of Poitier." However, the incident gave Thatcher's administration an unexpected gift that could be used to persuade Nissan. The French treatment had reminded the Japanese of how protectionist methods could be employed anytime in any member state and that Japanese industry must be firmly supported by the British government to counter such harsh actions. Thatcher sent Sir Patrick Jenkin—secretary of state for industry—to Tokyo to greet the new PM and MITI minister Sadanori

establishment of the company's UK investment, often against the wishes of his membership, who accepted the company's desire to invest overseas"; Wickens, 1987, p. 34. Wickens's view is typical of that of Ishihara and Japanese union leaders, who betrayed Shioji and sided with Ishihara. See Sect. 5 in Chapter 6.

[354] Mountfield, 2007b, p. 353.

Yamanaka. Nakasone named him minister because he was known as a hard-line negotiator and was nicknamed "kettle," for good reason.[355]

The two men met on 19 January 1983 in Tokyo. The official aim of the visit was to persuade the new government to make further efforts to ease the trade imbalance.[356] However, Sir Patrick also assured his Japanese counterpart that the British government would not employ protectionist methods, as the French had done in Poitier.[357] With the Japanese electronics industry operating in Wales, the British government was not in need of such measures. Seeing that Yamanaka was pleased, Sir Patrick referred specifically to Nissan and stated,[358]

> Anglo-Japanese economic relations have not at all improved. Should Nissan not launch its plant in Britain, the number of Japanese cars exported to Britain must be further limited.

It was up to the SMMT and JAMA to negotiate each year's VER quota, and neither the DTI nor MITI could directly intervene, but Sir Patrick understood the significance of referring to it. Sir Patrick was aware that his statement would attract the attention of Japanese media.[359] He was satisfied because this would also add pressure on Nissan.[360] MITI would be obliged to put pressure on JAMA, and Ishihara, as president of both Nissan and JAMA, would have to make a decision before long. Abe, who had been the minister in the former administration and knew the issue well, had been named foreign minister by Nakasone. Abe had assured the DoI before Sir Patrick's visit that MOFA was aware of Nissan's significance.[361] Regardless of how Kawamata and Shioji reacted, they were almost completely cut off at the highest political level from any possibility of rejecting the project.

[355] European Commissioner Étienne Davignon was known in Japan as having a similar character and was therefore a 'suitable' counterpart.

[356] TNA, PREM19/1073, Rhodes to Flesher, 18 January 1983; TNA, PREM19/1073, Private Secretary to Holmes, 6 January 1983.

[357] TNA, PREM19/1073, Cortazzi to FCO, 20 January 1983.

[358] Ibid.

[359] Ibid.

[360] TNA, T466/200, Mountfield to Lovell, 7 January 1982.

[361] TNA, PREM19/1073, Holmes to Coles, 5 January 1983.

On 21 January, Sir Patrick met Ishihara and his staff. With their agreement on local content of August and October the previous year in mind, Ishihara assured Sir Patrick that Nissan would commit to the agreement but once more asked for a flexible time limit to achieve the 80% requirement. Okuma hastily added that 80% referred to a goal to be aimed for but *not* a binding obligation. Sir Patrick nodded and assured the Nissan representatives that the British government would firmly back up Nissan should other EC member states retaliate.[362] He had in mind the case of Honda-Triumph, which had faced similar criticism but had been able to fend it off owing to the Triumph Acclaim—a licensed Honda Accord with a Triumph badge—achieving 80% local content.[363] France and Italy had warned that the Acclaim would be blocked should its local content fall under 80%.[364] The Honda-Rover collaboration was essential for the latter's future privatisation and could not falter.[365] Therefore, it was more than ever essential for Nissan to follow suit and adhere to the 80% requirement.

Sir Patrick did not miss the correct timing and made it clear that, if the necessary decisions were not immediately made by the Japanese, the British government would have to take a tougher line.[366] Kawamata, who had quietly listened to the discussion, was urged by Ishihara to respond.[367] Still showing reluctance, Kawamata assured Sir Patrick that he welcomed the British government's offered financial aid and would pursue the British project.[368] Sir Patrick bluntly replied that "the window would not be open forever." This was the phrase that the DoI had used when the negotiations had started in early 1980. Ironically, it was now Nissan's turn to hear it. Sir Patrick concluded that the best way to reinforce Anglo-Japanese relations was for Nissan to launch its plant. Should

362 TNA, PREM19/1073, Cortazzi to FCO, 22 January 1983.

363 TNA, FV22/134, Note of meeting with Honda, 10 March 1983. Honda and Rover signed a collaboration agreement in November 1981 that led to joint R&D of the Triumph Acclaim and Honda XX (Legend); TNA, FV22/134, Bowder to Mountfield, 1 June 1983.

364 Ibid.

365 TNA, FV22/134, Bowder to Lamont, 3 March 1983.

366 TNA, PREM19/1073, Cortazzi to FCO, 22 January 1983.

367 Ibid.

368 Ibid.

he reject the project, Kawamata would be blamed for worsening the bilateral relationship. Sir Patrick had once stated, "We have grown fonder of Honda but the kissing with Nissan is missing,"[369] but this was already in the past.[370] After the meeting, Sir Patrick once more asked MITI and MOFA to contact Kawamata to make sure that he had not changed his mind. He received a line from Sir Hugh in Tokyo that Kawamata had gradually changed course and was now pushing the plan forward.[371]

17 Another Retreat

Kawamata sent his man Kawai to London on 3 March 1983 to submit a "slightly" changed plan to the DTI.[372] Kawai proposed postponing production from 1985 to 1987, achieving one hundred thousand units of annual output in 1989 instead of sixty thousand in 1985, and deciding in 1989 whether two hundred thousand units of output was possible, but without promising that this quantity would be achieved in 1993 or 1994. Kawai also changed the plan of assembling mid-sized Violets to a plan to produce smaller segments. Just as it had in the early stage,[373] Nissan proposed a reduced plan and attempted to negotiate a compromise with the DTI. It was Kawamata's virtually last attempt at resistance.

It was the DTI's turn to lose patience. What had the two parties being negotiating for nearly three years? The DTI had made it crystal clear that production would start in 1985, that an annual output of one hundred thousand would be achieved in 1989, and that the output would ultimately reach two hundred thousand.[374] The most significant issue for the DTI had always been local content, but this issue had turned out to be the most disappointing. The DTI, however, decided to partly compromise with Nissan and admitted that local content should reach 80% in 1989 regardless of the number of assembled units. The understanding between the parties had formerly been 80% achievement when annual

[369] Cortazzi, 1998, p. 184.

[370] Ibid. Sir Hugh described Sir Patrick's call on Nissan as "little [progress made] with Nissan," but in fact his pressure did move the negotiation forward.

[371] TNA, PREM19/1073, Cortazzi to FCO, 22 January 1983.

[372] TNA, PREM19/1073, Spenser to Butler, 16 March 1983.

[373] See Sects. 11 and 12 of this chapter.

[374] TNA, PREM19/1073, Spenser to Butler, 16 March 1983.

output reached two hundred thousand. The DTI prioritised the level of local content rather than the timing of achieving that level or the desired output.[375] The DTI requested that the deadline of 1989 not be postponed any further.

Kawai resisted and appealed that it was impossible for Nissan's executive board to agree unanimously unless further financial aid was promised.[376] Kawamata's doubts were still not fully addressed.[377] The DTI rejected this appeal, replying that the initial offer of providing Nissan with 10% SFA would not be granted anymore.[378] The expected annual output had been considerably reduced, and therefore, the impact on creating jobs had diminished significantly. Adding further to the 10% aid was out of the question when Nissan was "trying to cut loose financial aid and local content requirements apart as if slicing salami."[379] Should the two elements be significantly changed or dismantled, the Nissan deal would be rejected at the cabinet meeting, and the negotiations would cease altogether.

To the DTI's relief, Kawai eventually agreed to achieve 80% local content in 1989, regardless of the annual output. The DTI estimated that it could seal the deal if a marginal amount of SFA was added in the final stage.[380] After Kawai returned from London, Kawamata wrote to Thatcher in April, both thanking her for the lease offer and requesting further consideration of RDG and SFA. Kawamata was consistent in his tactics, trying to postpone the achievement of local content and annual output as far as possible while struggling to obtain as much cash as possible from the British government. His efforts were unexpectedly—and unnecessarily—interrupted by diplomacy at the highest levels.

[375] Mountfield, 2007a, p. 112.

[376] TNA, PREM19/1073, Spenser to Butler, 16 March 1983.

[377] Mountfield, 2007a, p. 113.

[378] See Sect. 12 of this chapter.

[379] TNA, PREM19/1073, Spenser to Butler, 16 March 1983; Mountfield, 2007b, p. 362.

[380] Ibid.

18 The G7 Williamsburg Summit

The G7 Williamsburg summit took place in the US from 28 to 30 May 1983. Hosted by Ronald Reagan, the seven heads of government discussed a wide range of issues: global economic recession, growth, inflation, protectionism, reduction of governmental expenditure, development aid, and nuclear disarmament. Bilateral talks were held during the intervals. Thatcher and Nakasone met on the second day. The main issue was Japan's increasing trade surplus, but Thatcher did not miss the occasion to mention Nissan. Nakasone had already cooperated with Nissan's president Ishihara on the issue in September a year before, when Thatcher had visited Japan.[381] The issue was no secret between the two.

Thatcher stressed that Japan should rapidly increase its imports from Britain in sectors in which the latter held the competitive edge: whiskey, biscuits, chocolate, cigarettes, and aerospace products.[382] However, Japan importing biscuits would not fundamentally help the situation. The better solution was to import expensive industrial products or invest in Britain to launch plants. Nakasone could not disagree[383]; the only problem was the slow progress being made by the Japanese bureaucracy, both the government and private firms. Nissan's delay was no exception. Thatcher had to tell Nakasone,[384]

> I expect as I have up to now for Nissan to make an early decision. The project will promise Nissan profit and success and will bring both countries together ever closer.

In the following June, Thatcher would have to campaign for the general election, and she was in a rush to show progress. Although her popularity had increased after the Falkland crisis, unemployment had doubled since 1979 and was crucial for her constituents. Thatcher was brave enough to

[381] See Sect. 14 of this chapter.

[382] TNA, PREM19/1073, PM to Esaki, 27 January 1983. See also Sect. 14 of this chapter.

[383] TNA, PREM19/1073, Private Secretary to Holmes, 6 January 1983.

[384] TNA, PREM19/1073, Howe to FCO, 15 June 1983; Sato, 2012, p. 147.

refer to Nissan in the summit's host country, which also wished to see Japanese plants launched.[385]

Soon after returning to Tokyo, Nakasone "informed" Ishihara, "as planned,"[386] that Thatcher wished for Nissan's early decision.[387] It was Ishihara who injected the idea to use the summit as pressure against Kawamata owing to the high level of public attention.[388] Thatcher was immediately informed by Nakasone's secretary that her words had reached Kawamata. She thanked Nakasone for his help.[389] However, Kawamata came to know about the two PMs' conversation in Williamsburg through the next morning's newspaper, and the news struck him as a bolt from the blue. He felt that he had been cheated. Kawamata protested against Nakasone for such political manoeuvres regarding a "mere" private firm and its project. Nakasone did not apologise but ignored Kawamata's comments. Shioji, who for a decade had personally supported Nakasone becoming PM,[390] also felt betrayed. Immediately after the summit, Nakasone made excuses to Shioji that Thatcher had not specifically referred to Nissan, and he *was surprised* to find how the media had reported the meeting. Shioji soon found that this was not true.[391] If Britain openly employed political pressure to urge Nissan to make a decision, so would the UAW use Ronald Reagan, not only as diplomatic pressure but also to make local content requirements legally binding.[392]

385 On Nissan's US plant see Sect. 5 in Chapter 2.

386 Mountfield, 2007b, p. 359. However, after the summit, Nakasone and Ishihara, facing sharp criticism from Kawamata and Shioji, each blamed the other party for the Williamsburg summit incident. Shioji, 2012, pp. 247–251.

387 TNA, PREM19/1073, Cortazzi to FCO, 7 June 1983.

388 Sato, 2012, pp. 118–119.

389 TNA, PREM19/1073, Cortazzi to FCO, 7 June 1983.

390 Shioji, 2012, pp. 245–253; Kawakatsu, 2018, pp. 23, 131.

391 Shioji, 2012, pp. 252–253.

392 Sato, 2012, pp. 150–151.

After considering carefully, Shioji held an unusual press conference at *Keidanren* Press Club on 18 August 1983. He stated the unions' concern about the now unnecessarily politicised British project.[393] According to Shioji, for nearly a year, Ishihara had ignored the union's request that he share information on the project.[394] In the meantime, Ishihara had asked Nakasone to use all possible methods to back him up, but Nakasone had done almost all he could as PM.[395] MOFA, foreseeing that Nissan's failure to reach an agreement would deal a decisive blow to the already heated trade conflicts,[396] notified the British Embassy and asked for advice. The answer was for Thatcher to write to Kawamata. Any misunderstandings had to be amended immediately.

[393] Shioji, 2012, pp. 252–253.

[394] Ibid.

[395] TNA, PREM19/1073, Cortazzi to FCO, 16 June 1983.

[396] Ibid.

CHAPTER 5

The Deal: Financial Aid and Local Content

Abstract On 1 February 1984 the DTI and Nissan signed an agreement on 80% local contents, financial aids of RDG and SFA, and the timeframe of the plant's future expansion. The conflict within Nissan's management of whether putting priority on the US or the EC market had finally been amended. Accordingly the conflict among Nissan's unions were put down by dismantling its influence and purging its leader. Supported by Thatcher the DTI accommodated Nissan's request on "special treatment" of providing generous aids, but fell into conflict with the Treasury. Nissan had not decided on its plant location, but thanks to the reached agreement, which lacked legal binding, accelerated its selection of a suitable site.

Keywords Thatcher administration · Department of Trade and Industry · Treasury · Nissan · Local contents · Regional development funds

1 Introduction

Negotiations between Nissan and the Thatcher administration approached the final stages in late 1983 and 1984. Nissan's chairman

H. Suzuki, *Japanese Investment and British Trade Unionism*, New Directions in East Asian History, https://doi.org/10.1007/978-981-15-9058-0_5

Kawamata had turned to supporting the project but was still not confident about Nissan's heavy financial burden. The 80% British local content requirement was now a token, and the final issue was the exact amount of RDG and SFA Nissan would receive. The political pressure imposed by using the G7 Williamsburg summit had proved counterproductive, and now the "final obstacle" was the trade union leader, Shioji. The agreement was reached between the DTI and Nissan in February 1984, but the plant location had yet to be decided.

2 The 1983 General Election and Kawamata's Compromise

Thatcher celebrated a landslide victory in the general election of June 1983. Nissan's chairman Kawamata wrote to Thatcher to congratulate her soon afterwards. However, he did not forget to protest against her statement at the G7 Williamsburg summit in May.[1] Thatcher had openly asked Japanese PM Yasuhiro Nakasone to urge Nissan. Soon after receiving Kawamata's letter on 16 June,[2] Sir Hugh as ambassador and the DTI advised Thatcher to use the occasion to write back to Kawamata, referring to the negotiations. Thatcher agreed and wrote a short letter, but she neither apologised nor took back what she had said in Williamsburg. Instead, she explained her strong expectations for Nissan's decision, stressing,[3]

> The result of the general election and the continuation of my administration means that economic policies will continue as well, and this includes Nissan's negotiations.

Quite the opposite of what Kawamata expected, Thatcher openly questioned whether it was wrong for her to refer to Nissan at the highest diplomatic level.

Pressures against Kawamata both from Britain and within Japan intensified and reached a peak after the summit. Sir Patrick had not only himself put direct pressure on Kawamata in January but also asked MITI to follow

[1] Suzuki, 2015a, pp. 120–127.

[2] TNA, PREM19/1073, Tokyo to London, 10 June 1983.

[3] TNA, PREM19/1073, Howe to FCO, 15 June 1983.

suit.[4] Thatcher had done the same in May at the summit. MITI hesitated to react due to its preference for indirect guidelines controlling the automobile sector, which ran counter to openly applying pressure.[5] This time, MITI was obliged to take action because Thatcher and Nakasone had referred to Nissan at the highest level. MITI's automobile section called on Ishihara and forbade him to retreat from the British project.[6] This was not a real problem for him but was more a problem for Kawamata's. Again, the latter was ignored by the other negotiating parties, making him more furious than ever. In the following June, the stockholders' annual meeting was scheduled, at which Ishihara aimed to announce that he had struck a deal with the British government.[7] However, Kawamata's anger not only brought the British project to a halt but now risked Ishihara's presidency itself. If Kawamata insisted on his objection, Ishihara would have to resign.[8] The political and diplomatic pressure proved a failure with tangible results.

To mediate the clash, Sir Hugh apologised to Kawamata, saying that Thatcher had merely meant to state the significance of Anglo-Japanese economic relations.[9] Kawamata was not fully convinced by the British ambassador because he did not explain why a "mere private firm" should be referred to at a summit by heads of state. Thatcher had referred in Williamsburg to "Anglo-Japanese relations" instead of "Anglo-Japanese *economic* relations." Whether on purpose or not, this was understood by Kawamata as a political and diplomatic message. Upon immediate advice from the FCO and Sir Hugh, the DTI advised Thatcher to immediately refrain from any further political pressure.[10] Kawamata was gradually (and finally) starting to respond positively.[11] Thatcher concurred without delay. MITI's minister Yamanaka called on the DTI for his planned visit to

[4] See Sect. 16 of the previous chapter.

[5] See Sects. 2 and 3 in Chapter 2.

[6] TNA, PREM19/1073, Thompson to Coles, 11 July 1983; TNA, PREM19/1073, Cortazzi to FCO, 16 June 1983.

[7] TNA, PREM19/1073, Cortazzi to FCO, 14 June 1983; TNA, PREM19/1073, AJC to PM, 14 June 1983.

[8] TNA, PREM19/1073, Cortazzi to FCO, 16 June 1983.

[9] Ibid.

[10] TNA, PREM19/1073, Thompson to Coles, 11 July 1983.

[11] Ibid.

London in mid-July but the DTI politely declined a visit, observing that it was "not in the immediate national interests."[12]

The year 1983 was crucial for the Japanese automobile sector. The European Commission had monitored Japanese car exports to the EC, and Wilhelm Haferkamp—a former German trade unionist and Commission member—requested that Japan self-restrict exports.[13] An informal agreement capped exports at the levels of 1981 from 1983 to 1986.[14] The VER between Japan and the US made the Europeans feel that they had been sacrificed by the deal, which had been made at the expense of the European industry.[15] Nissan could not remain idle and continue to postpone its decision.

3 The Breakthrough

Nissan's annual stockholder meeting took place on 29 June 1983 in Tokyo. The year 1983 was memorable for Nissan. In April, president Ishihara was honoured by the emperor with the Grand Cordon of the Order of the Sacred Treasure, as his predecessor Kawamata had been in April 1975. In July, Nissan's exports reached 15 million units in total, and in August, the overall output reached 35 million. Last but not least, Nissan would celebrate its half-century anniversary in December. However, the British project was not concluded in time for the celebration. Shortly after the stockholder meeting, Kawamata sent Kawai, who had been promoted from managing director to senior managing director in June, to London on 6 July. Kawamata had given Kawai two plans to submit to Robin Mountfield, who had also been promoted from head of DTI's automobile division to deputy secretary of the DTI. Plan A was Kawamata's, and

[12] TNA, PREM19/1073, Coles to Spenser, 8 July 1983.

[13] Sigfrido Ramírez-Pérez, "The Automobile Industry: From the American to Japanese Challenge," in Éric Bussière, Vincent Dujardin, Michel Dumoulin, Piers Ludlow, Jan Willem Brouwer, and Pierre Tilly (eds.), *The European Commission, 1973–86; History and Memories of an Institution*, Brussels: European Union, 2014, pp. 274–275.

[14] Ibid.

[15] Ibid.

Plan B was Ishihara's.[16] Both plans had been approved by both Kawamata and Ishihara for the first time.[17] Ishihara had stubbornly opposed Kawamata's over-cautious plan but did not prevent him from forwarding it to Mountfield.[18]

Plan A proposed that production would start in 1986 as a "pilot plant" of knock-down kit assembly with a scale of twenty-four thousand units per annum. The pilot plant period was phase 1. With four hundred workers, the plant would produce twelve thousand units in 1986 and in the successive three years would produce twenty-four thousand units each year. The cars would be defined as made in Japan due to local content reaching only the minimum of 25%. Engines, gearboxes, and bodyworks would be imported as kits from Japan. The investment for phase 1 would be 51 million pounds, of which a maximum of 15% would be covered by RDG provided by the British government.[19] In addition to the automatically provided RDG, Nissan requested SFA covering 10% of phase 1 investment. Aid after 1987 would be negotiated between Nissan and the DTI at that point. Based on the assessment of phase 1, Nissan would decide in 1987 whether to proceed to expand the plant to full scale with 100 thousand units of annual output. If successful, this would become phase 2, with local content reaching 70% at the end of 1990 with an annual output of 81 thousand units. In 1991, the full output of 100 thousand units would be reached. To achieve the agreed upon 80% requirement for local content, press moulding and engine assembly facilities would be installed in the plant during this phase.[20] Owing to the high local content, Nissan would make all possible efforts to start exporting. At the end of 1990, Nissan and the DTI would negotiate whether the plant could proceed to phase 3,[21] with the aim of 200 thousand units of annual output. In summary, RDG would cover 10% of the investments in phase 1, RDG and

[16] Mountfield, 2007a, p. 113; Mountfield, 2007b, p. 360.

[17] TNA, PREM19/1073, "Note for the Record," Butler, 18 July 1983; TNA, PREM19/1073, Parkinson to Lawson, 15 July 1983; Mountfield, 2007b, p. 359.

[18] Shioji, 2012, p. 262.

[19] TNA, PREM19/1073, Butler to Spenser, 8 July 1983.

[20] Mountfield, 2007b, p. 352. On engine assembly requested by the SMMT, see also Sect. 8 of the previous chapter.

[21] According to Mountfield, phase 3 was the DTI's idea; Mountfield, 2007a, p. 113.

SFA combined would cover 10% in phase 2, and phase 3 would depend on future negotiations between the two parties.

Plan B was a reduced and restricted version without a pilot plant phase. This meant Nissan would launch a plant with 100 thousand units of annual output but would require RDG coverage of 15% and SFA of 25% of the overall investment. This meant that the British government would bear nearly half of the total 300 million pound investment.[22] Time and time again, Nissan had brought up a reduced proposal and disappointed the DTI.[23] Kawamata's tactic was to express Nissan's desperate need for financial assistance. For him, it made sense that British taxpayers be burdened with the cost of any production delay or damage in a British plant. However, for the DTI and Thatcher, this level of financial aid was never acceptable because providing that amount of aid for Nissan would cause alarm in the British public. It was a time when Thatcher was pushing her budget cut reforms through. Plan B also proposed that Nissan would aim to reach 70% local content in 1990 but did not refer to the 80% goal. This would leave open the possibility of engines being imported from Japan. Employment would reach one thousand in 1986 and would expand to the maximum of twenty-two hundred thereafter.

The DTI understood that the plans showed progress because Kawamata and Ishihara agreed with each other, although they did not see eye to eye, for the first time.[24] However, significant parts of the plan had been reduced from the initial announcement in January 1981. Plan B was almost out of the question. Local content and output fell far short of British expectations and, most significantly, any reference to an engine assembly facility had vanished. The DTI had just made certain with Honda and Isuzu that local content must reach 80%[25] and could not "discriminate" in favour of Nissan by accepting a lower ratio. Mountfield felt that both plans were a Hobson's choice and tried to extract the best from both.[26]

Cecil Parkinson, as secretary of state for trade and industry, took the two plans to Thatcher, and the cabinet had to make a choice. Parkinson

[22] TNA, PREM19/1073, Butler to Spenser, 8 July 1983.

[23] See Sects. 11, 12, and 17 of the previous chapter.

[24] TNA, PREM19/1073, Parkinson to Lawson, 15 July 1983.

[25] Ibid.

[26] Mountfield, 2007a, p. 113.

made it clear that Nissan considered the next round of talks to be the final stage, whatever the decision.[27] Kawai had specifically announced that Nissan refused any compromise on Plan B. The cabinet members understood that Plan B was the decoy to make the British government choose Plan A.[28] Thatcher decided that, although it was disappointing in specific aspects, Plan A was "value for money."[29] She estimated that once Nissan had begun production in Britain, even with a pilot plant, Nissan would proceed and expand its facilities, which would in turn benefit the British components industry.[30] The DTI expected future exports of British-made components to Nissan's plants worldwide.[31] Based on Plan A, the next (and final) round of talks was scheduled for July 1983.

4 The Final Round of Talks

Having sent Kawai to London, Kawamata felt that he had to write to Thatcher and once more raise the Williamsburg issue. The British media, especially *The Economist*,[32] had continuously and unjustly labelled him the one obstructing the project. Kawamata felt it unfair because as a business executive, his caution, in his mind, was totally rational. On 18 July, very shortly before the next round of talks, he sent a letter to London complaining that the project was too politicised.[33] Kawamata had warned Ishihara in January 1981 of the risk that Nissan's decision could slip out of their hands.[34] Nevertheless, Kawamata understood that Thatcher had made efforts to accommodate Nissan as much (in terms of money) as possible and was aware of increased unemployment in Britain. He could no longer postpone the decision but had to commit to a (political) decision.[35] At the same time, Kawamata decided to persuade his

[27] TNA, PREM19/1073, Parkinson to Lawson, 15 July 1983.

[28] TNA, PREM19/1073, Butler to Spenser, 8 July 1983.

[29] Ibid.

[30] Ibid.

[31] Ibid.

[32] TNA, PREM19/1073, "Note for the Record," Butler (FERB), 18 July 1983.

[33] TNA, PREM19/1073, Kawamata to Thatcher, 18 July 1983.

[34] See Sect. 6 of the previous chapter.

[35] Sato, 2012, pp. 137–140.

trade union counterpart Shioji to join him in giving the project the go-ahead.[36] Therefore, Kawamata assured Thatcher in his letter that Plans A and B were the best Nissan could offer and that he wished the next talks to resume with them. He wished the British government to offer as much aid and time as possible to accommodate his concerns about Nissan's heavy financial burden, which would last more than a decade after the launch.[37] Up to the final moment of his turn,[38] Kawamata had the mindset of a banker.[39]

Kawamata's letter did not reach No. 10 Downing through normal procedures. The negotiation between the DTI and Nissan was scheduled for a week later in Tokyo. There was not a moment to lose in rapidly responding. The British Embassy in Tokyo decided to breach the usual procedures and opened the letter at the point of receipt, without Thatcher's or the FCO's approval.[40] The contents were then telegrammed immediately to London, where they reached Thatcher's staff and the DTI in no time. Thatcher gave instructions to write back immediately. The DTI was still unsatisfied with the two Plans because they fell short of Nissan's first announcement in 1981, but neither were there sufficient grounds to reject them. Thatcher's answering letter was first written by the DTI's private secretary, welcoming Plans A and B but criticising Nissan's (and most of all chairman Kawamata's) delay in making a decision.[41]

After the draft was submitted to the PM's private secretary, Robin Butler, the DTI's complaints and criticisms were mostly deleted and replaced by gratitude to Kawamata and sympathy with his concerns.[42] Thatcher reminded Kawamata once more that, like it or not, British constituents were paying attention to Japanese investments and that they

[36] TNA, PREM19/1073, "Note for the Record," Butler, 18 July 1983; Sato, 2012, pp. 137–140. See also Sects. 6 and 7 of this chapter and Sect. 5 of the next chapter.

[37] TNA, PREM19/1073, Kawamata to Thatcher, 18 July 1983; Mountfield, 2007b, p. 358.

[38] TNA, PREM19/1073, "Note for the Record," Butler, 18 July 1983.

[39] Ibid.

[40] TNA, PREM19/1073, Cortazzi to Butler, 18 July 1983.

[41] TNA, PREM19/1073, Spenser (PS, DTI) to Butler (PS to PM), 19 July 1983.

[42] Ibid.

expected the PM to raise the issue when meeting Nakasone.[43] Upon advice from Butler, Thatcher added a short handwritten message of her personal gratitude to Kawamata at the end of the letter.[44] While waiting for the ink to dry, a telegrammed version was sent to the embassy in Tokyo, followed by the original letter, which arrived in Kawamata's office just a few days before the talks. Upon receiving Thatcher's letter, Kawamata was surprised and impressed that it had been answered so quickly.[45] Kawamata could have intended another delay by sending such a letter at the last moment, but in vain. The ball was immediately back in his court.

The two parties sat down for talks on 25 July 1983 in Tokyo. Plan A was the agenda.[46] It was a plan that left Nissan a possibility of withdrawing at the end of phase 1 should British-made components or labour–management relations cause serious difficulty. The cars assembled in this phase would be defined as made in Japan and counted as part of the limits of the Anglo-Japanese VER. Later that night, Kawamata, Kawai, and Ishihara held informal talks and decided on the essentials.[47] The decision to move from phase 1 to phase 2 would be made "by Nissan alone on its commercial judgement,"[48] a phrasing that would appear in the final draft of the agreement.[49] This meant that Ishihara had given up his idea of immediately launching a full-scale plant and compromised with Kawamata's plan, which left a veto right for Nissan to retreat. It was also decided that the final goal of achieving 200 thousand units of annual output would not be mentioned in the final draft.[50]

In phase 2, starting in 1987, Nissan would achieve local content of 80% within eighteen months after entering into full production. Nissan's promise of one hundred thousand units of output in 1990 meant it would double the output soon afterward. The estimated investment costs were

[43] TNA, PREM19/1073, Thatcher to Kawamata, 20 July 1983.

[44] TNA, PREM19/1073, Butler to PM, 19 July 1983.

[45] TNA, PREM19/1073, Cortazzi to FCO, 16 June 1983. TNA sources indicated that at this point, Kawamata became a fan of Thatcher. Mountfield testified that this occurred during the general election of 1983. Mountfield, 2007a, p. 113.

[46] TNA, PREM19/1073, DTI to PM, 3 August 1983.

[47] Mountfield, 2007a, p. 113.

[48] Ibid.

[49] See Sect. 8 of this chapter.

[50] Mountfield, 2007a, p. 113.

50 million pounds in phase 1 and 300 million pounds in phase 2. The majority or the whole of plant equipment would be arranged by a lease of the Bank of England. In the following August, the DTI and Nissan agreed that the latter would receive 10% coverage of investment by SFA in turn for promising 80% local content.[51] The DTI insisted that SFA be made available only in phase 2.[52]

5 The TUC Approves

While the DTI and Nissan were heading towards the final round of talks, the trade unions of both countries also intensified their contact. Nissan's chairman Kawamata had turned towards pushing the British project forward, and Shioji, who had cooperated closely with him, gradually followed suit. Before his decisive turn, Shioji aimed to secure his union members' employment in Japan. Nissan's union, *Jodousha-rouren*, adopted a position paper in August 1983 and clarified its view on the British project. Shioji held a press conference at the *Keidanren* Press Club to announce the unions' reservations. At the same time, Shioji maintained contact with his British colleagues to ensure that a single union agreement would be signed for the new plant. The TUC had also concentrated its efforts on accommodating Japanese investments, with priority for Nissan.

The Economic Committee of the TUC had launched its research on the British automobile industry in July 1981.[53] The first draft of the report was prepared by the Committee in January 1982, followed by consultation with experts and member unions during April and June. The second draft was completed within the same year, and the final draft was to be submitted to the TUC annual conference in 1983.[54]

The priority of the TUC report had shifted away from the Japanese newcomers and focused more on the four established assemblers in Britain—BL, Ford, Vauxhall, and Talbot.[55] The TUC targeted the three manufacturers—other than BL—and criticised that they had put less

[51] TNA, PREM19/1073, Parkinson to Lawson, 9 September 1983.

[52] Mountfield, 2007a, p. 114.

[53] See Sect. 9 of the previous chapter.

[54] MRCW, MSS, 292D/617/3, Carter to Lea, 14 September 1982.

[55] MRCW, MSS, 292D/617/3, Motor Industry Study, Economic Committee, TUC, 13 January 1982.

priority on the British market, reduced its outputs, and ignored development and contribution to British manufacturing. Ford in Britain assembled cars in Britain that constituted a mere 25% of Ford's overall output in Europe and, worse still, the output of Vauxhall-GM (Opel in Germany) and Talbot (Peugeot in France) constituted less than 10% of their total output in Europe. The TUC concluded that it was impossible to expect "non-British" assemblers to structurally reform British manufacturing.[56] In this context, the Japanese were called in, although with reservations.

The TUC perceived Japanese manufacturers in two ways: as a threat in the recent past but also a potential ally to reform British manufacturing. The Japanese as a "super-competitor" had worsened the circumstances of Britain's car manufacturing throughout the 1970s by drastically reducing production costs and improving productivity and quality with robotised plants. This drove European and American assemblers to fundamentally increase their investments in order to compete. These events coincided with the two oil shocks and economic depression, which shrank demands. Thus, Britain should accept the Japanese on its side rather than confronting them as outsiders. A chapter of the report was devoted to Nissan and raised three points. The first was high local content, the second was significant exports from the British plant, and the third was an assessment of Nissan's impact on the employment of the other four assemblers in Britain.[57] The TUC struck a balance between welcoming Nissan, although with conditions, on the one hand and addressing the problems and fears of other assemblers on the other.

The TUC's criticism was also directed towards the British government. Even the "free trade country," Germany, had directly intervened in the market and capped the Japanese market share at 10%. The DTI had left it to the industries, the SMMT and JAMA, to voluntarily set the annual limits. In the TUC's view, such reluctance to take action had led Ford, Vauxhall, and Talbot to import their own cars, assembled in other EC member states, to be sold in Britain.[58] The TUC's message was clear: If a manufacturer wished to sell cars in Britain, it should assemble them in Britain. British public opinion was firmly aligned with such views. The

56 Ibid.
57 Ibid.
58 Ibid.

TUC submitted the report to Mountfield in November.[59] Mountfield was pleased to see that the TUC had clarified its views and had rightly interpreted the significance of Nissan's arrival. This indicated that Nissan's desired single union agreement would not be contested or torpedoed by other unions that failed to sign it.

6 Shioji's Turn

While the TUC had defined its position on Japanese investment, trade unions in Japan were not yet unified in supporting the British project. Rather, it worsened the split. Shioji—as president of both Nissan's union, *Jidousha-rouren*, and the umbrella organisation JAW—called union leaders together on 18 August 1983. *Jidousha-rouren* adopted a position paper on Nissan's British project and announced its reservations at the *Keidanren* Press Club on the same day.

While stressing its unchanged support for Japanese manufacturers' overseas operation, *Jidousha-rouren* emphasised that its reservations were specifically about Nissan. There were four points, in order of priority.[60] The first was the overwhelmingly heavy financial burden.[61] The second, closely related to the first, was Nissan's loss of domestic market share in Japan, which had led to Nissan's financial difficulty. The third was a foreseen reduction in exports from Japan that would be caused by a new British plant. This was Shioji's counterargument to the TUC, which had been claiming that the cap of the Anglo-Japanese VER would be tightened once the British plant had entered into production. This would result in a double blow of Nissan reducing both domestic production in Japan and exports to the EC. Shioji's fear was also related to the prospect that Nissan cars made in Britain could face obstruction at the borders of other EC member states. The final point was the unusual and

[59] MRCW, MSS, 292D/617/4, Lea to Murray, 2 November 1983.

[60] MRCW, MSS, 292D/617/3, The All Nissan Motor Workers' Union of JAW (*Jidosha-rouren*), Our Position on the Project of Nissan to Invest in the UK, 18 August 1983. The name *Jidosha-rouren* is stated in a confusing way on this letter heading. The umbrella organisation JAW was *Jidosha-souren*, and Nissan's union was *Jidosha-rouren*.

[61] Kawakatsu, as one of the toughest critics (and attackers) of Shioji, claimed that the unions were wrong on this point and that the success of Sunderland was evident; Kawakatsu, 2018, pp. 128–129. He ignored the fact that although Sunderland turned out a profit before it was scheduled to do so, it took Nissan years to recover its investments, and it failed to reach its maximum output for more than a decade.

unnecessary political pressure coming from both the Japanese and British governments. Shioji was in agreement with Kawamata's claims on the final point. The paper was sent to the TUC on 1 February 1984.

Thatcher and the DTI had expected that Kawamata would persuade the "final obstacle," Shioji[62] but were now aware that the latter was not fully rejecting the project and that he had been confronting Ishihara for other reasons.[63] Now that Kawamata had decided to give the project the go-ahead, so would Shioji. Thatcher also understood that media coverage was an additional pressure urging his change of heart.[64] She was wrong. Like Kawamata, Shioji was misleadingly criticised as an opponent and was irritated by the criticism.[65] Shioji estimated that the launch of the British plant, if not coupled with a tightening of the VER caps, would cause little damage to employment in Japan.[66] In September 1983, after Nissan and the DTI had held talks in July in Tokyo,[67] Kawamata spoke with Shioji. In Kawamata's office, he explained his two-stage plan—Nissan's Plan A, which had been submitted to the DTI in July.[68] Shioji and the unions would not be able to support the plan in a short time, but Kawamata, well aware of Shioji's announcement at the *Keidanren* Press Club, asked Shioji to consider the plan carefully before Nissan executives officially consulted the unions.[69]

Before the unions could consider Plan A at all, Ishihara's people launched a negative campaign against Shioji and attempted to drive the unions and their members into division.[70] Shioji turned to supporting the British project when Ishihara, due to his own blunder, was obliged to support Kawamata's two-stage plan. Up to this point, Ishihara had

[62] TNA, PREM19/1073, DTI to PM, 16 September 1983; TNA, PREM19/1073, "Note for the Record," Butler, 18 July 1983; Mountfield, 2007a, p. 114.

[63] Ibid.

[64] TNA, PREM19/1073, DTI to PM, 16 September 1983.

[65] MRCW, MSS, 292D/617/4, Shioji to Evans, 25 November 1983; *The Guardian*, 14 November 1984.

[66] TNA, FO972/117, Foreign Policy Document No. 116, Labour Unions in Japan, 26 June 1984.

[67] See Sect. 4 of this chapter.

[68] See Sects. 3 and 4 of this chapter.

[69] Shioji, 2012, pp. 258–259.

[70] Ibid., pp. 259, 262.

opposed Kawamata's "tardy" plan, starting with a pilot plant of knock-down assembly. He wished to immediately begin full production in Britain.[71] Joined by one of Nakasone's secretaries, Ishihara mobilised staff and material from Nissan's Public Relations Division and attempted to involve Shioji in a scandal by photographing him with a girlfriend at Sajima Marina, a Nissan-owned yacht harbour.[72]

In May 1983, Ishihara had purged the executives in charge of personnel, who had close ties with Shioji, out of Ginza to Nissan's suppliers or affiliate firms.[73] Ishihara's man Taiji Hosokawa, who would later become Nissan's vice president in January 1986, was named managing director in charge of personnel. Soon after his arrival, negative campaigns and "re-education" on trade unionism took place in Nissan plants.[74] Shioji's number two and vice president of *Jidousha-rouren*—Haruki Shimizu—betrayed him and sided with Ishihara, leaking the unions' insider information.[75]

To drive the unions out of power, Nissan once more injected cash into publishers, especially Kodansha, to create negative images of Shioji and the unions.[76] Kodansha's tabloid *Focus* published an article in January 1984 that claimed Shioji was involved in a scandal.[77] Shioji had invited people to his yacht on 30 October 1983, but an "anonymous photographer" had shot a photo as if he was alone with a young girl at Sajima Marina.[78] Shioji and his yacht team found that the staff and a car of

[71] Ibid., p. 262.

[72] Ibid.

[73] Ibid., p. 334.

[74] Ibid., pp. 334, 376–379.

[75] Ibid., pp. 364–365, 372–373.

[76] Ibid., p. 333. Shioji testified that Nissan paid far more than Toyota's usual expenditure on public affairs. The annual amount reached 70 billion yen in 1986 so that anti-union and anti-Shioji articles would appear in the media; Shioji, 2012, p. 391.

[77] Shioji, 2012, pp. 4, 8; Kawakatsu, 2018, p. 161.

[78] Shioji recalled that the photographer was one of Nakasone's secretaries; Shioji, 2012, pp. 334–347. Kawakatsu recalled that it was he in a car borrowed from the Public Relations Division; Kawakatsu, 2018, pp. 160–165. Kawakatsu claimed that up to this point, he had *never* met Ishihara in person; Ibid., p. 170. In contrast, Shioji and Sato said that Nissan's anti-union sabotage and its spin were caused by an "Ishihara GPU," which coincides with Kawakatsu's secret team and its activity. Kawakatsu testified that he phoned Ishihara *after* his failed plot *for the first time* and apologised but was warmly

Nissan's Public Relations Division had been used.[79] The unions refused to discuss the British project until the truth was explained.[80] Hosokawa had no excuse to make,[81] and Ishihara as Nissan's president reluctantly issued an official apology letter to Shioji and read it himself at the labour–management consultation meeting on 12 December 1983.[82] The plot was counterproductive in gaining support for the project from the Japanese unions.

Shioji considered the letter insufficient. It reluctantly and vaguely stated that "some of the incidents pointed out by the unions could have occurred." He was persuaded by Kawamata that the letter was the highest level of apology and that he should officially accept it.[83] Shioji refrained from revealing the letter in public because it would damage Nissan's public image.[84] However, *Focus* published the article on 27 January.[85] Ishihara never gave up, and Shioji would be continuously targeted by Kawakatsu's team until his fall in February 1986.[86] In return for admitting the failed plot, Ishihara had to give way and accept Kawamata's two-stage plan.[87] Nissan announced its decision to launch a plant in Britain on 1 February 1984, ten days after the topical *Focus* was published.[88]

encouraged; Ibid., pp. 171–172. Ishihara stated, "Enough for Britain; it is not the only Europe. Other (European) locations would do (addition by the authour)"; Ibid., p. 179.

[79] Shioji, 2012, pp. 336–338.

[80] Kawakatsu, 2018, pp. 168–169.

[81] Kawakatsu, 2018, p. 169; Shioji, 2012, pp. 338–344.

[82] Shioji, 2012, pp. 262, 344–347. Kawakatsu testified that this meeting was held on 14 November; Kawakatsu, 2018, p. 166.

[83] Shioji, 2012, pp. 346–347. Kawakatsu denied Ishihara's official apology to Shioji, saying "it never existed"; Kawakatsu, 2018, p. 189.

[84] Shioji, 2012, p. 347.

[85] Ibid., p. 4. Kawakatsu claimed that he and Nakasone's secretary met for dinner and *by chance* found the girl who was with Shioji at the yacht; Kawakatsu, 2018, pp. 181–185. Up to this point, Kodansha had hesitated to publish the "scandal" article, fearing Shioji's counterargument that the girl was merely a friend of his daughter's; Ibid., p. 172.

[86] Kawakatsu, 2018, pp. 192, 194–246. See also Sect. 5 of the next chapter.

[87] Shioji, 2012, pp. 5, 8, 262, 353. Kawakatsu claimed that Plan A was Ishihara's idea and that the British project was saved by the tabloid article; Kawakatsu, 2018, pp. 188–189, 191.

[88] Shioji, 2012, p. 8.

7 The JAW and the TUC

Ever since he had launched the JAW and the Nissan union, *Jidosha-rouren*, Shioji had made efforts to communicate with local union leaders overseas to implement the Japanese style of trade unionism. He was cautious not to force changes from above.[89] The British project was no exception. The core of Japanese unionism was close and mutual consultation between management and labour. Management consulted unions before making any significant decisions concerning workers' employment, working conditions, and living standards. In turn, the union(s) would not take industrial action without previous notice. For Shioji and Japanese union leaders in the private sector, single union agreements were the best way to practice this mutual procedure.

Shioji's approach to the British unions was not an easy task. Where, when, and whom (not) to meet were sensible questions. British unions' attitudes were decisive for Nissan's choice of plant location. Wales had desperately lobbied Nissan and the DTI to get Nissan.[90] Late in 1983, the trade union leaders of Shotton had aimed to gain the status of a declining area. They aimed to increase the amount of aid they received under the regional policy.[91] Local industry and businesspeople opposed this because the status would create stigma and add to the negative images of the area. The North of England Development Council (NEDC) and the Tyne and Wear County Council reported this to Patrick Jenkin, who had switched from secretary of state of industry to secretary of state of environment in June 1983 but continued to act as a mediator between the North East and Thatcher.[92] Thatcher understood Shotton's move as providing an unfair advantage in financial aid designated for Nissan and rejected it.[93]

Far from giving up, the Wales Council of the TUC attempted to invite Shioji to Cardiff without notifying the TUC Executive Council. A single union agreement with Nissan would, however, be negotiated and signed not between a TUC regional council and Nissan's union, *Jidousya-rouren*, but between Nissan's negotiating team, which would become NMUK

[89] OISRH (Ohara Institute for Social Research, Hosei University) 3434–7641, Protocol of the thirteenth Annual Conference (JAW), 5–7 September 1984.

[90] See Sect. 9 of the previous chapter.

[91] MRCW, MSS, 292D/617/4, Lea to Murray, 2 November 1983.

[92] Lord Jenkin, in Conte-Helm, 1989, pp. xv–xvi.

[93] TNA, PREM19/1073, Ferdinand Mount to PM, 23 September 1983.

after a suitable site was selected, and a sectoral union alone. A meeting with Shioji could give the Nissan team the wrong message that the TUC unions were in conflict and could risk the deal itself. The invitation was cancelled by TUC executives who came to know about it through information coming from the DTI.[94] It was solely up to Nissan's team, but not Shioji, to negotiate the location.

To defend himself, Shioji had told TUC executives at an ICFTU meeting and Terry Duffy—the AUEW's general secretary—at the annual conference of the International Metalworkers' Federation (IMF) in autumn 1983 that he was still cautious about the British project[95] but did not totally reject the deal. This was soon reported at the AUEW Executive Council meeting on 25 October.[96] Nissan would give the go-ahead in no time, regardless of the location.[97] Duffy made certain with the executives that recognition of the AUEW as Nissan's (sole) negotiating partner and preparations for member recruitment at the new plant would progress without delay. It was also decided that as soon as Nissan decided on its location, the executive in charge of the region and Duffy himself would be responsible for reaching an agreement with Nissan.[98] An agreement between the AUEW and the TGWU was also necessary to ensure that the other unions would not yet again clash with each other to win the deal.[99]

In November 1983, shortly after avoiding the scandal plot, Shioji told his colleagues that he would support the British project.[100] Mountfield at the DTI soon came to know about Shioji's "official" change of heart.[101] The TUC executives met Japanese ambassador Hideo Kagami in Brussels in January 1984 and concurred.[102] For Ishihara, the clamorous and troublesome union leader was now worthless because Shioji had abandoned

[94] MRCW, MSS, 292D/617/4, Lea to Murray, 2 December 1983.

[95] MRCW, MSS, 292D/617/4, Lea to Murray, 2 December 1983; Suzuki, 2015a, pp. 141–142.

[96] MRCW, MSS.259/AEU/1/1/253, 25 October 1983, Executive Council.

[97] Ibid.

[98] Ibid.

[99] MRCW, MSS.259/AEU/1/1/254, Executive Council, 31 January 1984.

[100] MRCW, MSS, 292D/617/4, Lea to Mountfield, 27 January 1984.

[101] MRCW, MSS, 292D/617/4, Lea to Murray, 2 November 1983.

[102] Ibid.

his veto option on the issue. He could get rid of Shioji once the single union agreement was signed by a British union. His people, helped by Nakasone's staff, would once again plot to force Shioji to resign.[103]

In 1984, Shioji concentrated the JAW's efforts on international affairs. Its overseas operation expanded from research on car assembly to research on the production of local components and the improvement of Japanese employees' working standards outside Japan.[104] Local content requirements were not yet an issue for Japanese assemblers in the USA but were primarily raised by the British. Shioji made decisions in the previous year and started to mobilise the JAW to prepare for Nissan's British project.[105] Support for the British project was now in full swing. Seeing Britain's success, the USA would join in demanding local content for Japanese firms.

8 The Deal

Owing to Kawamata's change of direction, Thatcher's final push was to provide additional financial support for Nissan. However, this caused a serious split within the cabinet. As chancellor of the exchequer Nigel Lawson had made efforts to cut the budget, Thatcher now turned to him and insisted that they should pay Nissan extra. At the end, the DTI and the Treasury recommended a compromise: Nissan would receive additional aid through SFA, while future aid would be limited. The British components sector would be excluded as receivers, and aid for Nissan would not be allowed to exceed the agreed upon amount. The DTI and Nissan signed the agreement on production outputs, local content, financial aid, and the overall time schedule on 1 February 1984.

More than three years had passed since Nissan's first announcement in January 1981. The final points were the local content requirements and financial aid. There was still a risk that Nissan would turn its back on

[103] See Sect. 5 of the next chapter.

[104] OISRH, 3434-7641, Protocol of the thirteenth Annual Conference (JAW), 5–7 September 1984.

[105] Suzuki, 2015a, pp. 133–134.

Britain and seek other EC member states[106] should Thatcher's administration reduce the amount of aid afterwards.[107] However, how much should the British government compromise with Nissan? Nissan had requested 15% coverage by SFA but accepted the 10% cap. Further disappointment could lead to a dead end. Nissan raised taxation as a final issue. RDG was not charged tax, but SFA was, leading Nissan to request compensation for the "lost" amount.[108] Nissan was still asking for special treatment.[109] At the beginning of the negotiations, Thatcher, the Treasury, and the DTI had thought it unnecessary to accommodate Nissan with special treatment,[110] but now they were trying to find as much compensation as possible.

Chancellor of the exchequer Nigel Lawson opposed further aid, so Thatcher had to face a dispute.[111] In the Treasury's view, the planned aid was five times the average amount of similar projects and endangered the overall RDG budget.[112] The Treasury refused to provide any aid for Nissan in phase 2.[113] However, Sir Patrick Jenkin, when resigning his post as secretary of state for industry, had issued a letter to Nissan at the end of 1982 stating that the British government would provide Nissan with additional aid with maximum consideration, regardless of budget reforms to come.[114] Sir Patrick had done all he could to tie Nissan to the table when Thatcher's administration was reluctant to promise any SFA.[115] As a result, the change of minister did not end in Nissan abandoning the negotiations but rather accelerated them.[116] Fortunately, Sir

[106] TNA, PREM 19 1073, Parkinson to Lawson, 9 September 1983.

[107] TNA, PREM19/1073, DTI, "Nissan Project and Regional Assistance Changes," 2 September 1983.

[108] Ibid.; TNA, PREM19/1073, Young to Turnbull, 17 October 1983.

[109] TNA, PREM19/1073, Thompson (DTI) to Turnbull, 13 October 1983.

[110] See Sect. 11 in Chapter 4.

[111] TNA, PREM19/1073, Lawson to Parkinson, 12 September 1983.

[112] TNA, PREM19/1073, Lawson to Parkinson, 8 September 1983.

[113] TNA, PREM19/1073, Lawson to Parkinson, 20 July 1983.

[114] TNA, PREM19/1073, Thompson (DTI) to Turnbull, 13 October 1983.

[115] TNA, PREM19/1073, DTI, "Nissan Project and Regional Assistance Changes," 2 September 1983.

[116] Ibid.

Patrick had not promised a specific amount or the timing of payment,[117] but Thatcher could not afford to ignore the promise.

Lawson was also not able to ignore the issue from a different angle. In his mind, the DTI was leaning too far out to seal the deal.[118] Its desire to accommodate Nissan somewhere in Britain was understandable and acceptable in general terms, but the amount of aid was under Treasury jurisdiction and subject to its own rules and limits.[119] Lawson presented a thorough and critical review of the DTI's statistics. The Treasury estimated employment of 2,750 in the new plant, in contrast to the DTI's estimate of six thousand,[120] and accordingly, the adequate amount of SFA was approximately 87 to 112 million pounds.[121] This was still five times the average amount when calculating how much was necessary to create one job and was already too high an expenditure, risking the RDG budget.[122] Lawson thought that the DTI was overwhelmingly optimistic in expecting Nissan to actually purchase 80% of its components in Britain. The DTI was also ignoring the risk of French and Italian retaliation against Japanese cars exported from Britain.[123]

The DTI had to back off. Officials felt they could and should encourage the British industry by actively providing aid,[124] which had been a policy since the DoI but ran counter to Thatcher's budget cuts. In response to Lawson's criticism, the DTI agreed to strictly cap the aid for Nissan's "losses" caused by taxation.[125] Thatcher sided with this decision and made certain that future aid for the British components industry would be decided separately from aid to Nissan.[126] Lawson reluctantly accepted Thatcher's mediation. The Treasury and the DTI were in harmony regarding welcoming Nissan and not "discriminating"

[117] Ibid.

[118] Ibid.

[119] TNA, PREM19/1073, Parkinson to Lawson, 9 September 1983.

[120] Ibid.

[121] TNA, PREM19/1073, Lawson to Parkinson, 12 September 1983.

[122] TNA, PREM19/1073, Lawson to Parkinson, 8 September 1983.

[123] TNA, PREM19/1073, Lawson to Parkinson, 12 September 1983. See Sect. 10 in Chapter 6.

[124] TNA, PREM19/1073, Parkinson to Lawson, 9 September 1983.

[125] TNA, PREM19/1073, DTI to Lawson, 28 September 1983.

[126] TNA, PREM19/1073, Private Secretary to Spenser (DTI), 27 September 1983.

in favour of the firm with too-generous aid. Other assemblers, let alone other sectors, would rush to claim the same treatment. This would risk not only aid for the automobile sector but also Thatcher's reform itself. On the other hand, if Nissan's case failed, it would widely and negatively affect other Japanese investments.[127] In mid-September, Cecil Parkinson and Nissan agreed that the total amount of incentives provided for Nissan would be 100 million pounds, and this would not be affected by future budget cuts.[128] However, aid negotiated later would be subject to cuts, and the components sector would be excluded.[129]

The DTI and Nissan's team jointly prepared the draft of the "Memorandum of Understandings." As Okuma had asked Thatcher in October 1982,[130] Nissan once more requested that the memorandum not refer to an annual output of 200 thousand units.[131] The DTI aimed to refer to concrete numbers[132] but soon turned to accepting the request so as not to discourage Honda and other Japanese assemblers. Additionally, it respected Kawamata's careful approach of starting with a pilot plant, but the DTI insisted instead on referring to the plant's scale of 800 acres. This would indicate that the plant would ultimately reach 200 thousand units of annual output and appeal to the British public.[133]

On 1 February 1984, the DTI and Nissan signed the memorandum on local content, financial aid, exports, and the time schedule of each element.[134] Thatcher as PM did not attend the signing herself,[135] but she wanted another talk in person with Kawamata.[136] She and the DTI expected Kawamata—as chairman representing Nissan—to fly to

[127] TNA, PREM19/1073, DTI, "Nissan Project and Regional Assistance Changes," 2 September 1983.

[128] *Nikkei Business Daily* (Nikkei Sangyo Shimbun), 10 September 1986.

[129] TNA, PREM19/1073, Ferdinand Mount to PM, 23 September 1983.

[130] See Sect. 15 of the previous chapter.

[131] TNA, PREM19/1073, DTI to PM, 16 September 1983.

[132] TNA, PREM19/1073, Parkinson to Lawson, 15 July 1983.

[133] TNA, PREM19/1073, DTI to PM, 16 September 1983.

[134] MRCW, MSS 292D/617/4, Nissan Motor Co. Ltd., "Nissan News: Press Statement on Nissan's Plan to Build a Car Plant in the United Kingdom," 1 February 1984.

[135] TNA, PREM19/1073, Butler to Spencer, 18 July 1983.

[136] TNA, PREM19/1073, Private Secretary to Spenser (DTI), 19 September 1983.

London.[137] However, Kawamata refrained from participating in the ceremony. Memories of his meeting with Thatcher in September 1982 and the side effects of the G7 Williamsburg were still fresh.[138] He feared that another visit would be further politicised, which would make it impossible for Nissan to retreat from Britain. The DTI, having been especially cautious in the final round of talks, refrained from insisting. Ishihara proudly arrived in London instead. The gentlemen's agreement signed by Norman Tebbit and Ishihara was composed of thirteen paragraphs:[139]

> The Department of Trade and Industry ("The Department") on behalf of Her Majesty's government, and the Nissan Motor Co Ltd ("Nissan"), recognising their wish that Nissan should play an important and expanding role in the UK automobile industry in the mutual interests of Nissan and of the United Kingdom, have reached an understanding whose principal features include the following.
>
> Subject to a satisfactory outcome of negotiations with UK trade unions and local authorities, Nissan will commence design and construction of a car plant in 1984. The plant will be on a greenfield site of substantial acreage (probably around 800 acres) in a development area or special development area of the United Kingdom.
>
> The facilities will initially be operated as a pilot plant, with an assembly capacity of 24,000 units per annum based on the import of kits, and direct employment of between 400 and 500 people ("Phase 1"). During this phase, Nissan, in order to ascertain the feasibility of future development of the project, intends to gain experience in management and labour practices, sourcing of local components and other operating conditions in the United Kingdom. Production at the plant in Phase I will be treated as though these were built-up imports in the context of the discussions between the Society of Motor Manufacturers and Traders (SMMT) and the Japan Automobile Manufacturers' Association (JAMA).
>
> A decision whether to proceed to the next phase ("Phase II") will be taken by Nissan alone on the basis of its commercial judgement by 1987 in the light of its experience in operating the plant under Phase I. If Nissan

137 TNA, PREM19/1073, DTI to PM, 16 September 1983.

138 See Sects. 14 and 18 of the previous chapter.

139 MRCW, MSS, 292D/617/4, Heads of Agreement between the Department of trade and Industry and the Nissan Motor Company Limited, 1 February 1984; MRCW, MSS, 292D/617/4, Nissan Motor Co. Ltd., "Nissan News: Press Statement on Nissan's Plan to Build a Car Plant in the United Kingdom," 1 February 1984; Nissan, 1985, pp. 205–206.

does decide to proceed to Phase II, this phase would provide for an annual manufacturing capacity of at least 100,000 vehicles, and direct employment of around 2,700 people. Production under Phase II will commence by 1990, and 100,000 units will be reached in 1991. After Phase I, Nissan as a matter of course expects a substantial level of exports from the United Kingdom, and will use its best endeavours to achieve the same.

On completion of Phase II Nissan, solely on the basis of its commercial judgement, will decide whether to proceed with a further stage. If judged to be feasible, Nissan at that time would plan a further substantial expansion of its UK operations.

The above description of the project is based on the estimates made by Nissan on the assumption that sales objectives for the plant's output would be achieved as planned. If in the light of significant unforeseen changes in external circumstances or because of Nissan's experience of Phase I Nissan needs to consider substantial changes to Phase II the Department and Nissan will consult together in good faith about these changes in order to arrive at a mutually acceptable solution.

In Phase II of the project it is Nissan's firm intention to achieve a 60% level of local content on an ex-works price basis at the start of production, and to achieve a steady increase so that an 80% level of local content is achieved not later than the first half of 1991 and is maintained thereafter, and to achieve likewise the above levels of local content on any subsequent model. It is Nissan's intention to obtain even higher levels of local content wherever feasible. Equally, it is understood by the Department that Nissan cannot be held irrevocably to this timetable under circumstances of major technical or commercial difficulties recognised by the Department as being beyond Nissan's control.

Provided the agreed local content objectives are met, the Department confirms that the cars to be produced under Phase II should be regraded from the start-up of commercial production as of genuinely British make.

It is the mutual objective of Nissan and the Department to ensure that the project contributes to the development of long-term collaboration between Nissan and the local components and other supplying industries. Appropriate measures to this end will be taken by both parties. It is Nissan's intention to provide the maximum practicable opportunity for local manufacturers to compete for the supply of components, materials, services and machinery and equipment for the project.

The Department intends to use its good offices to the maximum practicable extent to facilitate all aspects of the establishment by Nissan of its UK manufacturing operations. The Department and Nissan intend to maintain the closest level of contact and cooperation to ensure the successful implementation of the project and the smooth operation of these Heads of

Agreement. Arrangement will be made for annual meetings for this purpose and to review the progress of the project, on the basis of information to be provided by Nissan.

The Department considers that the project and intentions outlined in these Heads of Agreement can be expected to make a significant long-term contribution to strengthening the UK economy. The Department therefore intends to make available to Nissan selective financial assistance of 11.72 per cent of the agreed eligible capital costs of Phase II of the project (equivalent to 10% of the estimated overall capital costs of the project), such assistance not to exceed 35 million pounds, in accordance with terms and conditions to be set out in an offer letter from the Secretary of State to Nissan.

These Heads of Agreement set out the intentions of the Department and Nissan and it is confirmed that the parties will implement these intentions in good faith. However, they are not regarded by either party as having legally binding status or as containing any statement giving rise to legal rights.

Signed at London in duplicate in the English and Japanese languages, both texts being equally authentic.

At the end of Nissan's draft, a paragraph was added stating that the firm expected to bring a new dimension to its relations with Britain since its cooperation with Austin.[140]

For Kawamata, the most significant part of the agreement was the statement "a decision whether to proceed to phase 2 will be taken by Nissan *alone* on the basis of its *commercial* judgement (emphasis added by the authour)." Kawamata insisted that this phrase be included and had told Nissan's executives that this was his last request.[141] Not Kawamata but his successors would make the decision whether to proceed.

RDG and 35 million pounds of SFA together covered nearly 30% of the overall investment costs, of which 50 million pounds were for phase 1 and another 330 million for phase 2.[142] The amount of RDG was not stated in the agreement but was orally announced by Tebbit. This was to prevent the image of an extraordinarily large amount of aid being paid

[140] MRCW, MSS, 292D/617/4, Nissan Motor Co. Ltd., "Nissan News: Press Statement on Nissan's Plan to Build a Car Plant in the United Kingdom," 1 February 1984.

[141] Shioji, 2012, pp. 264–265.

[142] *Nikkei Business Daily* (Nikkei Sangyo Shimbun), 10 September 1986.

to Nissan.[143] Although not precisely understanding the overall amount, the critics never missed the point.[144] The paragraph stating "the DTI intends to use its good offices to facilitate all aspects of the establishment by Nissan" meant the British government would counteract any doubts raised within the EC.[145] As requested by the DTI, Nissan also promised to launch an R&D centre in Britain.[146] Apart from the unexpected amount of aid and the rather tardy time schedule, Thatcher's administration was successful in persuading Nissan to fulfil the DTI's essential requests. The signing of the agreement was a milestone for the DTI for the successful negotiation, which Mountfield described later as "agonizingly protracted (for three years) on a knife-edge"[147] but which paid off. Thereafter, the agreement worked as a boost for Nissan in deciding on its plant location and signing a single union agreement with British trade union(s). The SFA was cleared by the Industrial Development Advisory Board in October.[148]

The confrontation between Ishihara and Shioji had continued until the last moment. A labour–management memorandum supporting the agreement was exchanged barely in time for the signing on 1 February. Ishihara had insisted that Nissan's decision to enter phase 2 be made solely by management. Shioji insisted that it required labour–management consultation *and* trade union approval.[149] The memorandum read,[150]

> Starting with an experimental pilot plant, Nissan decides whether to proceed or not based on its experience in the first phase.
>
> The decision to proceed to the next phase will be made by Nissan alone on a commercial basis.

[143] Suzuki, 2015a, pp. 146, 199.

[144] Garrahan and Stewart described "over 130 million pounds in public subsidies to employ some 3,500 people"; Garrahan and Stewart, 1992, p. 6. Mountfield described "RDGs [...] together with SFA of 35 million pounds [...] equivalent to 10% of the combined costs of Phase 1 and 2"; Mountfield, 2007a, pp. 114–115.

[145] Mountfield, 2007a, p. 115.

[146] Ibid.; Mountfield, 2007b, p. 351.

[147] Mountfield, 2007a, pp. 115, 119.

[148] Mountfield, 2007b, p. 362.

[149] Shioji, 2012, pp. 263–264.

[150] Ibid., p. 264.

The decision to proceed to the second phase will be decided after thorough consultation between management and labour takes place.

The memorandum confirmed Shioji's greatest concerns in the first and second points but avoided specifying exactly whether the unions would be able to influence the final decision.[151]

In March, Kawakatsu met president Ishihara "for the first time" in person and reported his team's secretive and "voluntary anti-union activities."[152] Now that the British project had been given the go-ahead, Shioji and his unions had to be silenced without delay. Kawakatsu requested Ishihara's official approval and backup in seducing union members to his side. The latter concurred.[153] A "shadow cabinet" was named among the executives, including Hosokawa,[154] to persuade chairman Kawamata's supporters to take their side, to uncompromisingly confront the unions and to separate the members from Shioji.[155] The new and official "shadow cabinet" soon discovered that Kawamata aimed to remove Ishihara and name his own man as the next president; if this plan did not succeed, he would regain power as president himself.[156] This discovery was decisive for Ishihara and Kawakatsu to launch a campaign on all fronts against Kawamata and Shioji. Workers at the plants in Yokohama and Murayama were propagandised to criticise Shioji's leadership.[157] The final struggle before the new British plant entered into operation was inevitably a morass.

[151] Ibid.

[152] Kawakatsu, 2018, pp. 194–196.

[153] Ibid.; Kawakatsu asked for 30 million yen for this renewed operation, and Ishihara immediately obliged.

[154] See Sect. 13 in Chapter 4 and Sect. 6 of this chapter.

[155] Kawakatsu, 2018, pp. 194–196.

[156] Ibid.

[157] Ibid., pp. 199–208. Referring to Akira Kurosawa's famous film, Kawakatsu nicknamed his team "the seven samurai"; Ibid., pp. 206–208. He enthusiastically crowned his team and activities with all possible heroic Japanese names.

CHAPTER 6

Plant Location Sunderland

Abstract The finalists of what was termed by the British unions as a "beauty contest" were Shotton and Sunderland. The former wished to accommodate Nissan because its steel industry was in decile and unemployment increased. Leftist unions remained influential and made Nissan doubt on whether its preferred Japanese unionism—single union agreement—could be implemented in the new plant. Sunderland had also suffered the decline of shipbuilding industry, but "fortunately" the influential union AUEW had signed single union agreements with Japanese multinationals in the region and was prepared for another. The plant celebrated its launch on 8 September 1986, where Thatcher herself was present. The TUC member unions fell into a serious split on such Japanese agreements.

Keywords Nissan · Sunderland · Shotton · Trade unions · Single union agreement · Japanisation · Amalgamated Union of Engineering Workers · TUC membership

1 Introduction

The DTI and Nissan had reached agreement on local content, financial aid, and the time schedule for both issues in February 1984. However, the

H. Suzuki, *Japanese Investment and British Trade Unionism*, New Directions in East Asian History,
https://doi.org/10.1007/978-981-15-9058-0_6

location of the new plant had yet to be decided. The decision depended upon Nissan's choice of a local trade union(s) as a wage bargaining partner. The question was which union(s) would accept the Japanese-style single union agreement, allowing solely one union in the plant. Nissan decided on 30 March 1984 to locate the plant at the former Sunderland airfield. The AUEW signed the deal with NMUK in April 1985.[1] It was no coincidence that the SEA of the EC was drafted and signed in the same year that the Sunderland launch event took place on 8 September 1986. The Japan-EC Elements of Consensus agreement of 1991, in which MITI and the European Commission jointly monitored Japanese car exports, terminated in 1999. Japanese exports were replaced, although not totally, by cars built in Britain. The advances in Anglo-Japanese relations had put an end to EC/EU member states' regulated free trade policy.

There were also downsides and contradictions to the success. The single union agreement was atypical in Britain and provoked wide debate then and afterwards. Specific aspects of Japanese unionism and "workaholic" lifestyles were critically debated. Beale pointed out the unions' weakened role and limits to adaptation,[2] while Garrahan and Stewart focused more on the (limited) local benefits, Nissan's dominance in the local economy, and the limitations of its "new" labour practices.[3] However, significant aspects of Japanese employment rules were not transferred into Britain. The extent of Japanisation was therefore limited, making the Sunderland operation successful. A hybrid Anglo-Japanese approach was invented between the British and Japanese unions,[4] regardless of Thatcher's known intention to introduce Japanese-style unionism into Britain. Toyota and Honda swiftly followed Nissan and launched their plants in 1992 with identical practices. The more Japanese plants were launched in Britain, the more the TUC unions fell into division on single union agreements, but this disagreement did not affect the successful operation of Sunderland (Chart 1) or any other Japanese plant in Britain.

[1] Suzuki, 2015a, pp. 155–157.

[2] Beale, 1994, pp. 172–184.

[3] Garrahan and Stewart, 1992, pp. 135–139.

[4] Nick Oliver and Barry Wilkinson, *The Japanization of British Industry; New Developments in the 1990s* (2nd ed.), Oxford: Blackwell Publishers, 1992, p. 219.

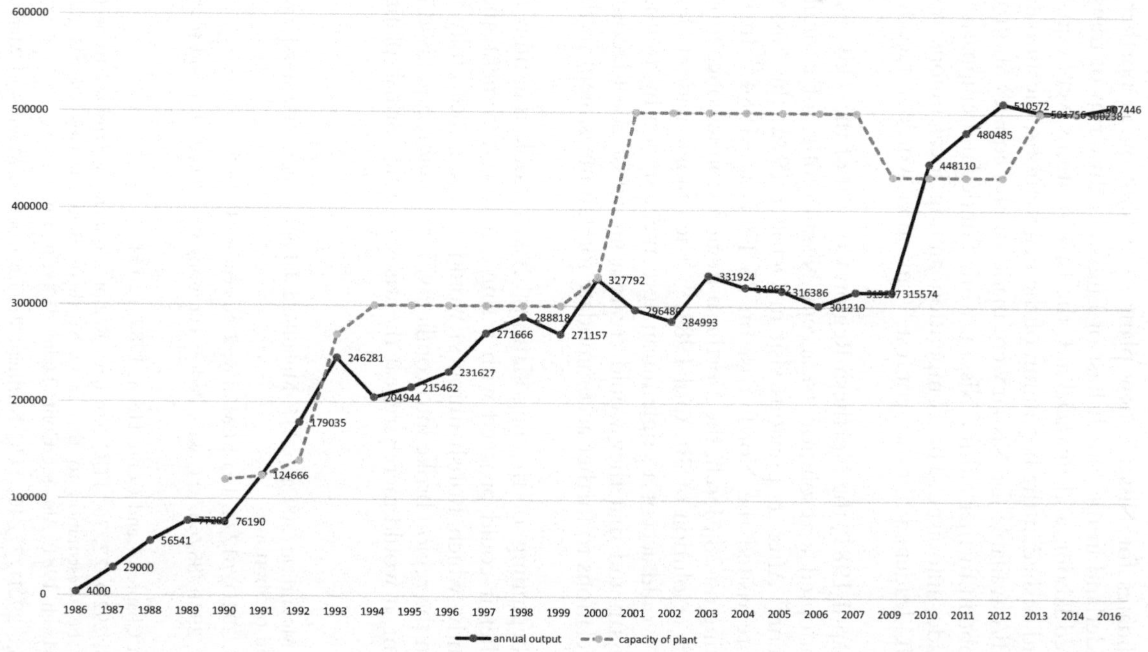

Chart 1 Annual output of Nissan Sunderland (units) (*Source* Industrial Journal [*Sangyou journal*]. 2018–1992. *Nissan; Group Activity of 2018–1992* [Nissan-jidousha group no jittai 2018–1992], Nagoya: IRC)

2 Sunderland

The final candidates for Nissan's new plant were Shotton in northern Wales and Sunderland in the North East of England.[5] In terms of transportation, skilled labour, and financial aid, the two locations were equal. As Thatcher had wished at the beginning of the negotiations, the amount of RDG and SFA available for Nissan were made strictly equal.[6] Shotton attempted to obtain further aid for Nissan, while Sunderland emphasised cooperative trade unionism. The competition among local unions was termed by TUC leaders a "beauty contest,"[7] in other words, a race for employment.

As early as April 1981, the Northern Region Council of the TUC had unanimously adopted a resolution to accept Nissan's offer of a single union agreement.[8] After its previous visit in October 1982, the Nissan team once more visited the North East on 25 February 1984.[9] In its executive meeting on 28 March, the Northern Region Council once more concurred in its resolution of 30 April 1981.[10] The unions made it clear that all unions would accept a single union agreement signed by another union with Nissan and that they would create a model of good labour–management relations to further accommodate foreign investment in the North East.[11]

From the beginning of the negotiations, Nissan took the time to examine whether it could proceed with a single union agreement and, most importantly, which British union(s) would accept it peacefully. If other unions in the region broke into conflict with the union organised in the Nissan plant, it would merely repeat the cases of other British plants.

[5] Ibid., p. 146; Mountfield, 2007a, p. 115. Mountfield did not mention why Sunderland was chosen instead of Shotton.

[6] MRCW, MSS, 292D/617/4, Lea to Murray, 2 November 1983.

[7] MRCW, MSS, 292E/85/667, "Coke's Perfect Harmony Goes Flat," date and source not stated.

[8] See Sect. 9 in Chapter 4 and Conte-Helm, 1989, p. 151.

[9] MRCW, MSS, 292D/77/36, TUC Northern Region Council, Appendix 2 to Secretary's Report to be Presentation to the TUC Northern Regional Council Executive Committee, 26 March 1981. Also see Conte-Helm, 1989, p. 146.

[10] MRCW, MSS, 292D/77/40, TUC Northern Region Council, Minutes of Meeting of the Executive Committee, 28 March 1984.

[11] Ibid.

Where the steel or automobile industry existed, the influential GMB or the TGWU would attempt to unionise the workers in the Nissan plant. This would not be the case in the North East, where the shipbuilding industry had declined and virtually vanished. The AUEW was the union that had organised workers in Japanese plants.[12] With 857,500 member workers, the AUEW was neither too weak to confront other unions' confrontation nor too much stronger and more "militant"[13] than the GMB and the TGWU. Nissan was confident in working with the AUEW. This was possible because Nissan started with a green-field plant and "green" labour.[14]

However, the AUEW had its own concerns. At the Executive Council meeting on 13 March, shortly after the visit of the Nissan team in February, concerns were raised about the "actual" amount of local content. The executives understood that it would "likely to be much less than the 80% quoted"[15] and that most of the components would be sourced from Japan.[16] Worse still, contacts made by G. Arnold and K.G. Cure with Japanese union leaders depressed the executives. They explained that "Japanese trade unions consisted of part of the decision-making in Britain and therefore maintain control of [the plant's] operation."[17] After giving up his resistance to the British project, Shioji had attempted to send Japanese component suppliers into Britain to the greatest extent possible.[18] For the British unions, the Nissan deal seemed to have opened up a new contradiction.

In March 1984, Nissan dissolved the feasibility study team in a preparatory office to launch the new plant. Nissan announced on 30 March that the plant would be located in Sunderland. The news was soon reported to the Executive Council of the AUEW by G. Arnold on 3 April.[19] On 6 April 1984, Nissan Motor Manufacturing (UK) Ltd. (NMUK) was

[12] For the case of NSK in Peterlee, see Sect. 9 in Chapter 4.

[13] See also Sect. 9 of this chapter.

[14] Oliver and Wilkinson, 1992, p. 278. The Japanese success in Britain was based on a better "fit" between manufacturing strategy and human resource strategy; Ibid.

[15] MRCW, MSS.259/AEU/1/1/254, Executive Council meeting, 7 February 1984.

[16] MRCW, MSS.259/AEU/1/1/254, Executive Council meeting, 13 March 1984.

[17] Ibid.

[18] See Sect. 6 of the previous chapter.

[19] MRCW, MSS.259/AEU/1/1/255, Executive Council meeting, 3 April 1984.

launched with 100% Nissan capital. The first president was Japanese—Toshiaki Tsuchiya—who became the first and last case of a Japanese president. The former Sunderland airfield, with 800 acres (3 million 240 thousand square metres), was sold to Nissan at a reduced price of 1800 pounds per acre. Construction was immediately begun. The Tyne and Wear County Council paved the land, and in July, the commencement ceremony took place. In November 1984, construction of the buildings started, and they were completed in December 1985. Plant equipment was installed, and now it was a question of recruiting workers.

3 The Single European Act

By the time the Sunderland deal was secured and the site went under construction, Thatcher's trusted man, Lord Francis Arthur Cockfield, had been sent to Brussels in 1985 as the vice president of the European Commission. Of the two British commission members, Thatcher sought to name Lord Cockfield—secretary of state for trade—as Christopher Tugendhat's successor, expecting him to become a "doughty fighter for Britain."[20] Doubts were raised about his inability to speak French, an indispensable capability for working in the commission, but Thatcher stuck to her choice.[21] The Labour nominee was Stanley Clinton-Davis, who was in charge of environmental, transport, and nuclear issues.

Lord Cockfield's role was to draft the White Paper "Completing the Internal Market" and the SEA.[22] The internal market, which had been defined in the Rome Treaty of 1957, was far from completion. Other than agriculture, very little had been done.[23] Internal tariffs had been reduced, but non-tariff barriers were still in play.[24] To realise a "real" single market,

[20] Wall, 2019, p. 291. Warlouzet pointed out a gap between Whitehall and Brussels. Thatcher expected to influence the negotiations through Lord Cockfield, while the Treaty of Rome forbade member states to give "instructions" to commissioners. Warlouzet, 2018, pp. 196–197.

[21] Ibid., p. 292.

[22] Warlouzet, 2018, p. 193.

[23] Wall, 2019, p. 336.

[24] Wilfried Loth, *Building Europe: A History of European Unification*, Berlin: Walter de Gruyter, 2015, pp. 276–277.

numerous national barriers to trade and services had to be abolished.[25] What had formerly been suggested by Sir John, MEP, in 1981 and consolidated by Whitehall in 1982 in the Japan report was now defined as the EC's desired policies and a common goal of the single market by Lord Cockfield.[26] In contrast to her fame as being anti-integration, Thatcher was counted as one of the founders of the single market because she had sent Lord Cockfield to Brussels.[27] Geoffrey Howe—foreign secretary—also supported the initiative.[28] Lord Cockfield acted with speed and, under the DG III's coordination, listed three hundred directives for removing physical, technical, and fiscal frontiers.[29] The commission played an essential role in drafting the SEA.[30]

Although disappointed in specific policy areas, the Thatcher administration perceived the content of the White Paper as surpassing British expectations of what the single market should look like.[31] British priorities were in the areas of removing physical and technical barriers to the free movement of goods, creating a free market in financial services and the transportation sector, and fully liberalising capital movements and established professions, especially accountants.[32] The first and second points would directly benefit NMUK exports to the continent. Nissan was more confident in having a stake in Britain. Once it entered into phase 2, the other member states would find it more difficult to reject exports of British-made Nissans.

The major achievement of the Intergovernmental Conference was that the SEA was agreed upon by all the member states, and without this agreement, the single market would not have existed.[33] The SEA was

[25] Francis Arthur Cockfield, *The European Union: Creating the Single Market*, Wiley Chancery Law, 1994, pp. 37–38.

[26] See Sect. 5 in Chapter 3 and Sect. 10 in Chapter 4.

[27] Loth, 2015, pp. 276–277.

[28] Warlouzet, 2018, p. 195.

[29] Éric Bussière, "Devising a Strategy: The Internal Market and Industrial Policy," in Éric Bussière, Vincent Dujardin, Michel Dumoulin, Piers Ludlow, Jan Willem Brouwer, and Pierre Tilly (eds.), *The European Commission, 1973–86; History and Memories of an Institution*, Brussels: European Union, 2014, pp. 271–276.

[30] Ibid., p. 276.

[31] TNA, FCO 30/6423, 24 June 1985.

[32] Ibid.; Warlouzet, 2018, p. 196.

[33] Wall, 2019, p. 328.

signed in February 1986, only seven months before the opening ceremony of the Sunderland plant. Although not stated specifically in the text, the SEA aimed to reinforce Europe's competitiveness against the US and Japan.[34] Although she fell into disagreement with Lord Cockfield, who took the issue further than she expected, Thatcher thought it right for Britain to sign the SEA because she wanted the single market.[35] Britain's role as a gateway for Japanese investments and car exports affected EC/EU policies.[36] In 1988, the European Commission and MITI initiated talks on regulating "Japanese" car exports that were later realised as a joint monitoring system in 1991.[37]

4 Recruiting Workers

In October 1984, Peter Wickens was employed as the director of personnel and information systems for NMUK. Formerly, he had worked for the Central Electricity Generating Board, Ford, Continental Can, and British Gas.[38] His job at Nissan was twofold. His first mission was to employ local workers, and his second mission was to train and educate them in Japanese ways of plant operation. Wickens testified afterwards that[39]

> [Nissan's] decision to recognise the [AUEW] came not from any assessment of the political tendencies of the unions, the numerical strength in the region or who would give [Nissan] the best deal but from our judgment as to which Union our employees were most likely to join.

[34] Warlouzet, 2018, p. 193; Loth, 2015, pp. 276–277.

[35] Wall, 2019, p. 332, citing Thatcher, 1993, p. 557.

[36] Mark Mason, "Elements of Consensus: Europe's Response to the Japanese Automotive Challenge," *Journal of Common Market Studies*, 32(4), 1994, p. 438.

[37] Ibid., p. 439; Christopher Kendall, "The Elements of Consensus: Liberalising EC-Japan Passenger Car Trade in the 1990s," in Keck et al., 2013, p. 229. On the Elements of Consensus, see the last section of this chapter.

[38] Wickens, 1987, p. xii.

[39] Ibid., p. 137

Nissan announced its recruitment of 22 supervisors, 40 team leaders, and 300 shop floor workers. To his surprise, 3500 candidates immediately applied for supervisor, 1000 for team leader, and 11,500 for worker positions.[40]

Wickens selected workers by prioritising an applicant's willingness to understand the Japanese style of equal working standards over individual job skills.[41] It was not an easy task because British and Japanese customs concerning both work and private life were different. Japanese people were more job centric, but one could not expect British workers to immediately think and act in Japanese ways. Japanese officials and businesspeople were confronted by doubts raised by Europeans and Americans about the differences. A MITI official sent to JETRO in London at the time received questions from the floor after speech about the Japanese appearing to sacrifice quality of life for their jobs.[42] Why would the British have to work like the Japanese in order to compete?[43] The question was not answered straightforwardly regarding how the British should adapt to Japanese way; instead, the official explained that Japanese workers were not expected to sacrifice their quality of life, and the aim was to strike a balance between finding meaning in a job and improving one's quality of life at the same time.[44]

Whether such answers filled the perception gap was doubtful. British public opinion was more critical of Japan and the Japanese than that in other EC member states. An opinion poll conducted in 1986 by *Nikkei* showed that the question "Do you think Japan is trustable?" was answered "Yes" by 72% of Spanish interviewees and 26% of French 26% but only by 7% of British respondents, which was by far the lowest percentage.[45] To the question "Is Japan an incomprehensible country?" 29% of the British respondents answered yes. To the question "Is Japan closed to outsiders?" 47% answered yes, and to the question "Has Japan fallen short in internationally contributing?" 72% answered yes. A self-proclaimed former Tory constituent wrote to TUC general secretary Len

[40] Ibid., pp. 180–181; Conte-Helm, 1989, p. 147.

[41] Wickens, 1987, p. 18

[42] Suzuki, 2015a, pp. 158–159.

[43] Ibid.

[44] Ibid.

[45] *Nikkei*, 15 May 1986; Suzuki, 2015a, p. 158.

Murry, "when the Jap (as stated in the letter) employ one, two British workers lose their job in BL."[46] The logic that the Treasury had employed during the early phase of negotiations[47] was twisted and used in public. Murry wrote back, in harmony with the DTI's views, that Nissan's entry would create new jobs. The wind was still against the new plant.

However, the critical voices were not merely directed towards the Japanese. The British were equally critical and uncompromising when judging British cars. Critics not only attacked British manufacturers but in time went after trade unions. A newly purchased BL car had to be sent for repair four times and after a total of four weeks of repair work was still not running well.[48] In other cases, rain dripped in, panels rusted, engines stalled when the headlights were turned on, windows fell in, door handles came off with a tug, and so forth.[49]

The critical tone was also directed towards the government. Thatcher was prepared to sell British brands, with Jaguar and RR at the forefront, to foreign manufacturers and investors. British unions demanded that the country "keep British."[50] These deals were seen as side effects of welcoming Nissan and Japanese investment. The unions criticised the government for "discriminating" against British assemblers while providing large subsidies for the Japanese.[51] Jaguar was sold to Ford in 1989 and then to Tata in 2008. Vickers had taken over RR's car assembly in 1973 and then sold it to Volkswagen/BMW in 1998.

5 Signing the Single Union Agreement

Nissan and other Japanese multinationals introduced, although not the full load, the Japanese style of employment and labour–management relations into Britain. The single union agreement allowed only one union to organise the workers in a plant and to collectively bargain for wage and working standards. The agreement was linked to several other

[46] MRCW, MSS, 292D/617/4, to Len Murray, 3 February 1984.

[47] See Sect. 12 in Chapter 4.

[48] MRCW, MSS, 292D/617/2, to Moss Evans, 26 October 1978.

[49] MRCW, MSS, 292D/617/2, to Moss Evans, 13 November 1978.

[50] MRCW, MSS, 292D/617/4, to Laird, 6 March 1986; MRCW, MSS 292D/617/4, Grantham to Willis, 10 February 1986.

[51] MRCW, MSS, 292D/617/4, Todd to Willis, 22 September 1986.

elements, such as the non-strike agreement, equal working standards for all employees regardless of job category, and flexibility.

The non-strike agreement restricted unions from striking while labour and management consulted at company councils and negotiated wages and working standards. This was *not exactly* a total ban of strikes but in Britain was[52] frequently misunderstood, including by Thatcher, as a ban.[53] Equal working standards not only meant workers with different job categories receiving the same wages but also all workers and executives wearing the same uniform and sitting in the same canteen, as in Japan. The flexibility of personnel relocation was closely related to equal working standards. Being paid equally meant workers were expected to be able to work flexibly in any job category in the plant. This was not a full instalment of the Japanese standard because it was limited to flexibility *inside* the plant and did not mean flexibility in the entire firm.[54] Workers employed at Sunderland would work solely in the plant and would not be relocated to other plants or affiliated suppliers far away. This was not the case for Japanese employees in Japan, where relocation took place flexibly at any time. Refusing relocation meant losing the job. Such strict Japanese terms were not exported to Britain.

The limited version of a single union agreement was still an unfamiliar custom for British trade unions. The TUC named its acceptance and adaptation Japanisation and new realism.[55] Cases before Nissan Sunderland were mostly from the Japanese electronics industry. Toshiba in Plymouth was the first to sign an agreement in April 1981 with the Electrical, Electronic, Telecommunication and Plumbing Union (EETPU).[56] Toshiba's union in Japan had strictly avoided preaching Japanisation from above, taking time with its British colleagues to mutually consult each other's rules and customs and jointly determine a suitable and agreeable "new Anglo-Japanese way."[57] The case of Panasonic (Matsushita-denki)

[52] Wickens, 1987, p. 148.

[53] Wickens termed it "a consensual atmosphere in which industrial action becomes unnecessary"; Wickens, 1987, p. 147.

[54] The Japan Institute of Labour (JIL), *International Labor Information* (*ILI*, Kaigai-roudou-jihou), 133, June 1988, Tokyo: The Japan Institute of Labour, p. 12.

[55] Garrahan and Stewart, 1992, p. 3.

[56] JIL, *ILI*, 111, August 1986, pp. 50–51.

[57] JIL, *ILI*, 88, September 1984, pp. 1–3.

in Cardiff was identical to that of Toshiba; Panasonic signed an agreement with the GMB and successfully produced 220 thousand colour televisions in 1984. Sharp and Sanyo (which later merged with Panasonic in 2011) signed agreements with the EETPU, and Sony signed an agreement with the AUEW.[58] Japanisation was not only about increasing British exports of Japanese products to the continent but also improving quality control.[59] The leading cases in electronics encouraged Nissan to take a similar path.

On 22 April 1985, NMUK and the AUEW, the latter represented by Duffy and Arnold,[60] signed the single union agreement. It was composed of four main points.[61] The first was that the sole union negotiating with management was the AUEW and that it would represent all workers in the plant—supervisors, team leaders, technicians, assemblers, administration staff, and so forth. The non-strike agreement followed as the second point. Before making decisions, management, and labour were to mutually consult on wages and working standards at company councils—or works councils in the cases of other Japanese firms[62]—consisting of ten men and women sent by both sides. Any mediation not resolved at company councils would be taken to the ACAS but could not be interrupted by industrial actions until talks were concluded. The third point was flexibility. All job categories inside the plant were divided into two

[58] JIL, *ILI*, 135, July 1988, pp. 13–16.

[59] JIL, *ILI*, 92, January 1985, pp. 1–4.

[60] MRCW, 807/Box19, vol. 2, Executive Council meeting, 22 April 1985.

[61] JIL, *ILI*, 100, September 1985, pp. 48–49. The JIL (*Nihon roudou kyoukai*) was formed as an organ of the Ministry of Labour in 1958 and carried out research on labour–management relations and working standards. In 1990, it was renamed the Japan Labour Research Organization (*Nihon roudou kenkyu kikou*), and in 2003, it became the Japan Institute for Labour Policy and Training (*Roudou seisaku kenkyu kensyu kikou*) attached to the Ministry of Health, Labour and Welfare. *ILI* was first published in January 1977 with the aim of reporting on labour–management relations and labour-related policies and law in countries where Japanese industry is present: Thailand, the Philippines, Indonesia, Malaysia, Korea, Brazil, Singapore, Hong Kong, and Australia. The hundredth volume, published in September 1989, expanded the journal scope and newly included regular articles on Britain, France, Germany, and the USA. The first article on Britain was about the Nissan Sunderland single union agreement. Sunderland was one of the largest test cases of Japanese trade unionism applied in Britain.

[62] Wickens, 1987, p. 141.

categories, manufacturing staff or manufacturing technician.[63] Employees were expected to flexibly perform any job in different sections and cooperate with management decisions to reorganise and restructure the plant. The fourth point was equal treatment. All employees worked under equal working standards—working hours, breaks, shifts, and extra payments. All staff, including executives, wore the same uniform and sat together in the same canteen. The Sunderland plant started as a new and unfamiliar entity in Britain. The agreement was reported to the Executive Council and the National Committee of the AUEW on the same day.[64]

Once the final and most obstructive issue had been resolved, Ishihara had no interest beyond pushing trade union leader Shioji out of the scene. There was not the slightest sense of no side in the confrontation. In September 1986, the opening ceremony of the Sunderland plant was scheduled, and Ishihara did not want Shioji to be present, alongside PM Thatcher and himself, as one of the founders. Joined by Nakasone's staff Ishihara plotted scandals around Shioji and successfully divided the union leaders and members into two camps, siding with either him or Shioji. Shioji's people either betrayed him or, if they insisted on siding with Shioji, were purged through salary cuts, redeployed, or sent to component suppliers.[65] Ishihara's anti-union intervention entered into full swing when he named Yutaka Kume as his successor in March 1985 and himself became Nissan's chairman after Kawamata.[66] Ishihara specified that Kume should succeed him with the same anti-union approach.[67] Shortly before the power change, Ishihara called Yoshikazu Hanawa back from Nissan USA and put him in charge of trade union issues.[68] Hanawa and Shimizu, of whom the latter was the union leader who had betrayed Shioji,[69] had both joined Nissan in 1957 and knew each other well.[70] Hanawa would

[63] Oliver and Wilkinson, 1992, p. 217.

[64] MRCW, 807/Box19, vol. 2, Executive Council meeting, 22 April 1985.

[65] Shioji, 2012, pp. 10, 357–365.

[66] Ibid., pp. 357–358.

[67] Ibid. Kawakatsu was treated coldly by Kume and eventually left Nissan in 1997, and his team was dissolved; Kawakatsu, 2018, pp. 261, 274–276.

[68] Shioji, 2012, pp. 357–358.

[69] See Sect. 6 in Chapter 5.

[70] Shioji, 2012, p. 365.

become Nissan's last Japanese president in 1996, shortly before Nissan was taken over by the French Renault.[71]

It was not only Nissan's union members who started to attack Shioji. Toyota's union proposed that the JAW force union leaders to retire at the age of 60.[72] Should this new rule apply, Shioji would, against his will, be forced to retire in January 1986. The rumour reached Shioji that Ishihara had asked Toyota's president to make its unions propose this rule.[73] A coup d'état to make Shioji resign was attempted at a Nissan-*rouso* conference on 22 February, but in vain.[74] Relieved that the plot had failed, Shioji carelessly visited a woman on the next day to advise her about a new job and was again caught by photographers of Kodansha's tabloid *Friday*.[75] This time, he was photographed alone with a woman. The "scandal" generated a negative image of Shioji.

On 25 February 1986, Shioji ended up resigning the presidency of Nissan's union, *Jidousha-rouren*, and he resigned that of the JAW on the next day. Trade union records that Shioji had stored in his office were burned to ashes in the Zama plant's incinerator.[76] Nissan's union, *Jidousha-rouren*, was dismantled in the name of realising a "more democratised union" and relaunched as Nissan-*rouren*,[77] and Shimizu became its first president. The influential union structure that Shioji had been building since 1962 was abandoned,[78] completing Ishihara's (and his successors') "dictatorship."[79] Thus, the British project weakened Nissan's unions in Japan.

[71] After a decade and a half of Carlos Ghosn's leadership, a Japanese executive, Hiroto Saikawa, was once more named Nissan's president in April 2017.

[72] Shioji, 2012, pp. 373–374.

[73] Ibid.

[74] Ibid., pp. 379–389.

[75] Ibid., pp. 390–391. Shioji's family was blackmailed until his resignation.

[76] Ibid., p. 6. Fortunately, Shioji had kept some of the records himself, which he later used to publish his memoirs in 2012, shortly before he passed away in February 2013. Former *Nikkei* journalist Sato's monograph on Nissan (2012) is based on Shioji's memoirs and an interview with him.

[77] Shioji, 2012, pp. 6, 391, 394–397.

[78] Ibid., pp. 11, 12, 394–397. Shioji described the change as the unions losing their ability to countercheck management; Ibid., p. 396.

[79] Ibid., pp. 13, 394. Inoue also described Nissan's presidency as a dictatorship; Inoue, 2019, pp. 4–6.

After witnessing his long-serving counterpart's fall, Kawamata passed away on 29 March. A few weeks before, 1 March had been his eighty-first birthday. To his family's surprise, Kawamata had renewed his driver's license a month before his death,[80] willing to stay behind the wheel, but in vain. The Sunderland launch event would take place without both men, symbolising the end of Nissan's post-war success as a mighty "unsinkable flagship"[81] based on cooperative labour–management relations. Nissan's market share in Japan decreased steadily and was absorbed by its dominant rival Toyota and the rising "small" Honda.

6 The Royal Couple in Japan

In May 1986, Prince Charles and Princess Diana visited Japan. It was the first time the Japanese public had seen the royal couple in Japan. "Diana fever" broke out all over the country.[82] News broadcasting and noontime television shows analysed Princess Diana's events and fashions every day as routinely as a weather forecast. The same clothing, shoes, and accessories would sell out immediately afterwards. The royal couple's visit marked a milestone of improved and deepened Anglo-Japanese relations. The Nissan deal was no exception.

Prince Charles and Princess Diana visited the Nissan Zama plant on 12 May. They were presented with the key for the first Bluebird to roll out of Sunderland's assembly line in the coming autumn.[83] The royal couple painted the right eye of the *Daruma*, a Buddhist tumbling doll, to bring good fortune to the new plant. In Japanese eyes, the ceremony meant that the royal family had welcomed Nissan's settlement in Britain. The same doll was transported to Sunderland and used once more in the opening ceremony.[84] The Bluebird was also symbolic for Nissan and Britain. Launched in 1959 and named by then president Kawamata, the Bluebird was a result of Austin's industrial cooperation with Nissan since

[80] Memorial Editing Committee of Nissan, *Kawamata Katsuji*, Tokyo: Nissan, 1988, pp. 213–214, 269.

[81] Sato, 2012, p. 10.

[82] Naotaka Kimizuka, *The Queen's Diplomacy and the Three Circles* (Jyouou-heika no gaikou-senryaku), Tokyo: Kodansha, 2008, pp. 296–297.

[83] Conte-Helm, 1989, pp. 148–149.

[84] Ibid., pp. 148–150.

1952.[85] Kawamata wished the car (and Nissan) to flourish worldwide and took the name from Maurice Maeterlinck's Nobel Prize-winning novel, *L'Oiseau bleu* (Bluebird). The Sunderland launch marked a new page in Anglo-Japanese relations, consolidating a new dimension, "Europe," into the establishment.

On the next day, the royal couple was invited to a lunch at Hotel New Otani in Tokyo hosted by *Keidanren* and Japanese business groups. Ishihara had named Yutaka Kume, who had been involved in the negotiations from the very beginning, as his successor in June 1985.[86] Ishihara himself became chairman of Nissan, and in April 1985, he became president of the Japan Association of Corporate Executives (*Keizai-doyukai*). At the lunch, Ishihara was seated next to Princess Diana. The two had a short conversation,[87] with Ishihara asking the princess whether she did not eat much. The princess politely replied that she was thin because she worked hard. Ishihara changed the subject and asked if she drove cars. Princess Diana replied that she loved driving but, due to the rules for the royal family, had driven only British cars and had not yet tried a Nissan car. Whether touching on the food issue was appropriate was questionable. Princess Diana had referred to the topic herself when visiting Panasonic's Ibaragi plant three days before. The latest high-vision television had displayed a goldfish to greet the royal couple. Seeing the fish, the princess had praised its beauty and commented that the goldfish seemed too large. The audience broke into affectionate laughter.[88]

7 The First Bluebird Assembled

The Sunderland plant assembled the first Bluebird/Auster in July 1986. In this phase 1 Nissan had signed contracts with 27 component suppliers in Britain and achieved the requirement of 20% local content.[89] The first

[85] See the Sect. 2 in Chapter 2.

[86] See the Sect. 4 in Chapter 4. Kume studied aero engines at the University of Tokyo and graduated in 1944, joining Nissan in 1946.

[87] *Nikkei Business Daily,* 14 May 1986.

[88] *Nikkei*, 10 May 1986.

[89] Conte-Helm, 1989, p. 148. Garrahan and Stewart raised doubt about the "local" content, pointing out that suppliers from the Sunderland Borough and the Northern Region were marginal; Garrahan and Stewart, 1992, pp. 52–52.

Bluebird was numbered "JOB 1." Freed of Kawamata's and Shioji's influence, on 15 August, Nissan and its union, Nissan-*rouren*, had abandoned their labour–management memorandum of January 1984[90] and decided to proceed immediately to phase 2 on 28 August.[91]

The Sunderland plant celebrated its opening ceremony on 8 September 1986. Thatcher as PM was present, along with Japanese Ambassador Toshio Yamazaki and Nissan President Yutaka Kume. Thatcher was satisfied and relieved to see the successful launch, six years and eight months after Nissan and the DoI's joint announcement. The *Daruma,* of which Prince Charles and Princess Diana had painted the right eye at the Zama plant, was placed in the ceremony. Thatcher and Kume painted the left eye together to celebrate their accomplishment.[92] Thatcher pressed the operation button of the welding line and proudly announced,[93]

> Workers at Nissan UK are well skilled. It will not take long before achieving better quality than Nissan in Japan.

Although showing hostility to British trade unions throughout the negotiations, Thatcher believed in the skills and potential of British workers.[94] Ambassador Yamazaki praised the history of exchanges between the North East and Japan ever since the Meiji era—the early decades of Japan's modernisation and its purchase of battleships. Kume, as Nissan's president, announced that the plant would enter phase 2 one year before schedule. The plant had been launched successfully and was now able to expand its capacities. However, significant protagonists were not present at the ceremony. Among the cabinet members and officials who had not been invited were Lord Patrick Jenkin and Sir Hugh Cortazzi,[95] let alone Labour MPs who had built a bridge between the DTI and the trade unions in the North East. Thatcher and Ishihara were in harmony about

[90] See Sect. 8 of the previous chapter.

[91] Shioji, 2012, pp. 397–398.

[92] Conte-Helm, 1989, pp. 148–150.

[93] *Nikkei*, 9 September 1986.

[94] Suzuki, 2015a, pp. iii, 164

[95] Cortazzi, 1998, p. 171.

excluding the centre-left people—including Shioji—and received criticism thereafter.[96]

In February 1987, Sunderland became the sole supplier of Bluebirds in Britain and started exports to Ireland. In the August 1988 press line, engine assembly and plastic moulding lines were launched and brought the ratio of local content up to 80%, equal to 420 million pounds worth of purchases.[97] Sunderland started exports of Bluebird to the continent in September 1988. Symbolically, the last remaining nationalised shipbuilder in Sunderland had closed in the same month.[98] In February the next year, Sunderland's total output reached 100 thousand units. In June, the leadership of NMUK was handed over by Toshiaki Tsuchiya to Ian Gibson.

Components supplied to Sunderland came from various firms operating in Britain. Japanese and Anglo-Japanese firms included Ikeda-Hoover for seats,[99] Hashimoto/Faltec for mouldings, Marley Kanto for dash panels, and TI Nihon (TIJ) UK and Calsonic for exhaust pipes.[100] All of these were Nissan suppliers that launched plants in Britain, following the parent firm. "British" suppliers included not only Lucas for batteries, Avon for radiator hoses, and SP Tyres for tyres but also the French Clarion and Michelin; the German Blaupunkt, Bosch, and Continental; and the Italian Magneti-Marelli.[101] "British" local content of Nissan cars made in Sunderland were a result of European integration and British membership in the EC/EU.

In May 1990, a new model, the Primera, replaced the Bluebird. Up to 80–90% of Sunderland Primeras were exported, heading to the EC, Yugoslavia, Poland, Czechoslovakia, and Taiwan.[102] The end of the cold war opened new markets in the former communist countries and created a global market. The Primera also became the first Japanese car exported

[96] Suzuki, 2015a, p. 165.

[97] Industrial Journal (*Sangyou journal*) (ed.), *Nissan; Group Activity of 1992* (Nissan-jidousha group no jittai 1992), Nagoya: IRC, 1992, p. 273.

[98] Garrahan and Stewart, 1992, p. 4.

[99] Nissan sold its stock in Ikeda Bussan in 2000, and the firm joined Johnson Controls.

[100] Industrial Journal, 1992, pp. 279, 289.

[101] Ibid.

[102] Ibid., p. 272.

to Japan from an overseas plant. The new model proved that British-made Nissans had a high reputation in Japan as a Japanese car that was fundamentally different from past efforts, with the European flavour of a saloon. The Micra/March would soon follow suit. Also in 1990, former chancellor of the exchequer Nigel Lawson and former foreign secretary Geoffrey Howe turned their backs on Thatcher, forcing her to step down as Tory leader and resign as PM.

While Thatcher left power and was succeeded by the pro-European John Major, Nissan Sunderland's success seemed unstoppable. NMUK made its first turnover of 18 million 400 thousand pounds in 1991, gaining British manufacturer status from the SMMT in April.[103] This was achieved one year ahead of schedule, based on Nissan's first feasibility study in 1981.[104] The Nissan European Technology Centre (NETC) opened an office in Cranfield in September 1991, aiming to internationalise Nissan's R&D.[105] In August 1992, the Micra joined the Sunderland line-up just in time for the launch of the new EU and its single market the next year. Now, Nissan was head-to-head with European rivals in the most competitive market for small cars. Two hundred million pounds were injected to add a new assembly line, coupled with further new employment and increased automation. Nissan aimed to reach an annual output of 300 thousand units by 1993, which would have helped the firm leap from a 4% market share in Britain to 10% by the millennium year.[106] In November 1993, the Micra won the European Car of the Year award, which was the first the honour had been granted to a "Japanese" car. It was a remarkable achievement not only of skilful and punctual assembly but also of joint Anglo-Japanese R&D in developing a new competitive model for the EC/EU market. The Micra proved popular not only in Europe but also back in Japan. The year 1993 was memorable for NMUK, which surpassed Rover and became the largest car exporter in Britain. The firm was honoured with the Queen's Award for Enterprise (International Trade/Export) for the third time since 1991.[107] Overall,

[103] Suzuki, 2015a, p. 166.

[104] Conte-Helm, 1989, p. 149.

[105] Industrial Journal, 1992, p. 7.

[106] Ibid., p. 272.

[107] Industrial Journal, 1996, p. 305.

car assembly in Britain had recovered and approached two million units per annum for the first time since 1972.[108]

8 Honda and Toyota Catch up

Honda and Toyota swiftly followed Nissan after seeing Sunderland's success in both assembly and export. Decisions for the hasty catching up were based on seeing the British government countering criticism and retaliation from the other EC member states. In July 1989, Honda announced that it was expanding its engine plant in Swindon into a full-scale car assembly plant. The plant assembled its first Accord in October 1992. The Accord was a model with a recent history embedded in Honda's collaboration with Rover under BL since 1980. The Swindon plant had an annual output of 250 thousand units by July 2001, when a second line was added. In the same year, the Civic Type R was exported from Swindon to Japan for the first time and sold out before delivery.

Among the three Japanese assemblers, Toyota was the last to join the trend. In April 1989, Toyota announced the launch of an assembly plant in Derbyshire and established Toyota Motor Manufacturing (UK) Ltd. in December. The construction of the Burnaston plant started in June 1990, and the first Carina was assembled on 16 December 1992, merely sixteen days before the opening of the EU single market.[109] Toyota successively launched an engine assembly plant in Deeside, North Wales.[110] Wales had lost the competition to win Nissan for Shotton but was able to win Toyota. In contrast to Toyota's success, Nissan experienced an ordinary loss for the first time in its post-war history in the same year.

It was not only Japanese car assemblers that followed Nissan's path. The Japanese components industry, with NSK and Yuasa as the forerunners, entered into joint ventures with British firms. Furthermore, Japanese investments in Britain continued to expand in the electronics industry. Fujitsu announced the launch of a semiconductor plant in Durham, which became the second-largest Japanese investment in the North East.[111]

[108] Mountfield, 2007a, p. 120.

[109] Mason, 1994, p. 438.

[110] Deeside not only supplied assembled engines for Burnaston but also exported hybrid engines to Japan.

[111] Conte-Helm, 1989, p. 172.

Fears that the EC would become a "fortress Europe" ran high and were partly confirmed by harsh reactions against Japanese cars made in Britain.[112] The exchange rate of the yen after the Plaza Agreement in 1985 was also a factor for Japanese industry accelerating overseas operations in Britain due to decreased price competitiveness when exporting from Japan. The CBI did not miss the occasion to persuade British firms to "either follow suit (with the Japanese *kanban* system) or go out of business, because more and more we are becoming part of a global market."[113] There was no option but to remain competitive.

The gateway that the Thatcher administration had opened for Japanese manufacturers bore fruit, resulting in her popularity soaring even higher in Japan than at home. Thatcher received the Grand Cordon of the Order of the Precious Crown from the Japanese emperor in May 1995. Her counterpart, Ishihara, was also honoured in both countries, receiving the Order of the British Empire from the queen in September 1990. He was honoured with the Grand Cordon of the Order of the Rising Sun from the emperor in April the next year. Ishihara's fame reached its height in Japan until Nissan was "dishonourably rescued" by Renault in 1999.[114]

9 Single Union Agreements in Britain

Typical of Nissan and Japanese firms' labour–management relations, single union agreements started to spread in other parts of Britain. They were viewed by foreign investors and multinationals as a sign of improved labour–management relations attracting investment into Britain. The image itself was controversial for the TUC and British unions. As the Nissan deal showed, on one hand, it meant the creation of new jobs. However, the downside was the unions' reduced influence and relative loss of workers' right to strike. The TUC and member unions started to question the AUEW and the EETPU about their single union agreements.[115]

The TUC had taken action in December 1985, eight months after the agreement in Sunderland, by adopting a guideline on negotiating and

[112] See the last section of this chapter.

[113] Conte-Helm, 1989, p. 172.

[114] See Sect. 3 of the next chapter.

[115] MRCW, 807/Box20, vol. 2, Executive Council meeting, 7 January 1986.

signing single union agreements. Before entering into negotiations, the union(s) should consult or reach agreement with other unions.[116] Within two weeks of notification, the TUC would advise the concerned unions on whether their negotiations respected the necessary procedures of the TUC and supply them with legal advice.[117] The TUC preferred to see its member unions not competing with each other in negotiating with management and agreeing with disadvantageous conditions. It aimed to prevent such competitions and conflicts under its mediation.[118] The so-called Bridlington Rules forbade unions to intervene in other unions' members and their membership.[119]

However, the TUC conflict mediation failed in several crucial cases. American multinationals swiftly followed Nissan's case. Coca-Cola Schweppes in Wakefield was successful in signing a deal with the AUEW (after 1986 called the Amalgamated Engineering Union, AEU).[120] However, the automobile sector was a different case, with not less than two thousand workers employed in one plant, making it difficult for the management to "choose" one union. In 1988, Ford in Britain announced the launch of an electronics plant in Dundee, Scotland, and negotiated a single union agreement with the AEU. The investment was estimated at forty million pounds.[121] However, the unions in the other twenty-one "old" plants countered this move because it breached their former agreements with Ford. This led to a dispute between the AEU and the TGWU.[122] The TUC was quick to attempt mediation between the unions, but Ford, reacting even more quickly, withdrew its announcement on 17 March 1988 and sought a new site in Spain.[123] One of the worst-case scenarios that the DoI had estimated in the early days of the Nissan negotiations became reality. If the unions insisted on traditional

[116] JIL, *ILI*, 135, July 1988, pp. 13–16; JIL, *ILI*, 111, August 1986, p. 51.

[117] JIL, *ILI*, 142, February 1989, pp. 9–12.

[118] JIL, *ILI*, 135, July 1988, pp. 13–16.

[119] JIL, *ILI*, 137, September 1988, pp. 21–23.

[120] Suzuki, 2015a, p. 169.

[121] JIL, *ILI*, 135, July 1988, pp. 13–14.

[122] Ibid.; MRCW, MSS, 292E/85/638, note for General Secretary, Ford Dundee (Report to Unions), date not stated.

[123] MRCW, MSS, 292E/85/638, news from the TUC, Ford Dundee, 17 March 1988.

wage bargaining and labour–management relations, investors would flee. It was a bitter lesson.

The EETPU also fell into conflict with leftist unions. At the TUC Convention in September 1987, the TGWU proposed banning single union agreements.[124] Ron Todd—general secretary of the TGWU—referred to such agreements as "*harakiri* (Japanese suicide)."[125] Arthur Scargill—president of the National Union of Mineworkers (NUM)—described them as a "TUC fudge."[126] The EETPU opposed the proposal and stated that it would leave the TUC should it be adopted.[127] In the same year, the EETPU confronted the TGWU about winning an agreement with Yuasa, a Japanese battery producer in Ebbw Vale, Wales. The TUC advised the EETPU to reject the agreement with Yuasa so that the TGWU could renegotiate a deal.[128] The EETPU reluctantly agreed.[129] However, in another deal with the Japanese Orion Electric, the EETPU refused mediation and suspended its TUC membership due to breaching the guidelines on single union agreements.[130] The EETPU was disaffiliated in September 1988.[131] There were two paths for the AEU, either to join the EETPU in leaving the TUC or merge with the EETPU and help its members regain TUC membership.[132] The two unions merged in 1992 and formed the Amalgamated Engineering and Electrical Union (AEEU), affiliated with the TUC. The incident showed the limits of the TUC's role in unifying the unions and its strategies.[133]

Regardless of disputes among British unions, the AUE/AEEU was eager to support the merits of single union agreements. The AUE in Wales issued a pamphlet titled *A Progressive Partnership* that emphasised successful cases with the Japanese in Britain: Sony and Meiki in Bridgend,

[124] JIL, *ILI*, 127, December 1987, pp. 76–77.

[125] Ibid.

[126] Ibid.

[127] Ibid.

[128] JIL, *ILI*, 137, September 1988, pp. 21–23.

[129] Ibid.

[130] JIL, *ILI*, 138, October 1988, pp. 13–16.

[131] JIL, *ILI*, 142, February 1989, pp. 9–12; Beale, 1992, pp. 183–184.

[132] JIL, *ILI*, 137, September 1988, pp. 21–23.

[133] Beale, 1992, pp. 183–184.

Nissan in Sunderland, Komatsu in Durham, and Sekisui in Merthyr.[134] Peter Wickens as Nissan's personnel director contributed his greetings, which read,[135]

> [...] We believed [the AUE] was the union that was committed to our philosophy of teamworking, flexibility, single status and an absolute dedication to quality. That belief has been totally fulfilled and we have worked well together ever since.

Toyota was swift to follow Nissan's path. On 31 October 1991, Toyota Motor Manufacturing UK signed the Recognition Agreement with the AUE. The elements of the agreement contained five points, similar to Nissan's case:[136]

> A single union for all employees from the shop floor to senior management.
>
> Single status for all employees, to break down the old, artificial barriers between the shop floor and the office.
>
> Independent conciliation and arbitration facilities, to deal with those few problems that cannot be resolved internally.
>
> National and local officials available at any time to assist in the development of smooth industrial relations.
>
> Provision of the flexible use of labour and the necessary training to maximise flexibility and productivity.

Honda was the last of the three Japanese assemblers. It was only in 2001 that the AEEU organised workers in Swindon.

Garrahan and Stewart, as critics of Peter Wickens, pointed out that there was "no really independent role" for the AUEW/AEU in Sunderland and that the AUEW was "[in] little sense [...] an independent

[134] MRCW, MSS.259/AEU/7/IG/11, AUE in Wales, *A Progressive Partnership*, date not stated but estimated to be before 1992 because it refers to Toyota in Burnaston and Deeside.

[135] Ibid.

[136] Ibid.

union" there.[137] Oliver and Wilkinson saw the Nissan case as influential in British industrial relations as a "fundamental transformation"[138] and "pioneer for the future,"[139] which not only applied to Sunderland but also had a wider impact on the British components industry.[140] In 1989, the lowest number of strikes since 1935 was recorded, and production losses due to labour disputes decreased by 40% over the decade.[141] Productivity in Britain started to improve.

It is still questionable to what extent trade unions and single union agreements played a role in the effective operation of Japanese plants. The organisation rate in Sunderland failed to reach 20% in 1989.[142] Workers tended to hesitate to join the AUEW,[143] which ironically realised a plant Ishihara had longed for in Japan. The more workers and employees were distanced from trade unions, the less they shared management's views in both the short and the long term. The same applied to Britain's EC/EU membership as an indispensable "condition" for the plant to stay in business, which was one of the core elements of the Nissan negotiations throughout. If Japanisation—close teamwork and mutual consultation—did take place to some extent, why was management's wish and hope to avoid Brexit not shared with workers and employees? The lack of exchanges and outreach both within Japanese plants and within the local society is in sharp contrast to the rich cultural exchanges between the North East and Japan, an aspect that Conte-Helm illustrated in detail.[144]

[137] Garrahan and Stewart, 1992, pp. 68–69, sited in Oliver and Wilkinson, 1992, pp. 218–219, 222. Garrahan and Stewart described company councils as "participation without power"; Ibid.

[138] Oliver and Wilkinson, 1992, p. 2.

[139] Ibid., p. 214.

[140] Ibid., 1992, p. 222.

[141] JIL, *ILI*, 149, July 1989, pp. 52–54.

[142] JIL, *ILI*, 148, July 1989, p. 69.

[143] Ibid.

[144] Conte-Helm, 1989, pp. 166–191.

10 Retaliation from the Continent: The Elements of Consensus

As soon as Sunderland Nissans reached the continent, the French government announced that it would define those cars as made in Japan.[145] French assembler Peugeot called Britain a "Japanese aircraft carrier" and "Japan's fifth island,"[146] proposing to ban Japanese plants in the EC.[147] On the British side, there was no doubt regarding whether Nissans assembled at Sunderland—or Burnaston-Toyota and Swindon-Honda—were made in Britain. The long debate over local sourcing bore fruit. The British government—and the European Commission[148]—countered the argument and put it down.[149]

A harsh attack from the continent followed with a European disguise. Britain sided with Japan when MITI and the European Commission's DG III (Internal Market and Industry) jointly monitored Japanese car exports under the Elements of Consensus during 1991 and 1999.[150] The agreement was negotiated simultaneously with the Japan-EC Joint Declaration (the Hague Declaration) of July 1991. The European Commission had asked MITI and MOFA to cooperate with the EC in allowing time for European assemblers to adapt to global competition and liberalisation. In concrete terms, it meant monitoring and controlling Japanese exports by each member state. Behind the scenes, the French government and assemblers had lobbied Brussels to control Japanese cars made in *both* Japan *and* Britain.[151] The German government initially showed reluctance but was urged by Volkswagen and ultimately sided with the French.[152]

On 17 July 1991, MITI vice minister Noboru Hatakeyama was approached by the European Commission during the Hague negotiations

[145] Mason, 1994, p. 438.

[146] Beale, 1994, p. 33.

[147] Mason, 1994, pp. 442–443. To circumvent such rigid opposition, the European assembler association was reformed as the Association of European Automobile Manufacturers (ACEA) in February 1991, and majority voting replaced unanimity; Ibid.

[148] Kendall, 2013, p. 230.

[149] Mason, 1994, pp. 444, 449.

[150] Suzuki, 2015a, p. 168; Kendall, 2013, pp. 231–235; Mason, 1994, p. 440.

[151] Kendall, 2013, p. 230.

[152] Ibid., pp. 442, 444.

to agree that MITI would accept a side letter restricting "Japanese" cars, which applied not only to those made in Japan but also those made in Britain.[153] Hatakeyama immediately rejected this deal, which breached GATT rules,[154] but then was asked to "silently admit" an "orally stated number of Japanese cars assembled overseas" as a request from French PM Édith Cresson.[155] This meant the agreement would not be stated in writing but would cap exports of British-made Japanese cars to the continent. The Commission stressed that this matter threatened the conclusion of the Joint Declaration. Hatakeyama also rejected the oral agreement but then was asked to reject it in a "more indirect manner." It did not target American manufacturers in Europe and was understood by the Japanese as discrimination.[156] Puzzled by the repeated attempts, Hatakeyama asked how a more indirect refusal would actually be expressed. No answer arrived until the next day. The Japan-EC Joint Declaration was signed in the Hague on 18 July. The European Commission had no option but to cut the Elements of Consensus off from the Joint Declaration and sign the former. The GATT was notified of the Elements of Consensus, which continued up to 31 December 1999.[157] British-made Japanese cars were excluded from the counts coming from Japan.[158] The consensus became an early case of the European Commission taking the lead in multilateral negotiations with external economic powers.[159]

NMUK launched a successful green-field plant in Britain and, owing to diplomatic efforts that realised the single market, was able to export to the continent. Nissan gained R&D knowledge and as a consequence developed new competitive models, not to mention helping Japan end

[153] Noboru Hatakeyama, *The Dramatic Trade Negotiations Over National Interests* (Tsusyokousyou wo meguru drama), Tokyo: Nikkei, 1996, pp. 198–222.

[154] Mason, 1994, p. 444.

[155] Hatakeyama, 1996, pp. 198–222.

[156] Ibid.

[157] Kendall, 2013, p. 230.

[158] There remained dissent on whether there was a cap. Commission Vice President Frans Andriessen attached an oral statement to the consensus that "assumed" that Japanese plants in the EC would assemble approximately 1.2 million units during the monitoring years, but his counterpart, Eiichi Nakao, denied this; Mason, 1994, pp. 446–450.

[159] Reuben Wong, "The Europeanlization of Foreign Policy," in Christopher Hill and Micheal Smith (eds.), *International Relations and the European Union* (2nd ed.), Oxford: Oxford University Press, 2011, p. 165.

trade conflicts with the EC member states. Nissan Sunderland is known for having achieved the highest productivity among European assemblers,[160] although its future was brought into question by the Brexit referendum in June 2016. Robin Mountfield later testified that Nissan's deal helped to improve the productivity and quality of the British components industry.[161] As Nissan's former adviser Lord Richard Marsh pointed out, Sunderland's success was made possible because the "attitudes and practices of both management and shop floor workers were markedly different from those traditional to the British motor car industry."[162] According to Lord Marsh, the Nissan deal showed a trade-off between Japan and Britain: "The British have many qualities, but the ability to adapt easily to new ways has not historically been the most obvious of them. In contrast one of the key elements in the economic success of Japan has been their ability to identify their weakness and adapt to new ways."[163]

Trade unions in both Japan and Britain were affected by the Sunderland deal. In Japan, the British project torpedoed Shioji's leadership and weakened Nissan's unions, which lost direct connections to management and were muted thereafter.[164] Shioji had not only built-up Nissan's unions but also unified the Japanese unions in the car sector under the JAW. His unionism, which showed little hesitation in taking industrial action, was more similar to that of British unions than the typical Japanese unionism in the private sector. The unification of Japanese unions under the umbrella Japan Trade Union Confederation (*Rengou*) in November 1989 was led by unions in the six private sectors: textiles, electronics, electricity, steel, transportation, and the JAW.[165] Ironically, the unification of

[160] See Takahashi, 2009, pp. 244–253; Mountfield, 2007a, p. 118; Uesugi, 2001, p. 143.

[161] Mountfield, 2007a, p. 119.

[162] Richard Marsh, "Foreword," in Wickens, 1987, p. x.

[163] Ibid., p. xi.

[164] Garrahan and Stewart quoted interviewees' phrases, "[to] put up or shut up," because losing the job (by expressing oneself) was out of the question when one had "a family, a mortgage, and 'debt in the car park'"; Garrahan and Stewart, 1992, p. 139.

[165] Ikuo Kume, *Labour Policy; Trade Unions in Post-War Politics* (Roudou seiji), Tokyo: Chuo-kouron-shinsha, 2005, pp. 242–251.

the private and public sectors made Japanese unions reduce their political lobbying influence.[166]

On the other hand, the British unions were also affected by the Nissan deal. Single union agreements containing a "non-strike" agreement were contested. The EETPU and the AUEW led the trend of accepting such Japanese deals. Leftist unions—with the TGWU and the NUM at the forefront—criticised the "new realism" and opposed the agreements as breaching the Bridlington Rules and abandoning workers' right to strike. The TUC attempted mediation, and the unions split, but single union agreements gradually spread in Britain, helped by the decline of leftist unions. Japanese investment in Britain acted as part of the global pressure for British unions to abandon traditional unionism and to transform them into a "cooperative" partner.

166 Ibid.

CHAPTER 7

Epilogue

Abstract Sunderland's operations proceeded before the schedule in fulfilling British local contents and accordingly exporting to the continent. The launch was a success and achieved its first turnover in 1991, gaining British manufacturer status from the SMMT the same year. While maintaining Britain's largest car exporter status, it failed to reach its maximum annual output throughout the 1990s. Due to its financial difficulties back home Nissan sought to reduce assembly costs, rather than reaching the maximum output, which brought Primera's local contents up to 90%. It was the new ruler Carlos Ghosn who boosted the output and immediately achieved the goal. But his arrival was paid harder in Sunderland than in Japan. British local contents were replaced by those of Renault, the prospect of hard-Brexit merely adding to uncertainty than improvement.

Keywords European Union · Economic Partnership Agreement · Brexit · Nissan · Local contents · Car exports · Single market · Export monitoring · Corporate governance · Carlos Ghosn

H. Suzuki, *Japanese Investment and British Trade Unionism*, New Directions in East Asian History,
https://doi.org/10.1007/978-981-15-9058-0_7

1 Nissan's Fall

As the Japanese bubble economy collapsed in the early 1990s, Nissan's records also started to falter. The last years of the twentieth century marked Japan's "lost decade," when land prices dropped sharply, banks suffered bad debts, and firms closed. The shiny days of post-war rapid economic growth were over, and the country of the rising sun turned out to be no more than an "ordinary" developed country in a slump, if not a slow decline. Nissan experienced ordinary loss for the first time in its post-war history in 1992.

Due to its over-ambitious overseas investment and simultaneous loss of domestic market share in Japan, Nissan's debt continued growing during the 1990s. The new and profitable Sunderland project sustained on its own in Britain, and the single market of the EU did little to prevent Nissan's fall. In 1995, Sunderland achieved its one thousand overall output since its launch, but in March the same year, the Zama plant in Japan closed. Nissan's domestic market share had reached 27% in 1984, but by 1994, it had fallen to 20.7%, barely reaching half of Toyota's.[1] Ironically, Toyota announced in the same month that it would expand its successful Burnaston plant in Britain. The 2,500 workers at Nissan Zama were made redundant, and the site was transformed into Nissan's technology centre.[2] Nissan's revival was postponed to the millennium years under French initiatives. A former employee at Zama wrote to Shioji, "We lost our Zama. All workers who dedicated their lives to Nissan lost their jobs. What is left with us are all the medals Ishihara received from other countries."[3] Shioji as a retired union leader could do little but bitterly observe Nissan-*rouren*'s powerlessness to protect its members' employment.[4]

[1] Shioji, 2012, p. 399.

[2] Currently, the site also accommodates a plant producing lithium batteries for electric vehicles with NEC.

[3] Shioji, 2012, p. 400.

[4] Ibid., pp. 15, 467–471. In his memoirs, Shioji recalled Ludwig Erhard, German minister of economy, and his visit to Japan in 1957 as forming the basis of trade unionism for him. Asked from the audience for advice on the Japanese economy, the minister answered that Japan should focus on increasing consumers' income and improving living standards as an engine for further economic growth. Then, and still, according to Shioji, Japan was a "queer country," compared to European countries because it prioritised

In contrast to Nissan's decline, Toyota announced the launch of a plant in France in December 1997, which became the first case of a Japanese assembler establishing a presence in France. Toyota's announcement was made two years before the final round of export monitoring under the Elements of Consensus expired.[5] In 2000, the Toyota Yaris/Bitz received the European Car of the Year award, the second case of a "Japanese" car winning the honour after the Nissan Micra/March in 1993. Like the Micra, the Yaris was jointly designed and developed between Japanese and European branches. The Valenciennes plant that produced the Yaris was launched in 2001. The trade conflict between Japan and the EC/EU member states, together with the expiration of the consensus of 1991, had finally drawn to an end. It was solved at the industry level but lacked formal diplomatic FTA/EPA arrangements between Japan and the EC/EU.[6] It was only on 5 July 2017 that the Japan-EU EPA was concluded.[7]

In contrast to Nissan's decline back home, Sunderland was successful in exporting the Primera and Mirca to the single market. Sunderland supplied the engines of the Nissan Vanette to its plant in Spain from 1992 onwards. The local content of the Primera was maintained at 83% and that of the Micra was maintained at 80%. Exports to the continent experienced a slump in 1993 and 1994, leading Nissan to consider alternative export outlets outside the single market, but in vain.[8] To reduce assembly costs in Britain, NMUK launched a supplier development team (SDT) at Sunderland. The SDT aimed to reduce costs by 30% by the millennium year, inviting suppliers into R&D to reduce the number of components.[9] As a result, the Primera's local content reached 90%.[10] What the British

corporate interests and industrial advances while paying little attention to living standards and working conditions.

[5] See the last section of the previous chapter.

[6] Hitoshi Suzuki, "The New Politics of Trade: EU-Japan," *Journal of European Integration*, 39(7), 2017a, pp. 875–889.

[7] Ibid.

[8] Industrial Journal, 1994, p. 281.

[9] Industrial Journal, 1998, pp. 275–276.

[10] Ibid.

components industry had requested at the beginning of the Nissan negotiations was now realised.[11] In pursuit of further cost reduction, Nissan sought to separate the Micra from the R&D of its sister model, the March, in Japan and develop it separately in Britain by using the Primera chassis.[12] Despite such efforts, the full annual output of 300 thousand units was not reached until the millennium year, when the Almera/Pulsar joined the line-up as the third car to be assembled at Sunderland.[13]

2 The Nissan-Renault Alliance

Nissan's financial crisis reached its peak in 1998. Under Yoshikazu Hanawa's presidency, Nissan rushed to find a partner who could finance the firm. Mercedes-Benz was at the top of the list, but the German giant delayed its answer and ultimately chose the American Chrysler as its new partner.[14] Shortly before Nissan's default, the French manufacturer Renault offered a deal. With the help of the French government's exceptional budget aid, Nissan was able to avoid bankruptcy with 2,000 billion yen of debt. Renault was a French assembler that Ishihara had described as a "small firm which Nissan thought to have purchased, but not the other way around."[15]

On 27 March 1999, Nissan and Renault announced capital tie-up, with the latter purchasing 36.8% of the former's stock and the former purchasing 15% of the latter's stock, but without voting rights in management. As the last Japanese Nissan President Hanawa put it, "Nissan had lost its vision of what to do" and now required "not a mere reform but a

[11] See Sect. 8 in Chapter 4.

[12] Ibid. Instead of this solution, the Micra was made into the Renault Clio's sister model under a decision by Carlos Ghosn. See the next section.

[13] Industrial Journal, 2000, p. 209.

[14] Hanawa testified that Nissan had negotiated with Renault from the beginning, and the negotiation with Mercedes-Benz was solely about Nissan Trucks; http://www.nissan-global.com/JP/HERITAGE/LEGENDS/LEGEND_10/index.html. Accessed on 21 August 2017. Inoue reported that the negotiations terminated due to Mercedes requiring all Nissan executives to resign before signing the merger, at which Hanawa went into a rage and rejected the proposal; Hisao Inoue, "A thought on the death of a Nissan executive and Nissan's 'real disease'" *(hitori no moto-kanbu no shi kara kangaeta Nissan no 'honto no byousou')*" 11 September 2019. https://news.yahoo.co.jp/byline/inouehisao/20190911-00142201/. Accessed on 8 October 2019.

[15] Sato, 2012, p. 20. See also Sect. 5 in Chapter 4.

revolution."[16] Thatcher had once expected Nissan to revolutionise British labour–management relations. Now, it was Nissan's turn to learn. Renault President Louis Schweitzer sent his best man, Carlos Ghosn, to Japan as Nissan's COO in June 1999. Ghosn had worked for Michelin and had come to be known as the (notorious) "cost-cutter" who had revived the formerly nationalised Renault.

Soon after arriving in Tokyo, Ghosn launched the Nissan Revival Plan. Rationalisation underwent the hardest way. Component suppliers tied to Nissan with the old *zaibatsu* connection were cut off, and the sourcing of components was made global to reduce costs. Nissan's truck assembly business was sold to the Swedish Volvo. Nissan's aerospace division—formerly a Prince Motor project—was sold to Ishikawajima-Harima in 2000, which formed IHI Aerospace, the largest Japanese aerospace engine manufacturer. Further rationalisation targeted car assembly. The Murayama plant—a Nissan heritage plant since its merger with Prince Motor in August 1966, assembling the Skyline and Gloria—had to close in 2004. After painful cost-cutting, Nissan rapidly recovered its profits and finished its payback in June 2003.

The ups and downs of Nissan in Japan started to affect Sunderland. It had taken more than a decade for Sunderland to achieve the full annual output of 300 thousand units. After the plant began assembling the Micra, the output reached 246,281 units in 1993, but it dropped to 204,944 in 1994 and 215,462 in 1995.[17] The local content of the Primera and Micra was maintained at 83 and 80%, respectively, but the plant failed to reach the output goal. Nissan sought to add a five-door estate car to the Primera and a Micra with a diesel engine, boosting the output to 271,666 units in 1997, 288,818 in 1998, and 272,000 in 1999,[18] but still fell short.

Ghosn's arrival in 1999 was a game changer, as Nissan ceased Japanese exports of the Almera/Pulsar to Britain and switched to local assembly at Sunderland from the millennium year on.[19] The plant now operated around the clock, and its output capacity was expanded to 500 thousand

[16] Uesugi, 2001, pp. 4–5.

[17] Industrial Journal, 1996, p. 307.

[18] Industrial Journal, 2000, p. 275.

[19] Industrial Journal, 1998, p. 269.

units per annum.[20] Results came immediately, and it achieved the highest annual output of 327,792 units in the same year.[21] A full model change of the Micra was scheduled for 2002, and an investment of 235 million pounds was injected into Sunderland.[22]

However, good news was inevitably coupled with bad news. British local content was seriously brought into question by Ghosn. His Revival Plan hit Sunderland harder than plants in Japan. Back home, Nissan asked component suppliers to reduce costs by 20% within two years. For Britain, this was increased to 30%, with the pound/euro exchange rate in mind.[23] Evaluation of the pound increased the exporting costs of assembled cars but reduced those of components imported from the continent. Ghosn had once considered terminating the assembly of the Micra at Sunderland and transferring it to Spain or Renault's plant(s) on the continent assembling the Clio but abandoned the idea due to the need for additional investments for such changes.[24] Costs did sink into British soil.

However, the crisis of British component suppliers was not far away. Ghosn decided to increase purchases of components from the eurozone.[25] 50% of the Primera components and 65% of the Micra components would be supplied from the continent.[26] The gentleman's agreement of 1984 was abandoned,[27] neither by a British or a Japanese decision but by a French choice. Once the Micra shared a chassis with the Renault Clio, the two cars had 95% of their components in common.[28] The percentage of British local content would fall, and the British components sector would need to confront its rivals on the continent head-to-head. Sunderland's achievement of an annual output of 500 thousand units was not free of costs and sacrifices.

Back home in Japan, Nissan revived within a few years thanks to Ghosn's strong but controversial leadership. Since 2009, Nissan's added

[20] Industrial Journal, 2002, p. 209.

[21] Ibid.

[22] Ibid.

[23] Ibid, p. 214.

[24] Ibid.

[25] Ibid.

[26] Ibid.

[27] See Sect. 8 in Chapter 5.

[28] Industrial Journal, 2002, p. 214.

value and investment per worker have surpassed those of Renault.[29] Nissan sold five million 516 thousand units globally in 2018, while Renault sold three million 884 thousand. Turnover amounted to 319 billion yen for the former and 424 billion for the latter,[30] of which two-fifths came from Nissan stock owned by Renault.[31] Sunderland has assembled the Note, the Juke, and the successful Qashqai/Dualis. In June 2013, Sunderland launched the assembly of the 100% electric car, the Leaf, which received the European Car of the Year award in 2011. It was the second car for Nissan and the third from a "Japanese" manufacturer to receive the honour, not to mention the first case of an electric vehicle.

3 Brexit, the Japan-EU EPA, and Carlos Ghosn's Fall

On 23 June 2016, the Brexit referendum resulted in 52% voting to leave the EU. While the RemaIn campaign gained support in large cities, Scotland and Northern Ireland, the Leave campaign kept a majority in Wales and rural areas across the country. Shortly before the referendum, Carlos Ghosn had announced that he opposed Brexit.[32] Regardless of Nissan Sunderland employing 6,700 workers in 2016—and Japanese multinationals employing a total of 140,000 in Britain[33]—65% of Sunderland constituents voted to leave in the 2016 referendum.

The striking news hit Japanese headlines the next morning. *Asahi-shinbun* reported that Brexit would affect the 1,380 Japanese firms operating in Britain due to Japan's relations with the EU being affected by reimposed tariffs.[34] Toyota expressed concern about its British plants, with 190 thousand units of annual output—of which three-fourths were exported to the continent—and local employment being affected by

[29] Liam Proud, *Reuters*, 20 November 2018.

[30] Jiji.com, "Comparison of Nissan and Renault's performance, May 2019 (*Nissan to Renault gyouseki hikaku*," 18 May 2019. https://www.jiji.com/jc/graphics?p=ve_eco_car20190518j-04-w490. Accessed on 8 October 2019.

[31] Liam Proud, *Reuters*, 20 November 2018.

[32] *Jiji-tsushin*, 29 September 2016.

[33] BBC, 5 September 2016. https://www.bbc.co.uk/news/business-37270372. Accessed on 8 June 2019.

[34] *Asahi-shinbun*, 24 June 2016.

EU tariffs.[35] Mitsui bussan refrained from comment on its North Sea petroleum business but hinted that its British strategy would have to be reconsidered.[36] *Reuters* estimated that the referendum suppressed Japanese GDP by 0.1 to 0.3%, possibly risking sending the Japanese economy back into deflation.[37]

A month before the referendum, PM Shinzo Abe had visited London and told PM David Cameron that he supported remaining in the EU.[38] At the end of June, he sent MOFA's top official, Shinsuke Sugiyama—vice minister for foreign affairs—to Brussels and London both to gather information on the EU and to confirm Anglo-Japanese relations.[39] Abe's concern was not only about Brexit's impact on Japanese firms and their investments but also about British commitments in the Pacific in terms of security issues.[40] In contrast to Nissan's "muted" attitude, the Abe administration was loud and clear about its reservations regarding hard Brexit. Japanese Ambassador Koji Tsuruoka told the BBC that Japanese multinationals would have to take all necessary solutions into consideration when post-Brexit Britain proved unprofitable, warning of the risks of plant transfers to the continent.[41]

In September, Carlos Ghosn told PM Teresa May that Nissan required compensation for tariff costs before making a decision on Sunderland assembling a new model.[42] Thereafter, a rumour spread that the government and Nissan had agreed on a "secret deal."[43] In October, Nissan and the May administration agreed on Sunderland assembling Nissan X-trail SUVs and British financial support of 80 million pounds (eleven billion yen).[44] The government feared that Nissan would move its plant

[35] Ibid.

[36] Ibid.

[37] *Reuters*, 24 June 2016.

[38] *Mainichi-shinbun*, 24 June 2016.

[39] Ibid.

[40] Ibid.

[41] BBC, 5 September 2016. https://www.bbc.co.uk/news/business-37270372. Accessed on 8 June 2019; *Sankei-shinbun*, 6 September 2016. Ambassador Tsuruoka was formerly in charge of the TPP negotiations.

[42] *Jiji-tsushin*, 29 September 2016.

[43] Ibid.

[44] *Jiji-tsushin*, 5 February 2019.

out of Britain and promised continued support after Brexit.[45] Sunderland would increase its output to 600 thousand units per annum.[46] May held talks with the heads of Japanese multinationals at No. 10 Downing on 8 February 2017, attempting to persuade them that Britain would maintain good relations with the EU by keeping tariffs and barriers as low as possible.[47] After the visit, Ambassador Tsuruoka rephrased his comments from the year before and emphasised that firms could not continue to do business in Britain should it be unprofitable, whether they Japanese or of any other nationality.[48]

There was reason for the Abe administration's uneasiness about Brexit and the future of Britain. The Japan-EU Economic Partnership Agreement (EPA) had been negotiated in the spring of 2011—shortly after the *tsunami* disaster in March—and was approaching its conclusion. Brexit was not in Japanese calculations. If Britain left the EU, tariffs on Japanese cars could be reimposed, whether made in Japan or in Britain. The EPA was signed in July 2018, and the parties agreed to abolish the average of 11% tariffs on Japanese cars entering the single market. If British-made Japanese cars were excluded from the EPA and therefore subject to tariffs, the profitability of Japanese plants in Britain would become questionable. The EPA was used as a bargaining chip by the EU and its member states against Britain[49] to show that the loss of membership would be unprofitable and diminish leverage in external (trade) relations. Moreover Article 8.11 of the EPA prohibits performance requirements on exports and local contents. The government will not be able to make Nissan promise likewise the case of the gentleman's agreement in 1984.

Shortly before the March 2019 Brexit deadline, the May administration announced that the Japan-EU EPA would not apply to Anglo-Japanese trade in the case of hard Brexit.[50] Japanese decisions were made quickly. Daiwa Securities reacquired its EU licence in Frankfurt and transferred its employees out of London.[51] Nomura Holdings moved to

[45] Industrial Journal, *Nissan; Group Activity of 2018*, Nagoya: IRC, 2018, p. 554.

[46] Ibid.

[47] *Jiji-tsushin*, 9 February 2017.

[48] Ibid.

[49] Suzuki, 2017a, p. 885.

[50] *Jiji-tsushin*, 22 January 2019.

[51] *Jiji-tsushin*, 11 March 2019.

Frankfurt, Mitsubishi UFJ to Amsterdam, and Tokyo Marines to Luxembourg.[52] Japanese banks maintained their offices in London due to its global status, but businesses related to the single market and single currency were transferred to the continent. The electronics industry was also quick to respond. Panasonic and Sony moved its European headquarters to the Netherlands, commenting that the firm could not maintain its European operation in Britain.[53]

As hard Brexit started to loom, the Japanese car industry responded. Toyota had announced in February 2018 that the next generation of the Auris/Corolla would be assembled in Burnaston,[54] but in March the next year, it announced a possible termination of assembly in the case of hard Brexit.[55] Necessary components in Burnaston were stocked for merely four hours of assembly, so just one shortage would bring the whole plant to a halt.[56] The Auris had failed to meet Toyota's expectations that it would boost its sales in the single market, and its name was therefore restored to the old, familiar Corolla. The unveiling of the next-generation Corolla scheduled in 2023 could be the time for Toyota to make a more crucial decision.

Nissan announced cancellation of the assembly of the X-trail at Sunderland; the car would be exported from its Kyushu plant in Japan instead.[57] The May administration responded that due to this retreat, Nissan should reapply for governmental financial aid.[58] Contradicting Nissan's denial, the media reported Sunderland's planned reduction of a maximum of four hundred workers, reducing the three-shift lines of the Qashqai and Leaf to two shifts.[59] This would mean that Sunderland's capacity would be reduced to its standard of the late 1990s, when it had fallen short of reaching its maximum output.[60] Profitability would once more come into

[52] Ibid.

[53] *Jiji-tsushin*, 22 January 2019; *Jiji-tsushin*, 20 January 2019.

[54] *Jiji-tsushin*, 1 March 2018.

[55] *Jiji-tsushin*, 7 March 2019.

[56] *Jiji-tsushin*, 20 February 2019.

[57] Ibid.

[58] *Jiji-tsushin*, 5 February 2019.

[59] *Jiji-tsushin*, 6 March 2019.

[60] See Sect. 1 of this chapter.

question should alternative export outlets not be found outside the single market.[61]

In response to the negative forecasts, Sunderland had taken its own initiative. In 2016, the plant had assembled 2,398,134 units of the Qashqai and surpassed the Micra's record, maintaining its status as the largest assembly plant in Britain.[62] NMUK has not officially stated the ratio of British local content, but it is estimated to be approximately 40%, with the rest imported from Germany, France, and Mexico.[63] The city of Sunderland sought to attract foreign suppliers before Brexit, planning to launch an industrial park (IAMP) of one million square metres next to NMUK by the end of 2018.[64] Nissan had preferred low-priced supplies from developing countries but, due to increased (labour) costs and disadvantageous exchange rates, once more turned to suppliers from developed countries.[65] An estimated investment of 300 million pounds (45 billion yen) would create 5,200 jobs at Sunderland.[66] A total of 910 million pounds would be injected to launch the industrial park, of which 42 million would be paid by the government for infrastructure.[67] Whether the new initiative will pay off after Brexit remains to be seen.

Carlos Ghosn's arrest on 19 November 2018 was a shock to all parties. Three days later, the Japanese and French ministers—Hiroshige Seko and Bruno Le Maire—agreed to maintain the Renault–Nissan–Mitsubishi alliance.[68] Nissan had aimed to reduce Renault's influence—and the French government's intention to merge the two firms—during and after president Hiroto Saikawa's coup d'état against Ghosn. However, Nissan's board of directors met and forced Saikawa to resign on 16 September 2019, accusing him of a financial scandal similar to Ghosn's. Nissan's unions failed to play a role, lacking the ability to urge management to meet standards of democratic accountability, let alone prevent

[61] This was once considered during the early 1990s. See Sect. 1 of this chapter.

[62] Industrial Journal, *Nissan; Group Activity of 2018*, Nagoya: IRC, 2018, p. 553.

[63] Ibid, p. 558.

[64] Ibid.

[65] Ibid, p. 559.

[66] Ibid, p. 558.

[67] Ibid.

[68] *Jiji-tsushin*, 23 November 2018.

such scandals.[69] For the sake of improving corporate governance, Nissan strengthened the role of outside directors to prevent similar scandals, but it is questionable whether they act any better as counterchecks than unions or civil societal organisations. Above all, national governments are in play in the Renault–Nissan–Mitsubishi alliance. On 11 October, Ghosn's predecessor, Thierry Bolloré, was also forced to leave his post as Renault's CEO. Whether Sunderland's output and its British local content ratio can improve has yet to be seen. As far as both the Japanese and French governments wishing to see the alliance continue, Nissan's supply chain would remain subject to Renault's decisions. The Spanish government announced on 28 May 2020 that Nissan decided to close its Barcelona plant where 3,000 jobs will be lost.

Last but not least, on 19 February 2019, Honda announced its intention to close its Swindon plant by 2021.[70] Swindon-made Civics—of which 55% were exported to the USA—would be replaced by exports from Japan and China.[71] By 2027—after eight years of the Japan-EU EPA entering into force—the 10% tariff on Japanese cars would expire,[72] making it easier for Honda to export from Japan. In 2018, Honda sold 140 thousand units in Europe, equivalent to (merely) 3% of Honda's overall global sales,[73] but this fell far short of Swindon's capacity of 250 thousand units of annual output.[74] Closure would result in a total loss of 3,500 jobs in Swindon.

Honda stated that the decision was *not* a result of the Brexit referendum but part of a global restructuring of its supply chain and branding, emphasising that its plant in Turkey was also scheduled to close, but Honda Motor Europe in Bracknell—the firm's European headquarters—would remain in business.[75] Gregory Clark, business secretary, expressed

[69] Not a single word of criticism on the scandals could be found on the unions' home pages. https://nissan-workers-union.or.jp/, http://www.ngu.or.jp/. Accessed on 5 November 2019.

[70] Bloomberg, 19 February 2019.

[71] Ibid.; *SankeiBiz*, 20 February 2019. Four-door saloon Civics were assembled in the US, while five-door hatchbacks were assembled in Swindon. Honda's decision to close Swindon hints that it would assemble whatever version it can in the US to circumvent the tariffs reimposed by Donald Trump. In this case, Britain is potentially the (worst) loser in the tariff wars between the EU and the US.

[72] *Jiji-tsushin*, 19 February 2019.

[73] Ibid.

[74] Ibid.

[75] *SankeiBiz*, 20 February 2019.

Table 1 World car production (1,000 units)

	2016	*2017*	*2018*
Canada	2,370	2,190	2,020
USA	12,180	11,190	11,310
Mexico	3,600	4,090	4,100
Brazil	2,160	2,740	2,880
Australia	160	0	0
Japan	9,200	9,690	9,730
Korea	4,230	4,110	4,030
China	28,120	29,020	27,810
Thailand	1,940	1,990	2,170
India	4,520	4,790	5,170
South Africa	600	590	610
Germany	5,750	5,650	5,120
Spain	2,890	2,850	2,820
France	2,090	2,230	2,270
UK	1,820	1,750	1,600
Italy	1,100	1,140	1,060
Russia	1,300	1,550	1,770

Source http://www.jama.or.jp/world/world/world_t1.html. Accessed on 2 March 2020 and modified by the authour

his deep disappointment, admitting that the decision would be devastating for the trained workers, committed employees, and their families in Swindon as well as the suppliers.[76] The BBC questioned whether the Japanese had lost faith in Britain.[77] On 6 March, Swindon workers gathered in front of the Parliament and appealed, "Honda, stay in the UK" and "#SaveHondaSwindon."[78] Japanese foreign minister Taro Kono warned on 27 June 2019 that Japanese firms in Britain would be threatened by a no-deal Brexit.[79] Anglo-Japanese relations have entered a new era, needing redefinition of the future while drifting in foggy conditions (Table 1).

[76] Bloomberg, 19 February 2019.

[77] BBC News, "Honda: Is Japan Losing Faith in the UK?" 19 February 2019.

[78] *Jiji-tsushin*, 7 March 2019.

[79] BBC News. https://www.bbc.com/news/av/uk-politics-48784175/brexit-japanese-foreign-minister-warns-against-no-deal. Accessed on 2 July.

CHAPTER 8

Conclusion

Abstract The Nissan-Sunderland deal was a milestone of improved Anglo-Japanese relations and played a role in putting an end to Japan-EC trade conflicts. Nissan was able to secure its access to the single market, followed up by Toyota and Honda. Whether the plant could remain profitable after Brexit would depend on its exports in- and outside Europe and R&D outputs. Local contents, which has been the core of British requirement throughout, was reduced by Nissan's new leader Ghosn after 1999. His fall showed that Nissan's corporate culture of lacking democratic counterchecks had not changed. Contrary to its early days in Britain the Japanese multinational lacked outreach and failed to prevent its undesired Brexit. The Japan-EU EPA added to Japanese and the EU's leverage in global trade, but for Britain it remains to be seen.

Keywords Anglo-Japanese relations · European Union · Economic Partnership Agreement · Brexit · Foreign direct investment · Car exports · Local contents · Nissan · Trade unions

The car industry has crowned the close ties of Anglo-Japanese relations, Nissan Sunderland was the prize example but is now being reconsidered. The Japanese had understood Britain's EC/EU membership as a token but were "betrayed." In British eyes, it was Nissan, whether due to its new

H. Suzuki, *Japanese Investment and British Trade Unionism*, New Directions in East Asian History,
https://doi.org/10.1007/978-981-15-9058-0_8

French leadership since 1999 or the global economy and ever-intensifying competition, that first abandoned good faith. The Nissan Sunderland deal was a pragmatic and issue-focused marriage between the Thatcher administration's trade and industrial policy of restructuring the British car industry—and trade unions—with its main focus on the EC/EU and Japan's structurally changing export policy of both the government and car assemblers. Japan slowly and gradually reduced exports from home plants and shifted towards local assembly in developed countries. The main cause of such decisions, for both Nissan and MITI, was to ease trade conflicts by reducing Japan's trade surplus. Ishihara was president not only of Nissan but also of JAMA and was in a rush for results. For Nissan alone, the British project, contrary to its own intentions under Ishihara's presidency, later gained more significance than "mere" exports to the single market. R&D in Britain/Europe helped Nissan improve its models' global competitiveness and strengthened the brand.

Sunderland never reached its maximum output throughout the 1990s, finally achieving it under Carlos Ghosn's leadership in the millennium year. However, the achievement was not free from sacrifices. The gentleman's agreement of February 1984 on 80% British local content was immediately abandoned and replaced with French/Renault supply chains. It is questionable to what extent investments were sunk in British soil. Car assembly has remained in Britain, but component supplies have remained to a lesser extent. Sunderland's competitors during the 1980s and 1990s were rival assemblers in other European countries. However, in the millennium years, the plant must compete more successfully than other plants within the Renault–Nissan–Mitsubishi alliance around the globe if it wishes to keep jobs in Britain. The same applies to other Japanese assemblers in Britain, but Honda has decided to slip away. Contrary to Nissan's initial intention, negotiating R&D and engine assembly in Britain secured extra jobs. From a Japanese point of view, the question still remains: Why would Japanese assemblers insist on operating in the single market and/or Britain when it contributes "merely" 10% of their global turnover? The American and Chinese markets together contribute more than half of their profits, which also surpass those in Japan. To what extent have British branches contributed to the brand image improvement and/or technological advance of Japanese multinationals?

The launch of Sunderland and its impact back home in Japan was less evident during the early years. The plant gradually increased its output, profited Nissan, and, as long as the 80% local content requirement was respected, benefited the British components industry and Japanese subsidiaries in Britain. The latter would, however, send royalty back home.[1] As trade union leader Ichiro Shioji warned, Nissan's British project—coupled with other overseas projects—threatened employment back home. This was concealed by the bubble economy until the early 1990s. As the bubble shrank and the Japanese economy stagnated, redundancy and unemployment increased and became visible, as was typified by the case of the Nissan Zama plant. However, the following "lost decade(s)" was explained instead as a consequence of the Bank of Japan policy of revolutionary reform of the Japanese economy along neoliberal lines by intentionally extending the stagnation.[2] Nissan's unions were rendered powerless during and after the Sunderland negotiations, resulting in the absence of grass-roots counterchecks against "dictatorial leaders" such as Takashi Ishihara and Carlos Ghosn.[3]

Japanese plants in Britain have caused a change in labour–management relations, but plants in Britain were not totally transformed into a "Japan in Britain." A new mixture of British and Japanese ways of labour–management relations was created. Single union agreements were implemented, but workers and employees were not forced to accept the full load of flexibility, similar to those in Japan. Nevertheless, the British unions were split over whether to accept Japanisation, centring around the debate over single union and "non-strike" agreements. The AUEW/AEU and the EETPU, which accepted the agreements, fell into conflict with the TGWU and other leftist unions. The EETPU walked out of the TUC. British unions struggled to adapt to the new realism.

Why locals voted to leave in the June 2016 Brexit referendum in constituencies where Japanese plants operate and to what extent trade unions' (diminished) role affected such results remains to be seen. Japanese multinationals and their management in Britain wished to remain in the EU, but consensus was lacking among local workers and employees. The Japanese style of labour–management consultation

[1] Garrahan and Stewart, 1992, pp. 7–8.

[2] Richard Werner, *Princes of the Yen; Japan's Central Bankers and the Transformation of the Economy* (2nd ed.), Carnforth: Quantum Publishers, 2018, pp. 14–19.

[3] Inoue, 2019, pp. 4–6 and Shioji, 2012, pp. 394–397. Inoue pointed out that Kawamata, Ishihara's predecessor, was also a dictatatorial leader who purged Ayukawa's men during his presidency and that this has been the corporate culture of the firm; Inoue, 2019, pp. 4–6, 71–79.

worked on shop floors, but there were no alternative methods ready for tackling the long-term strategic questions that would allow a firm to remain settled in Britain. Localisation efforts were made mostly in the short term and were job focused. In sum, the Japanese were keen on plant operation but were not (at all) ready to directly reach the British public and failed to do so, forgetting their own efforts during the 1980s to show that the Japanese were not arriving as "aliens."[4] The Japanese back home almost automatically assumed that Sunderland constituents, and many others where Japanese multinationals operate, would vote RemaIn.

Anglo-Japanese relations are entering a new stage. As the Nissan Sunderland deal has shown, Brexit is a loss for Japan, a country leaning too heavily on Britain, not only as a gateway to the single market but also as a watchdog for free trade, non-discrimination, and deregulation of the EU (and Japan!). To what extent it is a loss for the EU is not clear at this point, but member states on the continent have already benefited by accommodating Japanese branches transferring out of Britain. Britain's close relations with Japan are facing increased competition with France, not only in trade and investment but also in military exchanges and R&D on weapons.[5] Brexit has added to the EU's leverage in trade and industrial policy towards Japan. The Japan-EU EPA was concluded in 2018, not only with the intention of jointly countering US President Donald Trump's unilateral protectionism but also of putting pressure on Brexit negotiations,[6] reminding others that the loss of EU membership would damage trade, investments, and employment.

During the 1970s and 1980s, Japan sought improved relations with both Britain and the EC, but Britain became seriously divided over whether it belonged to Europe. Japan is potentially one of the countries most adversely affected by Brexit. If the EU and its member states cure Japanese losses, which is already taking place, Japan will increase its faith in the EU and have less faith in Britain, depending on the exact terms of a trade agreement between Britain and the EU. Anglo-Japanese relations

[4] Oliver and Wilkinson, 1992, p. xii.

[5] Hitoshi Suzuki, "Post-Brexit Britain, the EU, and Japan: The Car Industry, the Aero Sector, and Military Cooperation," forthcoming.

[6] Suzuki, 2017a, p. 885.

with the former's EU membership at its core are entering unfamiliar territory that needs re-definition, possibly leading to, as both countries stand, a "slow decline," especially in the case of hard Brexit.

Bibliography

Primary Sources

ACEU: Archive of the Council of the European Union.
CACC: Churchill Archives Centre, Churchill College, Cambridge University.
MRCW: Modern Records Centre, University of Warwick Library.
OISRH: The Ohara Institute for Social Research, Hosei University.
TNA: The National Archives.

Secondary Sources

Cockfield, Francis Arthur. 1994. *The European Union: Creating the Single Market*, Wiley Chancery Law.

Cockfield, Francis Arthur, José María Cuevas, Hans-Dietrich Genscher, Tuulikki Kannisto, Mario Monti, Lubomír Soudek, Sir Iain Vallance, and Karl von Wogau. 1996. *Is the Single Market Working*? Philip Morris Institute for Public Policy Research.

Cortazzi, Hugh. 1998. *Japan and Back and Places Elsewhere; A Memoir*, Folkestone: Global Oriental.

Hatakeyama, Noboru. 1996. *The Dramatic Trade Negotiations Over National Interests* (Tsusyokousyou wo meguru drama), Tokyo: Nikkei.

Industrial Journal (*Sangyou journal*). 1992. *Nissan; Group Activity of 1992* (Nissan-jidousha group no jittai 1992), Nagoya: IRC.

Industrial Journal (*Sangyou journal*). 1994. *Nissan; Group Activity of 1994* (Nissan-jidousha group no jittai 1994), Nagoya: IRC.

H. Suzuki, *Japanese Investment and British Trade Unionism*, New Directions in East Asian History,
https://doi.org/10.1007/978-981-15-9058-0

Industrial Journal (*Sangyou journal*). 1996. *Nissan; Group Activity of 1996* (Nissan-jidousha group no jittai 1996), Nagoya: IRC.

Industrial Journal (*Sangyou journal*). 1998. *Nissan; Group Activity of 1998* (Nissan-jidousha group no jittai 1998), Nagoya: IRC.

Industrial Journal (*Sangyou journal*). 2000. *Nissan; Group Activity of 2000* (Nissan-jidousha group no jittai 2000), Nagoya: IRC.

Industrial Journal (*Sangyou journal*). 2002. *Nissan; Group Activity of 2002* (Nissan-jidousha group no jittai 2002), Nagoya: IRC.

Industrial Journal (*Sangyou journal*). 2004. *Nissan; Group Activity of 2004* (Nissan-jidousha group no jittai 2004), Nagoya: IRC.

Industrial Journal (*Sangyou journal*). 2006. *Nissan; Group Activity of 2006* (Nissan-jidousha group no jittai 2006), Nagoya: IRC.

Industrial Journal (*Sangyou journal*). 2008. *Nissan; Group Activity of 2008* (Nissan-jidousha group no jittai 2008), Nagoya: IRC.

Industrial Journal (*Sangyou journal*). 2010. *Nissan; Group Activity of 2010* (Nissan-jidousha group no jittai 2010), Nagoya: IRC.

Industrial Journal (*Sangyou journal*). 2012. *Nissan; Group Activity of 2012* (Nissan-jidousha group no jittai 2012), Nagoya: IRC.

Industrial Journal (*Sangyou journal*). 2014. *Nissan; Group Activity of 2014* (Nissan-jidousha group no jittai 2014), Nagoya: IRC.

Industrial Journal (*Sangyou journal*). 2016. *Nissan; Group Activity of 2016* (Nissan-jidousha group no jittai 2016), Nagoya: IRC.

Industrial Journal (*Sangyou journal*). 2018. *Nissan; Group Activity of 2018* (Nissan-jidousha group no jittai 2018), Nagoya: IRC.

Ishihara, Takashi. 2002. *My Career and Nissan* (Watashi to Nissan-jidousha), Tokyo: Nikkei.

Japan Institute of Labour (JIL). *International Labor Information* (Kaigai-roudou-jihou), Tokyo: Japan Institute of Labour.

Kawakatsu, Noriaki. 2018. *Nissan's 2300 Secret Files; Seven Years' War of a Manager Against the "Absolute Power"* (Nissan-jidosha gokuhi file 2300), Tokyo: President.

Mountfield, Robin. 2007a. "Nissan's Investment in Britain: History of a Negotiation 1980–1984," in Cortazzi, 2007.

Mountfield, Robin. 2007b. "Course of the Nissan Neogtiation 1980–84," in Cortazzi, 2007.

Nissan. 1975. *Corporate History of Nissan, 1964–1973* (Nissan-jidouha shashi), Tokyo: Nissan.

Nissan. 1983. *The Path To The Twenty-First Century; Five Decades History of Nissan* (21 Seiki eno michi), Tokyo: Nissan.

Nissan. 1985. *Corporate History of Nissan, 1974–1983* (Nissan-jidouha shashi), Tokyo: Nissan.

NSK. 1991. *Towards Tomorrow, Towards The World: NSK's 75th Anniversary Commemorative Publication*, Tokyo: NSK.
Research Institute of Economy, Trade and Industry (RIETI). 2013. *The History of Trade and Industrial Policy, 1980–2000, Vol. 2, Commercial and Trade Policy* (Tsushou sangyou seisakushi 1980–2000 dainikan, tsushou sangyou seisaku), Tokyo: RIETI.
Shioji, Ichiro. 2012. *The Rise and Fall of Nissan; Testimony by the President of the Jidousha-rouren* (Nissan-jidousha no seisui), Tokyo: Ryokufu Publishing.
Thatcher, Margaret. 1993. *The Downing Street Years*, London: HarperCollins.
Wickens, Peter. 1987. *The Road to Nissan: Flexibility, Quality, Teamwork*, Basingstoke: Macmillan.

Books and Articles

Anzai, Takumi. 2014. *Keidanren; The Fall of Japanese Business's Headquarters* (rakujitsu no zaikai-souhonzan), Tokyo: Shinchosha.
Beale, Dave. 1994. *Driven by Nissan?: A Critical Guide to New Management Techniques*, London: Lawrence and Wishart.
Bussière, Éric. 2014. "Devising a Strategy: The Internal Market and Industrial Policy," in Bussière, et al., 2014.
Bussière, Éric, Vincent Dujardin, Michel Dumoulin, Piers Ludlow, Jan Willem Brouwer, and Pierre Tilly (eds.). 2014. *The European Commission, 1973–86; History and Memories of an Institution*, Brussels: European Union.
Bouneau, Christophe, David Burigana, and Antonio Varsori (eds.). 2010. *Trends in Technological Innovation and the European Construction: The Emerging of Enduring Dynamics?* Brussels: P.I.E. Peter Lang.
Coates, David (ed.). 1996. *Industrial Policy in Britain*, Basingstoke: Macmillan.
Conte-Helm, Marie. 1989. *Japan and the North East of England; From 1862 to the Present Day*, London: Athlone Press.
Cortazzi, Hugh (ed.). 2002. *Britain & Japan: Biographical Portraits*, Vol. 4, Abingdon: Routledge.
Cortazzi, Hugh (ed.). 2007. *Britain & Japan: Biographical Portraits*, Vol. 6, Honolulu: University of Hawaii Press.
Dower, John. 1986. *War Without Mercy: Race and Power in the Pacific War*, New York: Pantheon Books.
Garrahan, Philip, and Paul Stewart. 1992. *The Nissan Enigma: Flexibility at Work in a Local Economy*, London: Mansell Publishing.
Gilson, Julie. 2000. *Japan and the European Union: A Partnership for the Twenty-First Century?* Basingstoke: Macmillan.
Hayward, Keith. 1986. *International Collaboration in Civil Aerospace*, New York: St. Martin's Press.

Hook, Glenn and Hugo Dobson. 2007. *Global Governance and Japan: The Institutional Architecture*, Abingdon: Routledge.

Hook, Glenn, Julie Gilson, Christopher Hughes, and Hugo Dobson. 2012. *Japan's International Relations: Politics, Economics and Security* (3rd ed.), Abingdon: Routledge.

Inoue, Hisao. 2019. *Nissan vs. Ghosn; Two Decades of Dictatorship and Turmoil* (Shihai to antou no nijyu-nen), Tokyo: Bungei-shunjyu.

Iokibe, Makoto. 2011. *The Diplomatic History of Postwar Japan*, Abingdon: Routledge.

Johnson, Chalmers. 1982. *MITI and the Japanese Miracle; The Growth of Industrial Policy, 1925–1975*, Stanford: Stanford University Press.

Keck, Jörn, Dimitri Vanoverbeke, and Franz Waldenberger (eds.). 2013. *EU-Japan Relations, 1970–2012: From Confrontation to Global Partnership*, Abingdon: Routledge.

Kendall, Christopher. 2013. "The Elements of Consensus: Liberalising EC-Japan passenger car trade in the 1990s," in Keck et al., 2013.

Kimizuka, Naotaka. 2008. *The Queen's Diplomacy and the Three Circles* (Jyououheika no gaikou-senryaku), Tokyo: Kodansha.

Kumagai, Naoko. 2019. "Japan's Reconciliation in the Issue of Comfort Women with the Netherlands and South Korea: Pragmatic and Reflective Reconciliation," *Journal of European Integration History*, 25(1).

Kume, Ikuo. 2005. *Labour Policy; Trade Unions in Post-War Politics* (Roudou seiji), Tokyo: Chuo-kouron-shinsha.

Lord, Christopher. 1996. "Industrial Policy and the European Union," in Coates, 1996.

Loth, Wilfried. 2015. *Building Europe: A History of European Unification*, Berlin: Walter de Gruyter.

Mason, Mark. 1994. "Elements of Consensus: Europe's Response to the Japanese Automotive Challenge," *Journal of Common Market Studies*, 32(4).

Moriyama, Hiroshi. 2019. *Nissan's Past and Future; From Ichiro Shioji to Carlos Ghosn* (Koremade no Nissan, korekara no Nissan), Tokyo: 22 Century Art.

Noguchi, Yukio. 2019. *Post-War Economic History; Where Have We Failed* (Sengo keizai-shi; watashitachi wa dokode machigaetanoka), Tokyo: Nikkei.

Oliver, Nick, and Barry Wilkinson. 1992. *The Japanization of British Industry; New Developments in the 1990s* (2nd ed.), Oxford: Blackwell Publishers.

Owen, Geoffrey. 1999. *From Empire to Europe: The Decline and Revival of British Industry Since the Second World War*, London: HarperCollins.

Pardi, Tommaso. 2014. "Why Japanese Carmakers Have Been Struggling in Europe? Insites from the Nissan's FDI Negotiations," The 22nd International Colloquium of Gerpisa, *Old and New Spaces of the Automobile Industry*, Kyoto University, 6 June 2014.

Pardi, Tommaso. 2017. "Industrial Policy and the British Automotive Industry Under Margaret Thatcher," *Business History*, 59(1).
Pine, Melissa. 2012. *Harold Wilson and Europe; Pursuing Britain's Membership of the European Community*. London: I.B. Tauris.
Ramírez-Pérez, Sigfrido. 2014. "The Automobile Industry: From the American to Japanese Challenge," in Bussière, et al., 2014.
Rothacher, Albrecht. 1983. *Economic Diplomacy Between the European Community and Japan 1959–1981*, Aldershot: Gower.
Sato, Masaaki. 2000. *The Automobile Industry; The Making and Breakup of Alliances* (Jidousha gasshou-renkou no sekai), Tokyo: Bungei-shunjyu.
Sato, Masaaki. 2006. *Honda Myth; The Genius and His Wake*, Vertical.
Sato, Masaaki. 2008. *The Toyota Leaders; An Executive Guide*, Vertical.
Sato, Masaaki. 2012. *Nissan; Glory and Disgrace* (Nissan, Eikou to kutsujyoku), Tokyo: Bungei-shunjyu.
Shimokawa, Koichi. 1994. *The Japanese Automobile Industry; a Business History*, London: Athlone Press.
Stråth, Bo. 1996. *The Organisation of Labour Markets; Modernity, Culture and Governance in Germany, Sweden, Britain and Japan*, Abingdon: Routledge.
Südy, Zoltán. 2014. "Memoires on Japanese Investments to Hungary (*Nihon kigyou no tai-Hungary toushi no denkiteki-kousatsu*)," in Shuichi Ikemoto and Hiroshi Tanaka (eds.), *Japanese Multinationals' Entry Into The New Developing Markets in Europe; Perspectives from Central Europe and Russia* (Oushu shinkou-shijyou-koku eno Nikkei-kigyou no shinshutsu), Tokyo: Bunshindou.
Suzuki, Hitoshi. 2014a. "Negotiating the Japan-EC Trade Conflict: The Role and Presence of the European Commission, the Council of Ministers, and Business Groups in Europe and Japan, 1970–1982," in Claudia Hiepel (ed.), *Europe in a Globalising World: Global Challenges and European Responses in the "long" 1970s*, Baden-Baden: Nomos.
Suzuki, Hitoshi. 2014b. "The Rise of Summitry and EEC-Japan Trade Relations," in Emmanuel Mourlon-Druol and Federico Romero (eds.), *International Summitry and Global Governance: The rise of the G7 and the European Council, 1974–1991*, Abingdon: Routledge.
Suzuki, Hitoshi. 2015a. *Thatcher and the Nissan Sunderland Plant: The History of Negotiations 1973–86* (Thatcher to Nissan eikoku koujyou), Tokyo: Yoshida Publishing.
Suzuki, Hitoshi. 2015b. "From Trade Conflicts to "Global Partners": Japan and the EEC 1970–1978," in Pascaline Winand, Andrea Benvenuti, and Max Guderzo (eds.), *The External Relations of the European Union*, Brussels: P.I.E. Peter-Lang.
Suzuki, Hitoshi. 2015c. "Japan's Relations with the FRG and the GDR, 1966–1981 (Tou-zai-doitsu to nihon 1966–1981-nen)," in Yuichi Hosoya (ed.), *The*

History of Post-War Asian-European Relations (Sengo Asia-Europe kankei-shi), Tokyo: Keio University Press.

Suzuki, Hitoshi. 2017a. "The New Politics of Trade: EU-Japan," *Journal of European Integration*, 39(7).

Suzuki, Hitoshi. 2017b. "How British Corporate Interests and Their Views on Japan Were Transferred to Brussels. The Case of Nissan Sunderland Plant and the Single European Act," in Christine Bouneau and David Burigana (eds.), *Experts et expertise en science et technologie en europe des années 1960 à nos jours. Société civile organisée, démocratie et prise de décision politique*, Brussels: P.I.E. Peter-Lang.

Suzuki, Hitoshi. 2020, forthcoming. "Post-Brexit Britain, the EU, and Japan: The car industry, the aeronautical sector, and military cooperation," *Europe and the World*.

Suzuki, Hitoshi, and Izuru Makihara. 2019. "Japan-EEC/EU Relations, 1970–2005: Re-Emergence as Strategic Partners in Trade and Environment," *Journal of European Integration History*, 25(1).

Suzuki, Hitoshi, Yu Suzuki, and Yoshimi Igawa. 2019. "Japan and the European Union," in Finn Laursen (ed.), *Oxford Encyclopedia of European Union Politics*, Oxford: Oxford University Press.

Takahashi, Yasutaka. 2009. "Nissan's European Strategy: NMISA (*Nissan-jidousha no Europe senryaku* - NMISA)," in Yasutaka Takahashi and Shigemitsu Ashizawa (eds.), *The Strategy of the Car Manufacturer of Europe* (EU jidousha-mekaa no senryaku), Tokyo: Gakubunsha.

Takasugi, Ryo. 1984. *Full Gas to Hegemony; A documental novel on Nissan* (Haken eno shissou), Tokyo: Kodansha.

Tanaka, Toshiro. 1998. *Politics of the European Union* (EU no seiji), Tokyo: Iwanami-shoten.

Taylor, Robert. 2000. *The TUC: From the General Strike to New Unionism*, Basingstoke: Palgrave.

Uesugi, Jiro. 2001. *Nissan's Fall and Come-Back; Why Japanese Failed to Revive* (Nissan-jidousha no shippai to saisei), Tokyo: KK Bestsellers.

Ueta, Takako, and Éric Remacle (eds.). 2005. *Japan and Enlarged Europe: Partners in Global Governance*, Brussels: P.I.E.-Peter Lang.

Wall, Stephen. 2012. *The Official History of Britain and the European Community; Vol. II From Rejection to Referendum, 1963–1975*, Abingdon: Routledge.

Wall, Stephen. 2019. *The Official History of Britain and the European Community. Vol.III, The Tiger Unleashed, 1975–1985*, Abingdon: Routledge.

Warlouzet, Laurent. 2018. *Governing Europe in a Globalizing World; Neoliberalism and Its Alternatives Following the 1973 Oil Crisis*, Abingdon: Routledge.

Werner, Richard. 2018. *Princes of the Yen; Japan's Central Bankers and the Transformation of the Economy* (2nd ed.), Carnforth: Quantum Publishers.

Wong, Reuben. 2011. "The Europeanlization of Foreign Policy," in Christopher Hill and Micheal Smith (eds.), *International Relations and the European Union* (2nd ed.), Oxford: Oxford University Press, 2011.

Index

A
Abe, Shintaro, 86, 91
Abe, Shinzo, 86, 162
Advisory, Conciliation and Arbitration Service (ACAS), 89, 136
Agnelli, Giovanni, 36
Airbus, 41
Alfa Romeo, 37, 49
Amalgamated Engineering and Electrical Union (AEEU), 147, 148. *See also* Amalgamated Union of Engineering Workers (AUEW); Amalgamated Engineering Union (AEU)
Amalgamated Engineering Union (AEU), 65, 67, 68, 89, 115, 129, 146, 147, 148, 171. *See also* Amalgamated Union of Engineering Workers (AUEW); Amalgamated Engineering and Electrical Union (AEEU)
Amalgamated Union of Engineering Workers (AUEW), 7, 67, 68, 89, 115, 126, 129, 132, 136, 137, 145, 146, 148, 149, 153, 171
  Executive Council, 68, 89, 115, 129, 137
  National Committee, 137. *See also* Amalgamated Engineering Union (AEU); Amalgamated Engineering and Electrical Union (AEEU)
Amery, Julian, 70
Anglo-Japanese relations, 2, 3, 6, 25, 29, 31, 32, 47, 71, 79, 91, 92, 101, 126, 139, 140, 162, 167, 169, 172
Asahi-shinbun, 31, 32, 84, 86, 87, 161
Aston Martin, 46
Austin, 10, 13, 14, 27, 86, 122, 139
Australia, 27, 38, 50, 136, 167
Avon, 142
Ayukawa, Yoshisuke, 11, 13, 21, 171

H. Suzuki, *Japanese Investment and British Trade Unionism*, New Directions in East Asian History,
https://doi.org/10.1007/978-981-15-9058-0

B

BAe146, 86
Bank of England, 78, 108
Bank of Japan, 12, 13, 23, 56, 171. *See also* Japan, lost decade
BBC, 161, 162, 167
beauty contest, 128
Belgium, 16, 17, 26, 28, 30, 44, 64, 65
Blaupunkt, 142
BMW, 134
Bolloré, Thierry, 166
Bosch, 142
Botnar, Octav, 16, 44
Bretton Woods system, 22
Bridgestone, 17
Bridlington Rules. *See* Trade Union Congress (TUC)
Britain
  Anglo-Japanese relations, 2, 3, 6, 25, 29, 31, 32, 47, 91, 126, 140, 167, 169, 172
  as a Japanese gateway, 2, 3, 132, 172
  Brexit referendum of 2016, 1, 152, 161, 171
  British disease, 26, 27
  car assembling, 26, 27, 43, 57, 144, 170
  EC membership, 10, 16, 26–28
  Embassy in Tokyo, 47, 106
  Empire, 83, 85, 88, 145
  exports to Japan, 26
  exports to the Commonwealth, 27
  exports to the EC/EU, 28, 29, 102, 110
  imports from Japan, 10, 16, 18, 19, 26, 28, 31, 32, 45, 48, 50, 62, 79, 84, 95, 104, 109
  investment from Japan, 6, 7, 26, 28, 31, 34, 40, 47, 55, 75, 79, 80, 85, 88, 106, 108, 109, 132, 144, 153, 156, 162, 170, 172
  investment to Japan, 54, 70
  leaving the EC, 77
  pound/euro exchange rate, 59, 160
  prisoner of war, 29
  public opinion, 26, 29, 40, 46, 54, 60, 109, 133
  unemployment, 26, 29, 48, 105
British Leyland (BL)
  components, 2, 29, 33, 47, 48, 60–62, 88
  government aid, 46, 55
  market share, 28, 47, 61, 88
  nationalisation, 28
  Rover, 27, 45, 144
  Triumph, 27
British Leyland Motor Corporation (BLMC), 27
British Motor Holdings (BMH), 27
Bungei-shunjyu (Bunshun), 12, 13, 18, 81
Burnaston. *See* Toyota
Butler, Robin, 59, 83, 93, 94, 103–107, 111, 119

C

Callaghan, James, 32, 65
Calsonic, 142
Cameron, David, 162
Canon, 35
Cardiff, 89, 114, 136
Central and Eastern Europe, 89
Central Policy Staff, 33
Chancellor of Exchequer, 49, 116, 117, 143
China, 82, 166, 167
Chrysler, 45, 158
City, 23, 165
Clarion, 142
Clark, Gregory, 166

Clinton-Davis, Stanley, 130
Coca-Cola Schweppes, 146
Cockfield, Francis Arthur, 3, 5, 71, 130–132
co-determination, 47
Cold War, 40, 142
collaboration, 10, 12–14, 34, 46, 49, 70, 92, 121, 144
Commonwealth, 26
company council (works council), 135, 136, 149
components
  British, 2, 8, 13, 14, 29, 32, 33, 40, 47, 48, 55, 57–59, 61, 62, 73, 80, 85, 88, 105, 107, 116, 118, 144, 149, 152, 158, 160, 171
  French, 59, 160
  German, 29, 59, 66
  Italian, 59
  Japanese, 11, 12, 14, 28, 51, 58, 59, 61, 62, 64, 66, 73, 74, 89, 116, 129, 142, 144, 160
Confederation of British Industry (CBI)
  Japan policy, 5, 6, 34, 69, 79
  lobbying Brussels, 69
  lobbying Tory, 7, 70
Confederation of British Industry (CBI)
  Japan policy, 34
Conservative Party, 26, 34, 35
  Brighton Conservative Club, 70
Conte-Helm, Marie, 2, 30, 52, 57, 59, 63, 65, 66, 89, 114, 128, 133, 139–141, 143–145, 149
Continental, 132, 142
Cortazzi, Hugh, 3, 7, 10, 11, 35, 41, 47, 70, 79, 81, 85, 91–93, 96, 97, 101, 106, 107, 141
  Ambassador to Japan, 33, 47, 82, 100
Cresson, Édith, 151

D
Daily Mail, 55
Daily Telegraph, 32
Daiwa Securities, 28, 163
Davignon, Étienne, 69, 91
Deeside. *See* Toyota
Denmark, 30
Department of Industry (DoI), 29, 40, 44–49, 51–55, 57–66, 69, 71–81, 87, 88, 91, 92, 118, 141, 146. *See also* Department of Trade and Industry (DTI)
Department of Trade and Industry (DTI), 7, 28, 29, 40, 65, 76, 78, 87, 91, 93, 94, 100–109, 111, 114–120, 123, 125, 134, 141. *See also* Department of Industry (DoI); Department of Trade (DoT)
Department of Trade (DoT), 87. *See also* Department of Trade and Industry (DTI)
Diamond, 81
Duffy, Terry (Terrence), 67, 68, 115, 136
Duke of Edinburgh, 30, 31

E
Eaglescliffe, 51, 65
Economic Partnership Agreement (EPA). *See* Japan
Economist, 105
Electrical, Electronic, Telecommunication and Plumbing Union (EETPU), 135, 145, 147, 153, 171
  merger with AEU, 147, 171
  TUC membership, 147

Elements of Consensus, 1991, 126, 150
side letter, 151
European Car of the Year, 143, 157, 161
European Commission
DG III (Internal Market and Industry), 131, 150
export monitoring. *See* Elements of Consensus
subsidy ban, 150
European Communities (EC)
Japan-EC Joint Declaration (the Hague Declaration), 1991, 150, 151
law, 60
Rome Treaty, 130
European Economic Community (EEC), 2, 26, 27, 60, 70
European Free Trade Association (EFTA), 10, 15, 52
European Parliament (EP), 70, 71
European Union (EU)
Japan-EU EPA. *See* Japan
single currency, 164
single market, 3, 132, 143, 144, 156, 164, 172
tariffs on Japanese cars, 8, 18, 19, 26, 28, 161, 163
Evans, Moss, 67, 111, 134
export monitoring, 8, 157. *See also* Japan

F

Falkland crisis, 7, 40, 59, 78, 83, 84, 88, 95
Fanuc, 84
Fiat, 16, 36, 49
Financial Times, 51, 59, 63
flexibility, 135, 136, 148, 171
Focus, 112, 113
Ford in Britain, 48, 62, 109, 146
Dundee, 146
Foreign and Commonwealth Office (FCO), 47, 54, 72, 79, 81, 82, 85, 91–93, 95–97, 100, 101, 106, 107, 131
foreign direct investment (FDI), 28, 40
France, 16, 28, 30, 56, 65, 70, 75, 79, 90, 92, 109, 136, 157, 165, 167, 172
Fraser, Douglas, 43, 44, 57, 60
Friday, 138
Fry, Graham, 46
Fujinami, Takao, 43
Fujitsu, 84, 144
Fukuda, Takeo, 30
Furukawa, Miyuki, 38

G

G7 summit
Tokyo, 41
Williamsburg, 7, 82, 95, 100, 120
Garrahan, Philip, 20, 21, 35, 87, 123, 126, 135, 140, 142, 148, 149, 152, 171
GEC, 46
Geihinkan (State Guest House Akasaka Palace), 84
General Agreement on Tariffs and Trade (GATT), 18, 19, 80, 151
Kennedy Round, 18
Tokyo Round, 19
General Motors (GM), 11, 62, 83, 109
General, Municipal, Boilermakers and Allied Trade Union (GMB), 68, 87, 129, 136
Germany (Federal Republic), 17, 18, 27–30, 49, 63, 65, 70, 109, 136, 165, 167
Ghosn, Carlos, 8, 138, 158–162, 165, 166, 170, 171

Gibson, Ian, 142
Gilson, Julie, 2, 3
Ginza, 12, 20, 36, 46, 112
Giscard d'Estaing, Valéry, 54
Gorbachev, Mikhail, 40
green-field plant, 2, 6, 38, 45, 47, 62, 64

H
Haferkamp, Wilhelm, 102
Hanawa, Yoshikazu, 137, 158
Haneda airport, 84, 87
Harrier, 86
Harvard University, 20, 41
Hashimoto/Faltec, 142
Hatakeyama, Noboru, 150, 151
Heath, Edward, 27, 28, 82, 84
Hitachi, 12, 21, 46, 47
Hitotsubashi University, 13
HMS Prince of Wales, 29
HMS Repulse, 29
Höegh and Ugland Auto Liners, 16
Honda
  Accord, 24, 92, 144
  car assembler status, 18
  Civic, 23, 144, 166
  closure announcement of Swindon, 166
  Formula One, 18
  Honda Motor Europe, Bracknell, 166
  Marysville plant, 24
  Rover, 34, 45, 92, 144
  S600, 18
  Swindon plant, 144, 166
  T360, 18
  the US, 2, 23, 43, 166
  Triumph, 34, 92
  Turkey, 166
Hope, Robin, 46
Hosokawa, Taiji, 81, 112, 113, 124
House of Commons, 53, 55
Howe, Geoffrey, 95, 100, 131, 143

I
Ikeda-Hoover, 142
Industrial Bank of Japan (Mizuho Bank), 12, 23, 56
Industrial Development Advisory Board, 123
Ingleby Barwick, 51, 65
Internal Market White Paper, 71
International Confederation of Free Trade Unions (ICFTU), 19, 21, 53, 115
International Metalworkers' Federation (IMF), 115
Invest in Britain Bureau (IBB), 46, 48, 52, 59
Ireland, 26, 28, 66, 69, 79, 142, 161
Ise shrine, 31
Ishibashi, Shojiro, 17
Ishihara, Takashi
  anti-trade union, 35–37, 124, 137
  chairman of Nissan, 140
  coup d'état, 13, 138
  Order of British Empire, 145
  President of JAMA, 36, 37, 42
  President of *Keizai-doyukai*, 140
  President of Nissan, 3, 36
  President of Nissan-USA, 36
  rugby, 21
Ishikawajima-Harima (IHI), 41, 159
Ishizaka, Taizo, 18
Isuzu, 104
Italy, 28, 36, 49, 70, 75, 83, 92, 167
Iwakoshi, Tadahiro, 22, 23, 36, 42, 51

J
Jaguar, 27, 134
Japan

abuse of free trade rules, 2, 3
aliens, 172
bubble economy, 42, 156, 171
car industry, 6, 11, 17, 18, 25, 34, 41, 86, 152, 164, 169, 172
export drive, 2, 22
first year of my-car, 17
foreign direct investment, 28, 40
import tariffs on cars, 19
Japan-EC Joint Declaration (the Hague Declaration), 1991, 150, 151
Japan-EU EPA, 2018, 166, 172
lost decade, 156, 171
northern islands, 79
reconstruction, 2, 6, 10, 13
scapegoat, 80
trade unionism in, 5, 6, 35, 46, 64, 114, 136, 156
Trojan horse, 61, 63, 70, 79

Japan Association of Corporate Executives (*Keizai-doyukai*), 140
Japan Automobile Manufacturers' Association (JAMA, *Jikoukai*), 6, 10, 17, 19, 26, 32, 34, 36, 37, 42, 44, 51, 61, 72, 78, 91, 109, 120, 170
Japan Automobile Workers' Unions (JAW, *Jidousha-souren*), 6, 10, 19, 21, 43, 67, 74, 110, 114, 116, 138, 152
Japan External Trade Organization (JETRO), 133
Japan Institute of Labour (JIL, *Nihon roudou kyoukai*), 135, 136, 146, 147, 149
Japanisation, 87, 126, 135, 136, 149, 171. *See also* new realism
Japan National Railway (JNR), 31, 81, 82, 87
Japan Railway Company (JR), 82
Japan Trade Union Confederation. *See* Rengou (Japan Trade Union Confederation)
Japan World Exposition, Osaka, 30
Jenkin, Patrick, 52, 76, 87, 89, 90, 114, 117, 141
Jidousha-rouren, 19, 20, 110, 112, 138. *See also* Nissan-*rouren*
Jidousha-souren. *See* Japan Automobile Workers' Unions (JAW, Jidousha-souren)
Jiji-tsushin, 161–167
Joseph, Keith, 28, 52–54, 56–59, 61, 67, 68, 71, 74
just-in-time production, 74

K

Kagami, Hideo, 115
kanban, 145
Kasai, Yoshiyuki, 82
Katayama, Yutaka, 21, 36, 37
Kawai, Isamu, 57, 93, 94, 102, 105, 107
Kawakatsu, Noriaki, 20, 36–38, 53, 81, 82, 89, 96, 110, 112, 113, 124, 137
Kawamata, Katsuji
chairman of Nissan, 22
founder of renaissance, 17
Industrial Bank of Japan, 13, 23
President of JAMA, 36, 37
President of Nissan, 36
Vice President of *Keidanren*, 22
Kawasaki, 34, 41, 68
Keck, Jörn, 2, 3, 132
Keidanren, 18, 22, 31, 86, 97, 140
Press Club, 108, 110, 111
keiretsu, 74
King James I, 31
Kishi, Nobusuke, 11, 21
knock-down assembling, 14, 28, 79, 103, 112

Kodansha, 20, 81, 112, 113, 138, 139
Komatsu, 148
Kono, Taro, 167
Kota Bharu, 29
Kume, Yutaka, 46, 47, 55, 56, 137, 140, 141, 152
  President of Nissan, 141
Kurosawa, Akira, 124

L
labour–management relations, 10, 19, 33, 37, 42, 51, 55, 58, 64, 67, 69, 73, 74, 85, 107, 128, 134, 136, 139, 145, 147, 159, 171
Labour Party
  relations with the TUC, 64
Lawson, Nigel, 7, 103–105, 108, 116–119, 143
Le Maire, Bruno, 165
Leyland Motors, 27
Liberal Democratic Party (LDP) of Japan, 35, 38, 84
Llanwern, 51, 65
local content requirement
  30%, 77
  40%, 165
  80%, 7, 52, 53, 55, 58, 60, 71–73, 75, 81, 88, 92–94, 100, 103, 104, 107, 108, 121, 142, 157, 159, 170
  90%, 157
  American, 62
  British, 7, 8, 48, 51, 52, 60, 80, 88, 100, 116, 170
  of the EC, 52, 74, 80, 117
Lord Armstrong, 30
Lucas, 62, 142

M
Magneti-Marelli, 142
Major, John, 143
Manchuria, 11, 21
Mansfield, Michael, 43
Manx Tourist Trophy, 17
Marley Kanto, 142
Marsh, Richard, 90, 152
Massey-Ferguson, 50
Mastuoka, Yosuke, 21
May, Teresa, 162, 163
Mazda (*Toyo kogyo*), 18, 73
Meiji-McVitie, 35
Meiji University, 19
Meiki, 147
Memorandum of Understandings, 78, 119
Mercedes Benz, 158
Mexico, 14, 18, 85, 88, 165, 167
MG, 27
Michelin, 142, 159
Ministry of Defence, 79
Ministry of Foreign Affairs (MOFA) of Japan, 38, 55, 82, 84, 91, 93, 97, 150, 162
Ministry of International Trade and Industry (MITI), 11, 12, 17, 18, 38, 43, 44, 55, 80, 84, 86, 90, 91, 93, 100, 101, 126, 132, 133, 150, 170
  export monitoring. *See* Elements of Consensus
  export restricting. *See* voluntary export restriction (VER)
  reconstruction, 10
Mitsubishi, 12, 41
  alliance with Renault-Nissan, 165, 166, 170
Mitsubishi UFJ, 164
Mitsui Bussan, 46, 162
Morris, 27
Motor-Iberica, 49, 50
Mountfield, Robin, 3, 7, 10, 13, 16, 27, 29, 36–38, 41, 44–49, 51,

52, 55–60, 62, 65, 67, 71–78, 80–82, 86, 89–92, 94, 96, 102–104, 106–108, 110, 111, 115, 123, 128, 144, 152
Murray, Len (Lionel), 57, 63, 64, 110, 114, 115, 128, 134
Muskie Law, 23

N

Nakasone, Yasuhiro, 84, 90, 91, 95–97, 100, 101, 107, 112, 113, 116, 137
National Union of Mineworkers (NUM), 147, 153
neo-liberalism, 34, 40, 58, 171
NewCastle, 89
new realism, 135, 153, 171. *See also* Japanisation
New Zealand, 27
Nikkei, 12, 13, 18, 37, 42, 44, 81, 82, 86, 119, 122, 133, 138, 140, 141
Nissan
  agreement with AUEW, 7, 67, 68, 89, 115, 126, 129, 146
  Alfa Romeo, 37, 49
  alliance with Mitsubishi, 165, 166, 170
  alliance with Renault, 158, 165, 166, 170
  Almera/Pulsar, 158, 159
  Belgium, 16, 26, 28, 44, 64
  Bluebird/Auster, 7, 14, 16, 20, 61, 139, 140
  British manufacturer status, 8, 143
  Cedric, 86
  collaboration with Austin, 13, 14
  competition with Toyota, 144
  Cuernavaca plant, 14
  Datsun pickup truck, 42
  Datsun UK, 16, 38, 44, 45
  exports to Asia, 14
  exports to EFTA, 10, 16, 42, 119
  exports to the EC/EU, 2, 29, 102, 110, 126, 132, 143, 157, 169
  exports to the US, 11, 14, 17, 21–23, 26, 28, 36, 42, 43, 45, 102
  feasibility study (in Britain), 7, 43, 52, 53, 59, 68
  feasibility study (in the US), 23
  Germany, 17, 29, 49, 63
  Gloria, 159
  Hungary plant project, 16
  Juke, 161
  labour dispute, 2, 13, 77, 87
  Leaf, 161, 164
  merger with Prince Motors, 17, 159
  Micra, 8, 143, 157–160, 165
  MITI of Ginza, 12
  Motor-Iberica, 49, 50
  nationalisation, 28
  the Netherlands, 16, 28, 65
  Note, 161
  Oppama plant, 82
  Primera, 8, 142, 157–160
  Public Relations Division, 38, 112, 113
  Qashqai/Dualis, 161, 164
  Queen's Award for Enterprise (International Trade/Export), 67, 143
  Quicksilver, 49, 56
  R&D centre, 123
  Revival Plan, 159, 160
  Safari/Patrol, 50
  Sajima-marina, 112
  Skyline, 159
  Smyrna plant, 44
  Sunderland plant. *See* Sunderland (Nissan's plant in)
  Sunny, 16, 17, 28
  Teesport, 16
  Teesside, 44, 65

trade unions. *See* Jidousha-rouren
Tsurumi plant, 13
Vanette, 50, 157
Violet, 52, 61, 93
Volkswagen, 36, 49, 50, 63
Worthing, 45
X-trail, 162, 164
Yokohama plant, 12, 13, 20
Z, 21
Zama plant, 35, 49, 83, 138, 139, 156, 171
Nissan-*bunkai*, 19
Nissan-Datsun UK, 16, 38, 44, 45
Nissan European Technology Centre (NETC), 143
Nissan Motor Manufacturing (UK) Ltd. (NMUK), 7, 8, 44, 114, 126, 129, 131, 132, 136, 142, 143, 151, 157, 165
Nissan-*rouren* (Federation of All Nissan and General Workers' Unions), 20, 138, 141, 156. *See also* Jidousha-rouren
Nissan-*rouso*, 13, 20, 138. *See also* Jidousha-rouren
Nissan USA, 21, 137
Nomura Holdings, 163
non-strike agreement, 7, 135, 136. *See also* Japanisation
Northern Ireland, 69, 161
Northern Region Council (NRC), 68, 69, 89, 128. *See also* Trade Union Congress (TUC)
North Killingholme, 51, 65
North of England Development Council (NEDC), 114
Norway, 10, 15, 16
NSK Europe, 65
Peterlee plant, 65

O
Ohira, Masayoshi, 43
oil shock, 1973, 23
oil shock, 1979, 81
Okuma, Masataka, 23, 45–49, 52, 55, 56, 59, 65, 81, 82, 92, 119
Oliver, Nick, 126, 129, 137, 149, 172
Ooki, Saburo, 43
Opel, 62, 109
Organisation for Economic Co-operation and Development (OECD), 17, 18
over-capacity, 5, 6, 17, 33, 58, 69
Oxford University, 29, 151
Nissan Institute for Japanese Studies, 41

P
Panasonic (Matsushita-denki), 135, 140, 164
Cardiff plant, 136
Park, George, 65
Parkinson, Cecil, 103–105, 108, 117–119
Peugeot-Citroën, 62. *See also* PSA
Peugeot-Talbot, 62
Plaza Agreement, 1985, 145
Poitier, 90, 91
Prince Akihito (Emperor Akihito), 29
Prince Charles, 30, 139, 141
Prince Motor, 17, 159
Princess Diana, 139–141
productivity, 1, 18, 33, 46–48, 50, 57, 109, 148, 149, 152
PSA, 62. *See also* Peugeot-Citroën

Q
Queen Elisabeth II
coronation, 29
Japan visit, 6, 25, 29, 30
Queen's Award for Enterprise (International Trade/Export), 67, 143

R
rationalisation, 5, 62, 159
Reagan, Ronald, 44, 78, 95, 96
redundancy, 6, 171. *See also* unemployment
regional development grant (RDG), 7, 40, 58, 71, 72, 75–78, 94, 100, 103, 104, 117, 118, 122, 123, 128
Renault, 37, 138, 145, 158–161, 166, 170
  alliance with Nissan. *See* Nissan
  Clio, 158, 160
Rengou (Japan Trade Union Confederation), 152
Reuter, 161, 162
robotisation, 35, 68
Rolls-Royce (RR), 5, 27, 32, 34, 41, 134
Rover, 5, 27, 45, 92, 143, 144. *See also* British Leyland (BL)

S
Saikawa, Hiroto, 138, 165
Sakurauchi, Yoshio, 17, 46, 84
Sanyo, 136
Sasaki, Sadamichi, 23, 36
Sasaki, Yoshitake, 43
Sato, Masaaki, 12, 13, 17–24, 35–38, 43, 46, 49–56, 58, 59, 67, 76, 77, 81, 83–85, 95, 96, 105, 106, 112, 138, 139, 158
Scargill, Arthur, 147
Schweitzer, Louis, 159
Scotland, 69, 146, 161
screw-driver operation, 79. *See also* knock-down assembling
Sekisui, 148
Seko, Hiroshige, 165
selective financial assistance (SFA), 7, 40, 58, 69, 71–73, 75–78, 94, 100, 103, 104, 108, 116–118, 122, 123, 128
Seneffe, 44
Sharp, 136
Shimizu, Haruki, 112, 137, 138
shinkansen, 31
Shioji, Ichiro
  'scandal', 112, 113, 115, 138
  Harvard University Trade Union Course, 20
  labour aristocrat, 20
  President of the JAW, 10, 19, 67
  shadow emperor, 20
  Vice President of the ICFTU, 21, 53
ship-building industry, 30, 129
Shotton, 51, 65, 114, 128, 144
Showa emperor, 10, 29, 30
Single European Act (SEA), 5, 69, 71, 126, 130–132
single union agreement, 7, 47, 66, 67, 69, 74, 85, 87, 88, 108, 110, 114, 116, 123, 126, 128, 134–136, 145–147, 149, 153, 171. *See also* Japanisation
Soames, Christopher, 30
Society of Motor Manufacturers and Traders (SMMT), 7, 8, 26, 32, 34, 40, 48, 60–62, 72, 91, 103, 109, 120, 143
Sony, 47, 136, 164
  Bridgend plant, 66, 147
  Queen's Award for Enterprise (International Trade/Export), 67
Souhyou, 13, 19, 20
Spain, 50, 83, 146, 157, 160, 167
SP Tyres, 142
Stallingborough, 51, 65
Standard-Triumph, 27. *See also* British Leyland (BL)
Stevenson, Dennis, 66

Stewart-Clark, John (Jack), 70
Stewart, Paul, 20, 21, 35, 87, 123, 126, 135, 140, 142, 148, 149, 152, 171
strike, 27, 31, 48, 53, 74, 133, 135, 145, 149, 153
Subaru, 17, 36
subsidy, 7, 13, 51, 57, 62, 65, 69, 73, 123, 134
  ban of, 58, 150
  Japanese, 134, 171. *See also* regional development grant (RDG); selective financial assistance (SFA)
Sugiyama, Shinsuke, 162
Sunderland (Nissan's plant in)
  airfield, 7, 126, 130
  export to Czechoslovakia, 142
  export to Japan, 126, 132, 135, 142, 144, 157, 159, 160, 164, 166, 170
  export to Poland, 142
  export to single market, 131, 132, 143, 156, 157, 165, 170
  export to Taiwan, 14, 142
  export to Yugoslavia, 142
  first green-field plant in Europe, 62
  industrial park, 165
  land price, 156
  largest car assembling plant in Britain, 170
  launching ceremony, 132, 137, 141
  Nissan Revival Plan, 159, 160
  Phase 1, 103, 140
  Phase 2, 104, 141
  Phase 3, 104
  plant construction, 65, 77
Suzuki, 18
Suzuki, Zenko, 82, 84, 90
Swindon. *See* Honda
Switzerland, 30

T
tariffs
  abolishing of, 131, 163
  free of, 26, 28
  Japanese, 8, 18, 19, 26, 28, 161, 163, 166
  on assembled cars, 8, 160
  the EC, 26, 28, 29, 131
Tebbit, Norman, 55, 56, 58–63, 66–68, 72, 77, 120, 122
Thatcher, Margaret
  administration, 1, 7, 47, 48, 53, 62, 69, 71, 72, 76, 77, 83, 90, 99, 117, 123, 131, 145, 170
  anti-trade union, 35
  Cabinet Official Group on British Policy Towards Japan, 52, 79, 80
  fiscal reform, 40
  Grand Cordon of the Order of the Precious Crown, 145
  Iron Lady, 40, 83, 84
  Japan policy, 5, 34
  Japan visit 1977, 35, 36, 82
  Japan visit 1979, 41
  Japan visit 1982, 7, 22, 82, 84
  tiger, 41
  Tory leader, 28, 66, 82, 143
TI Nihon (TIJ) UK, 142
Todd, Ron, 134, 147
Tohoku University, 21
Tokugawa *shogun*, 31
Tokyo Marines, 164
Tory. *See* Conservative Party
Toshiba, 18, 135, 136
  Plymouth plant, 135
Toyota
  agreement with AUE, 148
  Aston Martin, 46
  Auris/Corolla, 164
  Burnaston plant, 2, 8, 144, 148, 150, 156

Carina, 144
Corolla, 17, 164
Deeside plant, 144, 148
GM, 11, 83
Valenciennes plant, 157
Yaris/Bitz, 157
Toyo-keizai, 81
Trade union
Britain, 3, 35, 37, 42, 46–48, 51, 52, 57, 66, 68, 73, 135, 141, 149, 152
Japan, 3, 5, 6, 19, 21, 22, 35, 71, 110, 114, 129, 152, 170, 171
trade unionism, 6, 35
the US, 20, 22
Trade Union Congress (TUC)
Bridlington Rules, 146, 153
Convention, 147
Economic Committee, 60, 64, 65, 89, 108
Executive Council, 89, 114
Northern Region Council (NRC), 68, 69, 89, 128
report on British automobile industry, 64, 108
Stockton, 57
Wales Council, 114
Transport and General Workers' Union (TGWU), 67, 68, 87, 115, 129, 146, 147, 153, 171
Treasury, 47, 48, 62, 73, 75, 77–79, 116–118, 134
Triumph, 5, 92
Acclaim, 92. *See also* British Leyland (BL)
Trojan horse, 60, 63, 70, 79
Trump, Donald, 166, 172
Tsuchiya, Toshiaki, 130, 142
Tsuruoka, Koji, 162, 163
Tugendhat, Christopher, 130
Tyne and Wear County Council, 114, 130

U
unemployment, 26, 29, 30, 48, 51, 52, 57, 69, 78, 80, 95, 105, 171
Union of Industrial and Employer Confederations of Europe (UNICE), 70
United Auto Workers (UAW), 20, 37, 43, 44, 57, 96
University of Tokyo, 19, 81, 82, 140
USSR, 17, 79

V
V2500, 41
Vauxhall, 50, 62, 108, 109
Vickers, 27, 134
Volkswagen, 36, 49, 63, 134, 150
Santana, 49
voluntary export restriction (VER)
Japan-Britain, 6, 26, 32, 34, 45, 60, 61, 79, 110
Japan-EC/EU, 2, 102, 110
Japan-US, 44, 102. *See also* export monitoring
Volvo, 159

W
wage bargaining, 33, 67, 88, 126, 147
Wales, 29, 41, 46, 48, 51, 65, 66, 69, 91, 114, 128, 144, 147, 148, 161
Wentloog, 51, 65
Wickens, Peter, 67, 87, 89, 90, 132, 133, 135, 136, 148, 152
Wilkinson, Barry, 126, 129, 137, 149, 172

Wilson, Harold, 27, 32

Y
Yamanaka, Sadanori, 91, 101
Yamazaki, Toshio, 141
Yuasa, 144, 147

Z
zaibatsu, 12, 159. *See also* keiretsu

The manufacturer's authorised representative in the EU is Springer Nature Customer Service Centre GmbH, Europaplatz 3, 69115 Heidelberg, Germany. If you have any concerns regarding our products, please contact ProductSafety@springernature.com

Printed and bound by CPI Group (UK) Ltd, Croydon, CR0 4YY

30/09/2026

02225451-0002